Living Justice

Living Justice

Catholic Social Teaching in Action: The Classroom Edition

Thomas Massaro, S.J.

ROWMAN & LITTLEFIELD PUBLISHERS, INC.
Lanham • Boulder • New York • Toronto • Plymouth, UK

ROWMAN & LITTLEFIELD PUBLISHERS, INC.

Published in the United States of America
by Rowman & Littlefield Publishers, Inc.
A wholly owned subsidary of The Rowman & Littlefield Publishing Group, Inc.
4501 Forbes Boulevard, Suite 200, Lanham, Maryland 20706
www.rowmanlittlefield.com

Estover Road
Plymouth PL6 7PY
United Kingdom

British Library Cataloguing in Publication Information Available

Library of Congress Cataloging-in-Publication Data:

Massaro, Thomas, 1961–
  Living justice: Catholic social teaching in action / Thomas Massaro. —
Classroom ed.
     p. cm.
  Includes bibliographical references and index.
  ISBN-13: 978-0-7425-5996-7 (cloth : alk. paper)
  ISBN-10: 0-7425-5996-3 (cloth : alk. paper)
  ISBN-13: 978-0-7425-5997-4 (pbk. : alk. paper)
  ISBN-10: 0-7425-5997-1 (pbk. : alk. paper)
  1. Christian sociology—Catholic Church. 2. Church and social problems—
Catholic Church. 3. Catholic Church—Doctrines. I. Title.
  BX1753.M354 2008
  261.8088'282—dc22   2007037766

Printed in the United States of America

∞™ The paper used in this publication meets the minimum requirements of
American National Standard for Information Sciences—Permanence of Paper for
Printed Library Materials, ANSI/NISO Z39.48-1992.

Contents

List of Tables   vii

Preface   ix

1 Social Justice and the Mission of the Church   1
   The Religious Motivation for Social Justice Efforts   3
   Social Mission and Church Morale   7
   Sharing "Our Best-Kept Secret"   8
   From "Charity Alone" to a Justice Orientation   9
   Looking Ahead   14
   Questions for Reflection   14
   Topics for Further Research   15

2 Going Public with Your Faith   17
   Bridging Two Distinct Worlds   17
   Tertullian's Question   19
   The Perils of the Crusading Spirit   22
   Religious Idealism: Its Contribution to Politics   25
   Maintaining a Delicate Balance   27
   Together on Pilgrimage   29
   Questions for Reflection   30
   Topics for Further Research   31

3 Inheriting the Tradition of Catholic Social Teaching   33
   The Documentary Heritage   34
   A Look Back to the Nineteenth Century   40
   Pioneers of Social Catholicism   43

	The Writing of the Social Encyclicals	46
	Questions for Reflection	52
	Topics for Further Research	52
4	The Sources and Methods of Catholic Social Teaching	55
	The Four Sources of Christian Ethics	56
	Universal Principles and Local Applications	75
	Questions for Reflection	76
	Topics for Further Research	77
5	Nine Key Themes of Catholic Social Teaching	79
	1. The Dignity of Every Person and Human Rights	80
	2. Solidarity, Common Good, and Participation	84
	3. Family Life	87
	4. Subsidiarity and the Proper Role of Government	89
	5. Property Ownership in Modern Society: Rights and Responsibilities	91
	6. The Dignity of Work, Rights of Workers, and Support for Labor Unions	95
	7. Colonialism and Economic Development	97
	8. Peace and Disarmament	103
	9. Option for the Poor and Vulnerable	112
	Questions for Reflection	116
	Topics for Further Research	117
6	The Role of Catholic Social Teaching Today	119
	A Blueprint? An Ideology? A "Third Way"?	119
	The Catholic Critique of Communism	126
	The Catholic Critique of Capitalism	129
	Applying Catholic Social Teaching in the Real World	134
	Commitments to Social Justice: Heroic and Ordinary	140
	Questions for Reflection	142
	Topics for Further Research	144
7	Future Directions for Catholic Social Teaching	145
	Four Continuities: Further Shifts in Emphasis	145
	Two New Challenges: The Environment and Globalization	158
	Spreading the Word about Catholic Social Teaching	171
	The Surprising Future	175
	Questions for Reflection	176
	Topics for Further Research	177
Annotated List of Resources for Further Study		179
Index		185
About the Author		191

List of Tables

Table 3.1.   Major Documents of Modern Catholic
             Social Teaching   35–36

Table 3.2.   Timeline of Key Events Shaping Catholic
             Social Teaching   51

Table 4.1.   A Sampling of Scriptural Texts Influential in
             Peace and Justice Communities   62–64

Table 5.1.   Key Texts for Nine Themes in Catholic
             Social Teaching   80

Table 5.2.   Categories and Criteria of Just War Theory   106–107

Table 6.1.   A Model of Moral Methodology Useful in
             Social Issues   135

Table 7.1.   Citations from Catholic Social Teaching
             Documents on the Environment   160

Table 7.2.   Models of Possible Christian Approaches to the
             Natural Environment   163

Preface

Encouraged by the popularity of a previous version of this book, I am delighted to offer this greatly revised and expanded Classroom Edition of *Living Justice: Catholic Social Teaching in Action*. This volume serves as a brief introduction to the tradition of Catholic social teaching. It is intended for use in the wide variety of college courses that treat topics regarding social justice and the Roman Catholic Church.

Admittedly, the subject matter of social ethics is complex, as this is the branch of religious thought that touches perhaps most broadly upon such diverse fields as economics, political science, sociology, history, law, and the behavioral sciences. Because students find themselves frequently bewildered by these complexities, I have made every effort to define and explain technical terms whenever they arise. No previous knowledge of theology, ethics, or theories of justice is assumed in the chapters that follow.

Perhaps this complexity explains how hard it has been to find an introduction to Catholic social thought that is at once informative enough for advanced students and easily readable. It is my hope that this thoroughly revised edition of *Living Justice* will fill the gap in a way that sparks student interest in this intriguing field. Hopefully, all readers will find in this book both an accessible, conversational tone and adequate intellectual rigor. The ultimate success of this volume will be measured not by how much ground is covered within these pages (I have deliberately kept this book brief so that it fits readily into many types of courses), but rather by how wide-ranging is the conversation promoted by these chapters.

Speaking of chapters, a word about the sequence of topics in the book is in order. The heart of the book consists of its three middle chapters: numbers three, four, and five. These chapters treat the historical background, sources, methods, and major themes of Catholic social teaching. They address questions like the following: Precisely which concerns about justice have led popes and bishops to write documents addressing the world beyond the doors of the church? How do sources such as scripture, natural law, social analysis, and various theological traditions contribute to the style and substance of Catholic social teaching? The middle chapters respond to these frequently asked questions and offer a list of nine major themes in the Church's social encyclicals and related documents.

Before addressing the "meaty" content of these middle chapters, most readers will find it important to set the stage for what is to follow. Thus, the first two chapters consider certain pivotal background questions about the various ways that faith traditions encounter and challenge the worlds of politics, economics, and social relations. How does religious faith (something often considered private or personal in nature) relate to the public affairs of a pluralistic society? What is the best way to describe the social mission of the Church? Expect in chapters one and two, then, a quick overview of the possibilities and limits of religious social ethics and the types of guidance Catholic social teaching offers to individuals and nations on complex issues. The book concludes with two chapters (six and seven) that sketch out several important concerns regarding the present and future role of Catholic social thought in the concrete circumstances of world events. This final unit contrasts the Catholic vision of justice with ideologies such as communism and free-market libertarian-style capitalism and then ventures some predictions about future directions and themes in Catholic social teaching. This book need not be read cover to cover in lockstep fashion. Indeed, it may be helpful to many readers to skip around the text among and within given chapters, depending upon reader interest and previous knowledge. Selective use of preferred sections is an excellent way to make maximum use of this book.

Note five further features of the book that are intended to make this volume as user-friendly as possible. First (actually, last in page order), a handy index facilitates quick searches for topics and proper names treated here. Second, eight tables provide at-a-glance summaries of historical and methodological points developed in the text. Third, I have provided an annotated list of selected books and web resources for further study that will probably be more useful to students than standard bibliographies of Catholic social thought. Fourth, a set of discussion questions for use in the classroom or in more informal settings appears at the end of each chapter. Fifth, each chapter concludes with a list of ten topics for further research. Instructors and students will be able to put all of these features to good use in a wide array of courses that introduce Catholic social teaching and apply it in various ways to pressing contemporary issues.

One of the great things about studying social justice, unlike many topics in theology, is that everyone has relevant opinions and probably at least a bit of experience. Even if you do not find yourself in agreement with all of the opinions and approaches presented in this book, whether they come from this author or from church documents, it will be easy to make informed judgments based on the principles and priorities you bring to this topic. There is plenty of room for honest differences of opinions and varying perspective on the proper goals and strategies for the improvement of society. Whether a given reader considers himself or herself a Roman Catholic, a member of another religious community, or a member of no particular religious denomination, the study of the tradition of Catholic social thought can foster profound reflection on the meaning of justice in our troubled world. Anyone concerned about the achievement of social justice is likely to make good use of this book, which is intended to invite all people into informed conversations about appropriate social priorities and principles of justice.

I wish to thank the many people who, over several decades now, have helped me understand and develop the ideas in this book, the many teachers, classmates, and students who took the time to debate with me the merits of various views of social justice. I am especially indebted to James Martin, S.J., Jeremy Langford, and Mark Kolakowski, who read the earliest versions of each chapter. Ross Miller and the wonderful staff of Rowman & Littlefield Publishers have offered nothing but encouragement through the long process of revising this text for classroom use.

I dedicate this book to my parents, Joseph and Nancy Massaro, who were my first teachers in the ways of justice, fairness, and concern for all people. They have joined their efforts to those of a multitude of believers, both laity and clergy, to practice, promote, and teach justice in a world so desperately in need of faith, hope, and love. As is written in the Book of Daniel, "Those who lead the many to justice shall be like the stars forever" (Daniel 12:3).

1

+

Social Justice and the Mission of the Church

The phrase "social justice" conjures up a wide range of images and associations. Depending upon who is consulted, the simple question "What is social justice?" might prompt answers that are abstract and theoretical, on one hand, or vividly concrete, on the other hand. Philosophers and economists might emphasize formulas and syllogisms for ensuring that each member of society receives the due amount of rewards and burdens. An average person on the street might be more inclined to list a bundle of indignities and hardships that nobody would have to undergo in a world that was more just. But whether the focus falls upon statistical measures of distributive shares or on simple acts of fairness and generosity between friends or even strangers, all common notions of social justice boil down to the goal of achieving a right ordering of society. A just social order is one that ensures that all people have fair and equitable opportunities to live decent lives free of inordinate burdens and deprivations. How can leaders and institutions ensure that access to the good things in life is extended to all members of society, without exception?

It seems that in every age social relations have been poisoned by disheartening realities such as ethnic hatred, racial discrimination, abject poverty, and similar sources of conflict and oppression. Throughout history, social commentators and ordinary citizens have expressed distress and even outrage about the state of the world. Impressive social reform movements have sprung up in many societies to enact social change and to advocate for improvements in the way that public affairs are conducted. Most often, these movements propose greater protections for the underdogs, that is, particularly disadvantaged members of society whose

1

lack of power makes them vulnerable to exploitation. Naturally, not everyone agrees about just how bad the status quo is at any given moment. However, it seems safe to say that any mature and morally serious person would notice significant inequities in society and would feel some impulse to do something about them.

Why, then, are so many people concerned with social justice, even when it will likely demand sacrifices on their part? While the easiest thing might be to adopt a policy of looking out for number one, it turns out that most people are actually quite eager to contribute in some way to the betterment of society, even if it does not directly or primarily benefit themselves. While it is not uncommon for such well-intentioned people to burn out a bit over the long haul or to be overwhelmed by the sheer enormity of social problems, most people are uncomfortable with simply burying their heads in the sand and ignoring the plight of the suffering. Since the status quo is clearly not acceptable, and since social injustices tend to persist unless concerted efforts bring unfair practices to a halt, the greatest challenge is to tap into those popular energies that already exist to set things right.

If it is true, then, that many people feel a common obligation to work to alleviate human suffering, the consensus about social justice for the most part ends there. Beyond this basic point of agreement lie many subsequent points of disagreement regarding the nature of justice, the causes of injustice, and the precise shape of appropriate responses to social problems. For example, disputes quickly arise when pondering the causes of deep poverty, even in affluent countries. Should most of the blame be attributed to the poor themselves, for example, for failing to take advantage of educational and employment opportunities? Or is it instead true that what really lies at the heart of the problem are the workings of larger social systems, such as economic and political structures that segregate struggling inner-city neighborhoods from the mainstream of society? In other words, are the poor most accurately portrayed as victims of unfair policies set by others or as culpable accomplices in their own marginalization?

These sweeping questions will be settled neither in this introductory chapter nor in this entire volume—in fact not in the entire body of Catholic social teaching documents, or anywhere else for that matter. But raising a few initial questions about the causes of poverty and the range of possible responses to social injustices is helpful in identifying one of the key qualities of social ethics. As is the case with any field of inquiry that involves morality and ethical reasoning, social ethics is an especially open-ended endeavor, one that resembles more an art than a science. In investigating this tradition of reflection on social justice, expect to encounter many ambiguous areas, where precise answers are elusive and the proper responses to dilemmas are far from obvious. Even reasonable people of good will frequently disagree on which priorities to embrace and on how to apply moral principles to specific situations. Acknowledging this ambiguity in no way means that social ethics is hardly worth studying. Rather, it simply serves as a reminder of what anyone who follows public affairs and current events already knows: that it is wise to expect lively debates on hot-button topics such as how to achieve social justice.

THE RELIGIOUS MOTIVATION FOR SOCIAL JUSTICE EFFORTS

As noted above, the natural pull to engage in acts of charity and social justice touches many people—probably a majority, possibly even everyone at some point in their lives. Some of these efforts turn out to be heroic in nature, while others seem rather ordinary in scope. Every year millions of people make many different kinds of commitments to the advancement of social justice. They might volunteer on a weekly or monthly basis to help provide social services at a local community center. They might work at a soup kitchen or homeless shelter, assist through clerical support at a drug-counseling program, answer phones at a crisis hotline, serve as foster parents, or offer their EMT skills at a local volunteer fire department. They might use a portion of their inherited or earned wealth to establish a charitable trust or foundation to alleviate poverty.

People who have less time or money to give might resolve to make a conscious effort to respond just a bit more often and more generously to those heartrending letters of solicitation from charitable organizations. Or they might choose to go beyond financial assistance and part-time volunteering to make a deeper commitment, perhaps giving a year or more of their lives to service work for and with the least fortunate members of society, whether in their native land or overseas. Others deliberately accept lower-paying careers with a service dimension because they want to make a positive difference in the lives of others—and so they become public service attorneys instead of corporate lawyers or administrators of nonprofit organizations instead of corporate executives. Nobody gets rich working in inner-city schools or doing community organizing, but this kind of work attracts an often surprising number of talented young people.

It is safe to say that the decisions of such generous people would receive applause from just about any audience; it simply warms our hearts to learn of selfless efforts that benefit the least fortunate members of society. We can all agree that the world would be a better place if more of us more often made decisions like those described above. Nobody wants the problems of poverty, homelessness, inadequate health care, and under-funded legal assistance for vulnerable populations to continue unchecked or to worsen in the future. To be human is to have a heart that is moved by stories of desperate need and crying injustices. Humanitarian responses to people in crisis are practically instinctual.

While all of us would like to see less suffering and more social justice in the world, an interesting question quickly arises: Why do some people choose to get involved while others do not? What ideas or motivations impel certain members of society to make especially significant sacrifices of their time, energy, and money to help others and to improve society? What gives some people the energy and loving-kindness to perform generous actions and undertake altruistic projects that most people approve of but fail to tackle themselves? While all of us have the frequent experience of our hearts going out to the needy, why is it that some of us reach out in ambitious ways to our neighbors in need while others do not?

There are many secular-minded humanitarians in our midst who are motivated by genuine concern for other people. These people may explain their compassionate response to suffering and injustice in terms of a desire to assist the project of human development, the cause of human rights, or the well-being of a specific nation, region, city, or ethnic group. They may gladly line up under any number of banners, such as "secular humanism," the "human rights movement," "feminism," "Black Power," or even "universal solidarity." Some of these people may resist all attempts to label the sources of their social concerns, preferring to steer clear of being identified with any specific cause, ideology, or philosophy. They may be satisfied with the simple explanation that their work for justice is merely a response to a personal inner calling they feel to "give something back" and "do one's duty to others."

Many people, however, are eager to identify their charitable works with their religious beliefs. They are quite articulate about why they perform philanthropic activities: to do the will of God in the world, to promote the sacred dignity of the lives of their neighbors in need, to spread the Gospel in a concrete way, to reflect the love of God to other children of God, to be a witness to Jesus Christ and the Kingdom of God while here on earth. Religiously motivated people sometimes direct their energies toward church-based activities and work with agencies and programs that are obviously religious, such as Catholic Charities, the Saint Vincent de Paul Society, Pax Christi, Covenant House, or the Salvation Army. At other times, similar efforts may be motivated by religiously inspired ideas but do not proceed under the auspices of any church or religious institution. Agencies such as Bread for the World, Interfaith Worker Justice, and Witness for Peace fall into this category of advocacy groups that are religiously inspired but not affiliated with a specific faith community.

When religious people who are engaged in the work of social justice talk about what motivates their activities, they usually connect these acts of *love of neighbor* with the *love of God*, which is at the root of the life of faith. As Dorothy Day, the founder of the Catholic Worker movement, says on the final page of her autobiography, *The Long Loneliness*, "We cannot love God unless we love each other." These words echo several sayings of Jesus, who closely unites our response to the needs of our neighbor to our relationship with God, a relationship that supports and justifies all we do on earth.

This connection between heavenly and earthly realities is tricky business. Recognizing within oneself a desire to respond to God's call to build a more just world is only the beginning of a long journey of discernment. How can anyone know which actions are authentic responses to God's love? How does one choose between alternate ways of donating time, money, and energy in good works? Should priority be given to responding to the immediate needs of the least advantaged, or is it better to focus on long-range solutions that cannot be accused of functioning as mere band-aids? How widely should the net of concern be cast? These are obviously difficult questions to address. The good news is that we are not alone in our attempts to answer them.

In a sense, we are standing on the shoulders of giants, at a vantage point where we can take advantage of many traditions of reflection on these perennial questions. The wisdom of past ages can guide our vision and help us to come up with adequate answers. In fact, every religion and every secular ideology has an implicit or explicit way of addressing these very questions. There are well-formulated sets of answers for Marxists, utilitarians, libertarians, Hindus, Jews, Muslims, Mennonites, and Lutherans. This book will focus on just one tradition: Roman Catholicism. Over the past century or so, the Catholic Church has developed a body of social teachings that has grown increasingly insightful, challenging, and sophisticated in helping to shape the personal and collective responses of people of faith to social concerns such as poverty, violence, and injustice.

Each chapter of this book explores a particular aspect of the intellectual resources of Catholic social teaching: what it says, why it makes these claims, and how we can apply these insights in everyday life. Even if studying the message of Catholic social thought will not dramatically change what you are doing in the name of social justice, it will at least deepen your reflections on the "why" questions. Familiarity with the ethical stances articulated by popes and bishops may allow you to get a better grip on your own motivations and strategies for engaging in social activism and charitable work.

The story of the Church's involvement in social justice is a story of growth, much as a small seed sprouts from its modest beginnings to become a living and flourishing organism. Over the past few generations, Catholic clergy and laity have been growing in the direction of a more socially responsible stance toward political and economic issues that affect the lives of all people. It is reassuring to note that Catholics are not alone in this regard. There is a remarkable convergence among people of many different faiths and in diverse religious communities that have been walking along parallel paths in recent years. In both their basic concern about promoting justice as well as in the specific content of their social teachings, religious voices from various traditions have been echoing one another in recent decades, calling for many of the same reforms and advocating many of the same measures.

Ecumenical and interreligious collaboration in the area of justice has become so palpable and robust that a revealing slogan has been coined: "Where doctrine divides, the practice of pursuing social justice unites." In other words, even while the world's many religions remain at odds on theological questions, religious approaches to social justice have a way of bringing many diverse believers together. This is especially obvious when it comes time to stop theorizing about what should be done and to get down to rolling up our sleeves and engaging in serious work for service and social change.

Still, significant differences remain among the approaches of members of different religions, including the various branches of Christianity. It is indeed comforting to find overlapping messages on social justice from religious leaders, but it would be naive to claim that these leaders are in complete agreement about everything. Even when we agree that certain practices and structures are wrong, that lamentable situations of injustice exist in our world, there remain a wide variety of possible responses. Some people, for example, are inclined to be passive, resigning themselves to the status quo, at least for the time being. To justify their stance, they may cite core beliefs about "God's providence" or their confidence in eventual vindication.

Others become extremely impatient and can imagine no constructive course of action except immediate (and perhaps violent) revolution, advocating a sharp break from current ways of conducting "business as usual." The vast majority, however, find themselves somewhere between these two extremes of passive endurance and utter enthusiasm for overthrowing systems. As these people try to cling to what is helpful in the present socioeconomic system even while working for gradual improvement, they make use of whatever sources of inspiration and explanation they can find in traditions of thought about proper social order. They find inspiration in the words and actions of those who have gone before them seeking to discover fitting paths to justice and social responsibility. It is especially with these people in mind that this book about Catholic social teaching is written.

SOCIAL MISSION AND CHURCH MORALE

After offering the above reflections regarding the broad appeal of religious social thought in general, a few words are in order about the role of Catholic social teaching within the life of the contemporary Roman Catholic Church, in a more specific way. It is no secret that many adult Catholics have been feeling somewhat alienated from the institutional Church, particularly in recent years. For a variety of reasons, and against the backdrop of often painful personal experiences, millions of Catholics harbor some degree of doubt about their attachment to their parish, their diocese, perhaps even the entire structure of Roman Catholicism. Startling revelations about clergy misconduct and grave mistakes made by bishops and other church officials have led many observers to conclude that the Church may in recent years have squandered much of its moral credibility. Previously observant Catholics may experience diminishing enthusiasm for participating in parish activities, perhaps even staying away from liturgy and worship for long periods of time. Entire families sometimes waver in their practice of the faith, some even to the point of no longer identifying themselves as Catholics.

The causes of this malaise are complex and no doubt vary from person to person and place to place. Some people may be impatient or distressed by a seeming preoccupation of church authorities with questions regarding theological orthodoxy or church finances or other particular issues of limited interest. Many thoughtful Catholics find themselves depressed and exhausted by frequent conversations about the declining number of priests and nuns, the uncertain future of parish life, and an overemphasis on divisive issues such as inclusive language in the liturgy, the necessity of an all-male and all-celibate priesthood, and ecclesiastical politics in general. Endless debates over the fine points of arcane doctrine and the exercise of ecclesiastical discipline seem irrelevant to these people, especially when their hunger for a deeper union with God is not being fed by the sermons they hear Sunday after Sunday or the various programs that are supposed to nourish parish life.

The mere act of turning to the topic of Catholic social teaching, of course, does not automatically solve the problem of declining church morale. It certainly does not settle all the debates over church practices and policies, each of which demands serious attention in every locality. But there is an immense benefit in refocusing religious energies to the world beyond the front door of the church—to the struggle for social justice that affects people around the world, not just a limited circle or a few elites. Becoming more aware of the great issues of the day—from hunger to the plight of refugees to environmental crises to the cessation of war—has a way of putting into perspective the squabbles that take place within the walls of the institutional church. Many Catholics who find their energies for church life flagging have received great encouragement from learning more about the Church's principled and often courageous stances on peace, justice, and human rights. This is especially true of younger Catholics who, in survey after survey, express a rather high regard for the role of active service in their religious commitments. Members of the Millennial Generation (those born after 1979) consistently reflect the opinion that helping the poor and outcast is as central to the practice of their faith as the life of the sacraments or the doctrinal articles found in creeds. This is a generation whose understanding of discipleship includes a healthy dose of concern for social justice.

Catholic social teaching, then, can serve as a unifying force, a banner under which believers may rally even if they remain somewhat divided on certain matters about the internal life of the Church. Even allowing for some differences of opinion between liberals and conservatives over how to apply the message of Catholic social teaching to concrete problems, it is a promising possibility to look to the Church's teaching on economic, political, and social issues with pride and hope.

SHARING "OUR BEST-KEPT SECRET"

When outsiders think of the Roman Catholic Church, many images and ideas routinely come to mind. For example, they may identify the Catholic Church with the face of a prominent pope, bishop, or saint, or they may recall the sweet smell of incense, the beauty of a stained glass window, or the soothing melody of Gregorian chant. It is unlikely, however, that many would make such a quick association between Catholicism and the notion of social justice. For this reason, Catholic social teaching has often been called "our best-kept secret." In fact, some people are astonished when they first hear of the Church's commitment to justice throughout the world. How can an institution like the Catholic Church, long associated with a *conservative* approach that resists change and looks to the past, have been delivering for so long a *progressive* message that challenges the prevailing global economic and political order to be more just? Part of the mission of Catholics today is to expose this "secret" and share the riches of this tradition with the wider community of concerned people.

The sharing of this secret has already started in ways that may not be obvious. In fact, many of the laudable social institutions and practices that Americans and others take for granted today have their roots in teachings and activities of the Christian community, including the Catholic Church. For example, the complex system of hospitals and modern health care from which we all benefit sprang from charitable works that were sponsored by churches, both Protestant and Catholic, in previous centuries. Modern labor unions and group insurance policies are an outgrowth of various activities of guilds and sodalities, agencies through which members of the medieval Church practiced mutual support, often under direct religious auspices. Groups of religious sisters and Protestant laity were the most active pioneers in establishing orphanages and child welfare agencies. Further, churches organized the first schools in the United States and in many other lands, and much of our educational system at all levels is still religiously affiliated. It was the church that cared for low-income families before there were public social service agencies. The contemporary social work and nursing professions grew out of the efforts of church personnel, largely nuns and laywomen, Catholic and Protestant alike, to assist families in need of resources, expertise, and healing.

For good reason, then, the Church has frequently been called the "godmother of the nonprofit sector." The Church continues to have significant impact on the shape of all these activities and professions as well as various social movements for justice, civil rights, and a more humane world. In fact, there is a recurring historical pattern by which assorted laudable efforts begin with religious motivations and zeal and then come to be regularized and routinized in the form of secular institutions. This is a beneficial, constructive aspect of the Church's service to the world and in no way diminishes the Church, as long as we remain conscious of the way these developments are a credit to the Church and its efforts at advancing social justice in our world.

FROM "CHARITY ALONE" TO A JUSTICE ORIENTATION

So far, this chapter has employed the terms charity and social justice almost interchangeably, as efforts to reform society and assist the less fortunate have been praised without reference to the specific conceptual orientation they display. Before proceeding further, however, it is necessary to introduce a distinction in the way we refer to such laudable efforts. While it would be an exaggeration to sharply separate the two, it is helpful to categorize certain undertakings as primarily works of *charity* and others as primarily works of *justice*. A review of historical trends in church social ministries supplies the best point of entry to this distinction.

Over the past few decades, the Church has witnessed a significant shift in how it understands its mission to contribute to the fight against poverty. To illustrate this point, compare the Catholic Church of the nineteenth century to the Church of today. In the United States and Europe, the work of the Church in the earlier era emphasized the role of charitable efforts as being the key to its social mission. In those years, the Church attempted primarily to inspire "works of mercy" among its members, especially those with the financial means to assist their less fortunate neighbors. According to that approach, charity was an unsystematic, episodic, and largely personal issue. The most church officials felt they could do was to appeal to the private consciences of individuals and perhaps fill in the cracks by sending missionaries and members of religious orders to attempt to meet some of the more desperate needs that were not being met through the generosity of anyone else. The heroic efforts on the part of many groups of religious sisters in this era are especially to be commended. These members of women's religious orders selflessly founded and staffed orphanages, schools for the children of immigrants, and various charitable agencies that supplied food, clothing, housing, and other forms of assistance to millions.

The Church of today continues to do many of these same good works, but it supplements its charitable activities with additional undertakings that contribute to the promotion of justice. The contemporary Church speaks about issues and undertakes efforts that were unheard of a century ago. The United States Conference of Catholic Bishops in Washington, DC, for example, includes an office dedicated to lobbying members of Congress and the executive branch of government. The purpose of these advocacy efforts on the part of the Bishops' Conference is not to win special favors for the Church, as if Catholic religious leaders were just another special interest pushing a selfish agenda. Rather, the goal is to encourage influential government officials to enact programs that will advance the causes of peace, public morality, and social justice.

By maintaining a presence on Capitol Hill, the American Catholic bishops seek to serve as advocates for the less privileged members of society—low-income families, the homeless, recent immigrants. These are the same demographic groups that, in previous eras and according to the older model of *charity alone*, the Church assisted primarily through direct relief, as the conduit for donations of money, goods, and services. The difference is that today, according to the newer model of church activity that emphasizes *justice in addition to charity*, more church efforts consist of indirect attempts to change social structures (including civil laws and government budget priorities) so that all people may have a better and fairer chance of living a good life.

Church lobbying to advocate fairer laws may seem like a controversial and indirect way to advance social justice. In fact, even the Church's modest activities along these lines strike many as either ineffective or overly provocative, perhaps as threatening to violate the boundaries that prudently divide church and state, a topic to be taken up more fully in chapter two. But a more direct and less contested set of efforts for justice is organized under the auspices of the Catholic Campaign for Human Development (CCHD). Since 1969, this organization has been funded and overseen by the U.S. Catholic bishops. The CCHD is dedicated to education and self-help programs designed to support the achievement of greater social justice in localities around the country. The overarching goal is to empower all people to participate fully in the life of society so that no one is deprived of the freedom and rights so often take for granted. Every year, the CCHD assists projects such as rural cooperatives in Appalachia, adult education programs for migrant farm workers, and community-based micro-enterprise projects that provide jobs in inner cities, on Indian reservations, and in areas suffering from high unemployment.

From its beginning, the CCHD has been a source of hope for those who often seem forgotten. Some impressive victories against injustice and inequality have been achieved by encouraging people to work together on the local level. Such involvements have grown into an important component of the Church's ministry of justice, as it provides the financial and logistical resources to empower people to improve their lives through building up the local community and breaking the cycle of poverty and dependence.

Besides lobbying activities and the CCHD, there are other examples that illustrate how the Church's response to poverty and injustice has shifted in recent decades. Older approaches have been retained, but have also been mixed with newer ones. There are certainly many points of continuity with the past, such as the Church's constant concern for the well-being of the least advantaged, its call for personal conversion toward care for others, and the willingness to perform direct service to the poor in moments of crisis or dire need. But there are also striking elements of change. For example, contemporary observers now enjoy an expanded view of what is needed to foster total human development. As a result, religious people today are committed to creating a social environment as well as a physical environment that is healthy for humanity. The result is a broader sense of what efforts are appropriate for the Church to undertake in its mission of service to the Gospel and the world.

To its existing belief in the benefits of charity, then, the Church has in recent decades added a commitment to justice. Where charity tends to involve individuals or small groups of people acting to meet the immediate needs of others, work for justice involves a more communal and even global awareness of problems and their potential long-term solutions. Where the notion of charity calls to mind voluntary giving out of one's surplus, the notion of justice suggests that there is an absolute obligation to share the benefits of God's creation more broadly than is witnessed in the present order.

Because justice makes demands upon all people to practice social responsibility, it is impossible to ignore its call to work through large institutions, including government, to change the structures that perpetuate poverty and keep the least powerful members of society from achieving their human potential. That the Church has begun to reflect on the underlying structures that breed injustice, to speak of the demands of justice, and to advocate changes on the local, national, and international levels is indeed a great advancement. The Church's commitment to structural change is a relatively new face of her awareness of her social mission.

This does not mean that the Church has somehow abandoned the way of charity or hands-on, neighbor-to-neighbor assistance; by no means has the Church announced that love comes up short. Rather, church leaders, documents, and agencies have discovered a unity between love and justice, two virtues that complement one another in remarkable and encouraging ways. In a world that is growing ever more complex, it is becoming increasingly obvious that love travels best through well-worn routes known as social structures and institutions. Recent decades have witnessed an enhanced awareness in church circles of how the well-being of the most vulnerable depends upon the fairness of these structures and institutions. Simultaneously, the church has committed itself in recent decades to the transformation of the world, so that social progress unfolds for the benefit of all God's children. Direct works of charity and the somewhat indirect efforts for social justice each advances this agenda in its own distinct way.

As it often does, the Church is offering a both-and solution to what is often portrayed as an either-or option. In other words, there is no need to choose between justice and charity. Rather, many options emerge in seeking the best way to combine heroic acts of love with a clearheaded view of the importance of justice regularized and routinized in fair institutions that respond to the needs and dignity of all. Indeed, many of the praiseworthy activities carried out by generous people on behalf of less fortunate members of society display a combination of the charity and justice orientations. Financial donations, acts of political advocacy, volunteer work in educational endeavors, involvement in outreach programs, and direct assistance to the poor—all exist on a wonderful continuum that stretches between charity and justice efforts.

Interestingly, the great civil rights leader Martin Luther King, Jr., coming from his own background as a Baptist clergyman, echoed these same insights in the course of his impressive ministry. Without any explicit reference to Catholic thought or practice, he often exhorted his listeners to combine traditional charitable activities with the commitment to empowerment ("a hand up rather than a handout") that so characterizes the justice orientation. On one occasion he challenged his audience with these words: "True compassion is more than flinging a coin to a beggar; it understands that an edifice which produces beggars needs restructuring."

Through such bold pronouncements, the civil rights leader gives more eloquent expression of an orientation to justice than has probably ever appeared in any document of the Catholic Church.

Perhaps the most vivid and dramatic instance of Dr. King's appeal to these themes came in his very last sermon, delivered in Memphis on the night before he was assassinated in April 1968. In that famous talk, sometimes called the "I've Seen the Promised Land" sermon, King invokes the familiar parable of the good Samaritan in the tenth chapter of the Gospel of Luke. Recall that the protagonist in this story told by Jesus falls among robbers as he makes his way along the road from Jerusalem to Jericho. Dr. King, who had visited Jerusalem and trod that same road, details for his audience how dangerous that path can be. Because of distinctive geographical features of that particular corner of the Holy Land, it has for centuries been, as King described it, a "wandering, meandering road. It's really conducive for ambushing." While holding back no due measure of praise for the generous good Samaritan who treated the wounded victim of the crime, Dr. King nevertheless appealed for a deeper analysis of what had gone wrong and a more complete response to the situation. Memorably, he quips that the superior response would be "to organize a Jericho Road Improvement Association" to prevent further victimization.

This insight of King's, namely "that it is better to deal with the problem from the causal root," is a crucial underpinning of the justice orientation. While a charitable response to a victim's suffering is always appropriate and welcome, in the long run the only fully adequate response is to strive for structural improvements to prevent future harms. This same point was frequently underlined by Saint Alberto Hurtado, a Chilean Jesuit of the early twentieth century who was known for his extraordinary work among the very poorest people in his country. His most famous saying is usually translated, "Injustice causes many more wounds than charity alone can heal." Whether we learn it from Dr. King or Saint Alberto or both, the lesson remains apt. The band-aids we apply to victims of injustices are more effective when they are accompanied by efforts at corrective surgery to address root causes of problems. Great progress comes when people of good will commit themselves to addressing the deeper structures that cause social ills, beyond whatever commendable efforts they make in charitable activities that respond to the most immediate human needs.

It would, of course, be wise to avoid an exaggerated sense of the importance of any particular human efforts for justice. No matter how well the Church fulfills her mission to justice, the imperfect conditions of this sinful world will always leave us falling short of the righteous order of God's kingdom. No amount of effort on the part of humans will ever transform social conditions into a utopia or paradise. The ultimate basis for human hope is always bound up with God and can never rest solely on human efforts. At the same time, however, it would be unwise to over-look the importance of continued fidelity to the Church's mission to do justice. As the 1971 Synod of Catholic Bishops in Rome boldly declared in its major document *Justitia in mundo* (Justice in the World):

> Action on behalf of justice and participation in the transformation of the world fully appear to us as a constitutive dimension of the preaching of the Gospel, or, in other words, of the Christian mission for the redemption of the human race and its liberation from every oppressive situation. (no. 6)

LOOKING AHEAD

This chapter has offered an initial description of the importance of Catholic social teaching in the life of the Church. The remainder of this book attempts to explain what the Church says about the social, political, and economic realities of our world. Chapter two describes some major features of the dialogue between the Church and the world, between the life of faith and the public life of a secular community such as a nation. Chapter three investigates the history of Catholic social teaching and ex-plores some of the historical forces that shaped its development. Chapter four describes the sources and methods of Catholic social thought, pre-senting a simple picture of where it derives its principles and how it makes its judgments about the contemporary world. Chapter five exam-ines in greater detail the content and central themes of this message that the Church brings to the world. Chapter six brings Catholic social teach-ing into dialogue with other common schools of thought that serve as its rivals and critics. Finally, chapter seven concludes this study by speculat-ing about future directions and priorities that are just beginning to emerge in Catholic social teaching.

QUESTIONS FOR REFLECTION

1. Do you know anyone who participates in philanthropic activities without any underlying religious motivations? How would you characterize his or her motivations?
2. Which parts of the Bible, or which figures in Christian history, seem to inspire the Church in its mission to justice? How would your an-swer be different if that question ended with the phrase "its mission to charity"?

3. What factors contribute to the low profile of Catholic social teaching? Would the Church be much different if it were not "our best-kept secret"?
4. Have you ever experienced (firsthand or through reports) any projects that were ecumenical or interreligious in nature? If so, what are the major obstacles to such cooperation? Does this experience leave you mostly optimistic or mostly pessimistic about prospects for praying and working together with people of many faiths?
5. Does the shift in church social action from a model of charity to a more thoroughgoing justice orientation make you uncomfortable in any way? What are the dangers and how can the church avoid them?

TOPICS FOR FURTHER RESEARCH

1. The American practice of volunteering in civil society—trends and comparisons
2. Social justice teachings of other faith traditions, such as in various world religions
3. The school of thought called secular humanism—its meaning and how it developed
4. The human rights movement—its relationship to religious thought
5. Justice and charity—how these two concepts are related in the thought and writings of various figures
6. Love of God and love of neighbor—how these two are related in the works of various theologians and spiritual writers as well as in Scripture
7. The process of secularization—how various institutional sectors were spun off from unitary religious establishments
8. Ecumenical and interreligious cooperation in social justice endeavors
9. Comparison of religious attitudes on the part of various generations of Christians
10. The Catholic Campaign for Human Development—its history and purposes

2

+

Going Public with Your Faith

The commonsense distinction between public and private is deeply ingrained in a majority of people. Most children learn at an early age that certain topics are suitable for public conversations and others are to be kept strictly private. It would be a matter of bad manners and a source of potentially great embarrassment, for example, to reveal to a wide audience the details of what goes on in the private recesses of a household. Although outsiders may be amused when "kids say the darnedest things," nobody denies that certain topics (such as which chemicals we use on our graying hair and which bedclothes we choose to wear or not wear) should remain off limits in public conversations.

The purpose of this chapter is to address a few of the host of questions that arise when pondering the public role of religious faith. Where should believers in the world today draw these lines? Is the subject of the life of faith something to be kept entirely private? Recall the old saying that there are two subjects that should never be broached in polite conversation: religion and politics. This chapter presents a challenge to the wisdom of that traditional adage. It suggests that a mature and socially responsible faith will not only insist that both topics be addressed, but that genuine disciples must never shy away from the controversial task of addressing religion and politics together.

BRIDGING TWO DISTINCT WORLDS

Talking about religious and political matters in the same breath makes most people a bit nervous; the great majority of people are much more comfortable segregating these two topics into separate compartments. Further, it is clear that the modern world has by and large benefited from the historical process by which religious matters have come to be differentiated from political affairs. As far back as prehistoric times, societies began to appoint religious leaders—often called priests, shamans, or holy men or women—who were distinct from their chieftain, king, queen, or village leader.

For many reasons, this division between religious and political office makes good sense; it allows both fields to benefit from the specialized knowledge of those who concentrate on one human endeavor. The skills required to lead congregations in prayer and rituals or to console the bereaved in time of mourning, for example, do not readily translate into the world of treaty negotiation, law enforcement, or public finance. Setting up clear lines of demarcation allows both religious and political leaders to fulfill appropriate roles and carve out proper spheres of legitimate authority. Only the foolish person would claim competence in all arenas, and only an imprudent society would entrust one person with the full range of both political and religious duties.

But this separation of functions is not the final word on the relationship between the spiritual and political lives of people. Just as mayors sometimes need to consult with pastors of churches in local troubled neighborhoods and just as religious prophets have traditionally sought to bend the ears of kings, dialogue between the spiritual and the temporal worlds benefits each sphere and is necessary for the well-being of both church and state. On some issues, it is easy to recognize how the concerns of secular and religious leaders overlap and converge, as the borders between the two tend to blur in day-to-day life. Matters of public policy invariably have moral dimensions in which religious leaders have a real stake. Conversely, religious organizations like churches invariably find themselves involved in activities with political implications and in which public officials have a legitimate stake. Thus, the way we organize our political lives is never completely sealed off from our deepest spiritual values and our picture of ultimate eternal truths.

The interplay of religion and politics has been a constant concern of Christianity throughout its history. In response to rather mischievous questioning along these lines, Jesus himself addressed the issue in a somewhat oblique way. Recall his claims that his kingdom is not of this world (John 18:36) but, at the same time, his followers are to "repay to Caesar what belongs to Caesar and to God what belongs to God" (Matthew 22:21; see also Luke 20:20–26). Saint Paul recommends that we adopt a stance of obedience to civil authorities (Romans 13:1–7), but elsewhere in the New Testament (for instance, Revelation 13:1–10), government is portrayed as demonic in nature—at the very least not to be trusted and perhaps even to be resisted with all one's might.

The early centuries of Christianity found the members of Christian communities attempting to live within a Roman Empire they at once admired and feared. Government certainly had the power to persecute them in the most violent ways, and it certainly did so, albeit on a sporadic basis. Yet the early Christians were also aware that government could be a force for immense good in the world. After the conversion of Emperor Constantine early in the fourth century and the eventual establishment of Christianity as the official religion of the empire, for example, popes, bishops, priests, and lay Christians forged a rather cozy (some claim, too cozy) relationship with government officials, even to the point of using the structures of the Roman Empire to spread Christian belief to new corners of the world. Even today, a lively debate continues to rage over the relative merits of the Constantinian style of Christendom. While few observers would advocate a return to the crass "throne and altar" arrangements of medieval Europe, there is still considerable support in many countries for religion to retain certain privileges and to maintain some official status, either in the form of "established churches" or in other versions of favorable legal recognition. On the other side of the spectrum are voices calling for the public life of modern nations to be stripped of practically all religious influence, so that in the interest of state neutrality the government would enforce a "naked public square" free of undue privileges for any and all religious groups.

TERTULLIAN'S QUESTION

Amidst some years of uneasy relations between the early Church and the Roman Empire, a North African Christian named Tertullian asked a simple but provocative question: "What has Jerusalem to say to Athens?" His inquiry was metaphorical, not geographical in nature. The Greek city of Athens represented all the treasures of secular culture, including the great traditions of learning and the arts that came from pagan figures such as Homer, Sophocles, Plato, and Aristotle. Jerusalem, capital of the Holy Land, sacred to the Jewish tradition, the city whose streets Jesus had trod, stood for the heritage of biblical faith and religious piety. At the start of the third century, Tertullian's reflections raised questions still relevant and controversial today: How can and should Christians hold together in creative tension their citizenship and their discipleship? How can someone simultaneously participate in the life of the Church and remain a participant in a secular culture that resists and even rejects the demands of faith?

Tertullian's question opens up a rich and complex debate about the relationship between faith and culture, between church and world, between the demands of religious affiliation and those of full participation in political life. It has prompted Christians across many centuries to take an inventory of their deepest loyalties as citizens and as believers. Do we identify more with our secular culture or with our religious commitments? To what extent is it necessary to make a choice between these two aspects of our lives?

When people consider Tertullian's question and survey their own reactions, two patterns of response tend to emerge. On one hand, there are those who emphasize the possibilities for harmonious fusion between faith and culture, between the Gospel and the world as we know it. Call this the both-and option. A person of sincere Christian faith, it seems to these people, can function quite well in the public world, marked as it is by pluralism and a great variety of value systems. Religious people can blend right in with others without undue tension or discomfort. In public life, there is no reason why believers cannot readily make common cause with non-Christians, for the relevant values are in the end not all that different. Dialogue and mutual understanding between Gospel and culture, between the church and the secular state, are possible and indeed promising endeavors.

The other set of potential answers to Tertullian's question belongs to those people who judge modern culture in an entirely different light. They hold the either-or type of opinion and are much more pessimistic about the prospects for successfully balancing Christian identity with membership in secular society. They emphasize the inevitability of deep, even radical conflict between the two. This stance is sometimes referred to as the "sectarian option" and includes hostility on the part of some people of faith to nonreligious sources of wisdom, extending to a distrust of science, academic philosophy, and the school of social thought called secular humanism.

While great care must be exercised not to exaggerate or caricature this approach to social life, the sectarian option is most evident in the lifestyles of entire communities that attempt to live apart from modern influences. One familiar example is found in the Amish people of Southeastern Pennsylvania. The Pennsylvania Dutch, as they are sometimes (quite inaccurately) called, deliberately shun a majority of modern conveniences and technological advances that most people take for granted. They do not make these choices out of an idle romantic nostalgia for the past but as a matter of principle, based on the same beliefs that lead them to avoid as much contact as possible with government, the court system, and the military. Other adherents of sectarianism are prompted by their beliefs to withdraw from the wider society in smaller, less noticeable ways. For example, they may choose to educate their children privately or to boycott elections or print and electronic media because they judge the cultural mainstream to be somehow antithetical to their personal religious values. Very often these points of highly principled behavior reflect biblically grounded obligations, such as refusing to cooperate with any use of violence or coercive force and refraining from swearing oaths to anyone but God.

Most Catholics today have considerable difficulty imagining a life of withdrawal from the social mainstream as practiced by followers of the sectarian option. The dominant approach within the Catholic Church features an ethic not of separatism but of *social engagement*—a willingness to become deeply involved in society despite an awareness of the flaws and injustices of the present social order. If social institutions are found to be corrupt, then the proper response is to take on some responsibility for transforming structures and procedures to make them measure up to reasonable standards. If there is something disturbing about the dominant culture of an age, Catholics usually do not ask how quickly they can find an exit route to flee the disaster, but rather, how they can contribute to reforming the objectionable features and practices of society so that it better reflects their religiously grounded values.

According to this ethic of social engagement, the two most extreme answers to Tertullian's question ("nothing" and "everything") are both misguided and potentially dangerous. To claim that Jerusalem has *nothing* to say to Athens would amount to giving up the struggle before it begins. It would be irresponsible to deprive society of the contribution of religiously motivated persons whose ideas and energies are the potential basis for much needed activism and social movements for great improvement. To take just a few examples from U.S. history, where would American society be if religious groups had not agitated for an end to slavery (in the Abolition movement), to extreme militarism (the peace movement), to racial injustice (the Civil Rights movement), and to extreme poverty (the fight against hunger, homelessness, and illiteracy)?

Each of these movements witnessed the formation of an effective coalition for social change, and religious groups were key partners in all these coalitions. On some occasions, religious leaders even played a dominant role, but they were always willing to make common cause with people motivated by secular reasons for the transformation of society toward greater justice and compassion. Sometimes the rhetoric of the resulting coalition borrowed religious language to advance the cause; words like "covenant" and phrases like "good Samaritan" and "my brother's keeper" become rallying points even for atheists working for change. Examples from other cultures and ages would confirm the conclusion that Jerusalem clearly has something of great significance to offer Athens.

Just as it would be inaccurate to claim that Jerusalem has nothing to offer Athens, it would also be unwise to suggest that Jerusalem has *everything*

to say to Athens. In other words, it would be misguided and even dangerous to claim that religious messages should dictate the terms of public policy or social institutions in a complex, pluralistic society. Even those who
look favorably upon the way religious traditions inspire greater morality
and justice in society wisely recognize the limits of religious influence on
the workings of politics. To forget this insight is to risk sliding into a situation of crass theocracy—literally the "rule of religion," where public policy
proceeds at the beck and call of religious leaders. Even assuming that a
given society could agree on the matter of precisely which religious leaders
speak with the necessary authority to determine social priorities and strategies, there are numerous weighty reasons to avoid this outcome.

Already noted above is the way this failure to distinguish between religious and political functions deprives society of the benefits of special-
ization in distinct spheres of activity. The next section examines a second
objection to an exaggerated public role for Jerusalem: the way a theocratic
approach misapplies religious zeal and idealism to the political world of
realism and compromise.

THE PERILS OF THE CRUSADING SPIRIT

Religion evokes the deepest aspirations of the human spirit for meaning
and proper order in the universe. In the contexts of both personal life and
the affairs of the wider society, religious zeal possesses remarkable power
to inspire people to make great sacrifices and undertake heroic efforts to
achieve laudable goals. Reading stories of the lives of the saints, for example, serves as a reminder of some of the commendable achievements
that have been inspired by faith commitments. On this micro level of individual lives and face-to-face relations, it is easy to reach the conclusion
that immense good has been done in the name of faith.

History books, on the other hand, give us a more balanced account of
the positive and negative influence of religious motivations on the larger,
macro level of society, especially on political affairs. In a world threatened
by terrorism, it is of course hard to forget the power of religious extrem-
ism to feed violence and hatred in the present moment. But it is somewhat
startling to realize how practically every age of human history has witnessed destructive and violent behavior justified by religious reasons.
Throughout history, people of many faiths have used the name of God to
promote and justify their self-serving goals—political agendas, commercial gain, or military conquest. While some of these abuses stemmed from
cynical opportunism on the part of religious or political officeholders, others may be attributed to leaders who were quite sincere in their expres-

sion of religious motivations but applied religious ideas in inappropriate ways to advance misguided political agendas.

Perhaps the most stunning examples of religious commitment gone awry are the Crusades. Literally, the word *crusade* refers to "an effort that unfolds under the shadow and protection of the cross" (the Latin word for cross is *crux*, the root word of crusade). The word has taken on the connotation of any militant struggle undertaken for reasons of religion or deeply held ideological beliefs. In the late medieval world, popes and bishops of Western Christianity preached fervent sermons in an attempt to inspire knights, peasants, and even children to take up arms, make mass pilgrimages to the Holy Land or other regions on the edge of Christendom, and defeat nonbelievers in combat that was supposedly divinely sanctioned. Muslims and Jews were demonized as infidels against whom any means of warfare was justified. The authority of God's will, as interpreted by officeholders in the Christian church, was invoked as the wellspring of these repeated efforts to claim sacred places for Christ at the point of a sword.

Other episodes in Christian history display the same logic of limitless violence in service to a divinely sanctioned cause. Most notable among them is the Inquisition, a centuries-long effort to uphold orthodox belief by subjecting suspected heretics to investigation, imprisonment, and even torture to defend the purity of the faith. Without a doubt, the Inquisition represents one of the darkest chapters in the history of the Catholic Church.

Lest anyone think this perversion of religious motivation is limited to Christianity, however, it is instructive to note how the peculiar notion of "holy war" has been applied throughout history by numerous religious groups, from the Muslim *jihad* to extreme forms of Jewish Zionism and Hindu separatism in the Indian subcontinent. The only things these groups have in common are a zealous devotion to a particular notion of divine will and enough power to exert their geopolitical will through force of arms. The core contents of authentic faith that are (with rare exceptions) oriented toward peace, love, and respect for others come to be twisted by temptations toward greed, hatred, and distrust of the alien—motives that unleash unspeakable outbursts of violence and terrorism against innocent persons caught in the crossfire. Americans were reminded of this horrible dynamic by the terrorist attacks of September 11, 2001. These unspeakable atrocities were perpetuated by a terrorist organization (Al Qaeda) that cited selected principles of the religion of Islam to justify its extremist agenda of hatred. The damage done is multiplied in instances when these misguided religious energies capture the apparatus of government and apply the coercive power of a state for inappropriate ends.

Two instructive episodes in the history of the United States also reflect this dynamic of the misapplication of religious zeal to politics, but on a more limited scale than the medieval Crusades. The first is the growth of the concept of Manifest Destiny, the notion that our nation somehow received a divine mission to spread its territorial control and distinctive way of life from the Atlantic to the Pacific, to become a continental power under the approving eyes of God. On the surface, this patriotic idea seems acceptable enough until one thinks back to the geographical realities of the early decades of the new nation, when this ideology was beginning to blossom. The extreme version of Manifest Destiny ignored one key inconvenient fact: the land over which the fledgling nation seemed destined to expand was by no means vacant territory. The area that now comprises the western United States was populated by Native Americans and residents of Mexico, and both groups had prior claim to the millions of square acres of land our American forebears so coveted.

Although Manifest Destiny was not a formal theological doctrine of any specific Christian denomination, this religiously based ideology helped provoke the Mexican War of 1846 to 1848 and the numerous violent campaigns that nearly exterminated the tribal peoples usually referred to as American Indians. Although historians differ in interpreting the significance and degree of culpability for some of these developments, these sad episodes demonstrate that American Christians are by no means immune from the logic of the crusade. The doctrine of Manifest Destiny that justified U.S. land grabs to expand this nation was a product of religious zeal that entered the world of politics only to leave destructive and regrettable effects in its wake.

A second example from American history involves much less violence, but it does round out the picture of the problems inherent in bringing a crusading religious spirit into large-scale politics. Near the top of the agenda of many religious leaders in the United States about a century ago was the campaign to outlaw the production and consumption of alcoholic beverages. Starting in the nineteenth century, religious forces, especially in conservative Protestant denominations, teamed up with others to form effective coalitions such as the Anti-Saloon League and the Women's Christian Temperance Union. These coalitions, first on the state level and subsequently nationally, won impressive legal victories to restrict the availability and use of liquor.

To support the cause of temperance, a range of arguments, both theological and practical in nature, were spelled out: the evil effects of intoxication on family life and public morals; the unconscionable waste of valuable grain, time, and money on the production of alcohol, at drinking establishments, and in pursuit of associated vices; the corruption of wanton escapism and alcoholic excess prohibited by several verses of the

Bible. Congress eventually passed, and in 1919 the states ratified, the Eighteenth Amendment to the U.S. Constitution outlawing the "manufacture, sale, or transportation of intoxicating liquors" throughout the United States. However, fourteen years later, in 1933, the Twenty-first Amendment reversed the earlier attempt to enshrine in our nation's laws the religious and moral objections to drinking.

What went wrong with Prohibition? On one level, we find this simple technical answer: criminalizing alcohol produces no deterrent effect on actual levels of drinking, but merely fosters greater control on the part of organized crime over this and other vices. The law also suffered from selective enforcement, as legal authorities charged with implementing the ban often looked the other way out of disinterest or because they were bribed into doing so. Ultimately, what made Prohibition unworkable was its faulty underlying assumption that it is possible to legislate morality regarding particular behaviors that much of the population considers acceptable. Most people considered drinking to excess a sin but not necessarily a crime. In the absence of a firm consensus that any drinking at all (not merely imbibing to the point of intoxication) should be criminalized, civil law turned out to be too blunt an instrument to enlist in this battle against immorality. Paradoxically, the temperance crusade was perhaps the most intemperate social movement in U.S. history. Its insistence that we should all be teetotalers turned out to be an unrealistic expectation when it confronted the actual realities of law enforcement and public opinion.

The lessons to appropriate from the brief experiment with Prohibition are clear. Beware of the religiously inspired crusading spirit, for it often trails in its wake a temptation to forget some important commonsense considerations. No matter how persuasive and desirable a given cause for social improvement might appear, it is still necessary to consider all the relevant political realities, including the likely consequences of making sweeping changes in public policy. Even if religious or humanitarian arguments seem convincing that the world would be a better place if a given vice or pattern of human behavior were eliminated, it is still wise to retain a healthy skepticism about employing the force of law for social engineering of any stripe, no matter how sincerely motivated.

RELIGIOUS IDEALISM: ITS CONTRIBUTION TO POLITICS

As history amply chronicles, the world of politics is an arena dominated by the necessity of compromise and mutual adjustment to opposing voices. Even when a given party or movement can muster a majority, it is important to consider the opinions of the minority and to consult broadly before acting through the political process. A crusading spirit often short-circuits the prudence necessary for wise governance. Such cautionary observations might raise doubts that this leaves any room at all for religious contributions to public policy debates. This section argues for the continued relevance, indeed the indispensable importance, of such religious contributions. Religion offers one thing the political process requires but can find in no other place: ideals.

It is no embarrassment to say that religion offers politics the perspective of a utopia, a place that does not actually exist but nevertheless provides us with standards for judging the political order that does exist. Under the influence of theological principles and the religious imagination, people of faith have consistently supplied ordinary politics with indispensable portrayals of ideal order, virtue, and pure motivation that have served the common good in many cultures and contexts. Religion lends these ideals to the political order in various ways. Religious institutions (churches, mosques, synagogues, faith-based nonprofit organizations, and others) witness to ideals by living out values such as love and compassion, thereby setting an example for others. Religious leaders and intellectuals share ideals by knowing and exposing sources of social wisdom contained in their traditions of reflection upon life in society. This is precisely the purpose of contemporary Catholic social teaching in all it says about peace, justice, and social cooperation for the common good.

The one thing that remains out of bounds for religious leaders as they aspire to share the utopian ideals of their visions of proper social ordering is any direct attempt to control the social order by actually wielding political power. Holding political office or overseeing the actual making of laws in the name of one's religion is usually understood to be overstepping the proper boundaries between faith and politics. To use the language introduced by Tertullian once again, Jerusalem has a legitimate role in advising Athens but should not rob Athens of its proper authority. Excessive entanglement in the political process on the part of religious leaders would be as inappropriate as a coach or team chaplain jumping off the bench and running onto the playing field, encroaching on territory where such figures do not belong during the game.

To state this insight another way, there is a legitimate autonomy of the secular realm that must be respected if religious leaders are to remain true to their calling and mindful of their precise mission. Recognizing and articulating this truth was among the most significant contributions of the Second Vatican Council (or Vatican II) to the Catholic understanding of the role of politics in our complex, pluralistic world. Vatican II was a worldwide gathering of thousands of church leaders (primarily bishops) who met in Rome in several sessions from 1962 until 1965. One of the final documents it approved is titled "Pastoral Constitution on the Church in the Modern World," often known by the first three words of its Latin version, *Gaudium et Spes*. In paragraph 36 of this document, the Council Fathers affirm that there is a "rightful independence of earthly affairs" which the Church must respect. In recognizing the limits to direct church control of these areas, Vatican II echoes the exhortation of Jesus to render unto Caesar the things that belong to Caesar.

This insight applies to the realms of science, the arts, and all fields of secular learning, as well as politics. The proper division of labor affects the overall relationship between clergy and laity as well as between church and state. As that same Vatican II document states in paragraph 43:

> Let the lay[persons] not imagine that [their] pastors are always such experts, that to every problem that arises, however complicated, they can readily give [them] a concrete solution, or even that such is their mission.

This part of the message of the Second Vatican Council is a restatement of lessons that many cultures and thinkers have discovered at various points in history. Indeed, Catholic authorities appear to have been relative latecomers to this precept of prudence. Religious values in general, and the moral teachings of the Church in particular, are to serve as important guides to the political activities of lay Christians and others, but ultimately the political world operates in ways that are independent of religious authority.

MAINTAINING A DELICATE BALANCE

In noting the distinctions between the world of faith and the arena of politics, the paragraphs immediately above may give the impression of favoring the sectarian position, the either-or option where faith and culture are radically at odds and the best response for people of sincere faith is to live apart from secular society. Upon closer inspection, however, that is not at all the message of Catholic social teaching, even in those moments when it takes pains to acknowledge the necessity of some degree of separation between faith and secular culture. Nowhere in the Church's teaching on social issues is there any support for a sectarian option. Neither papal encyclicals nor statements of bishops offer encouragement to those who, like the Amish, decide to insulate themselves from the modern world for the purpose of preserving their own personal purity from the threat of secular infection.

The contemporary Church has consistently called upon Catholics to practice social responsibility by involving themselves in the messy world of politics and modern culture. Many of the documents of recent Catholic social teaching amount to calls to action featuring eloquent exhortations urging the faithful to launch and sustain serious efforts to improve today's world. In fact, Church leaders and documents on many occasions have singled out *apathy* as the most pressing enemy of proper social engagement. This word refers to the perennial human hesitation to get sufficiently involved in worldly affairs, a temptation to stay on the sidelines and to set aspirations for social improvement too low.

When the Church does, on occasion, sound warnings about inappropriate involvements in politics, as it has on such issues as the status of liberation theology, it is merely attempting to navigate the tricky waters of defining its overall mission in a proper and balanced way. While the struggle for social justice will remain an indispensable part of the Church's work for as long as humans inhabit a world marked by sin, the mission of the Church can never be reduced to this one aspect. The essential task entrusted to the Church is to evangelize—to preach the Word of God and to proclaim God's Kingdom to a world in need of hope. There will always be a delicate balance between the two places where this hope is found: the hope that lies in human history; and the hope that lies in the Kingdom of God.

These two locations of hope must be kept in sharp focus, for there is no substitute for either one. If all human hope is located one-sidedly in God's Kingdom, then the focus becomes excessively otherworldly, and the temptation to cease caring about social issues rears its ugly head. In the very process of recognizing the truth that ultimate human purposes and the fullness of justice will always exceed the grasp of any human society, placing all human hope in the next world may lead to a needless abandonment of hope for progress in the present order. Going too far down this road runs the risk of spiritualizing away the real-life issues of grinding material poverty and injustice that threaten the lives of millions who remain in need of new opportunities and even liberation. But, conversely, if all human hope is reduced to a this-worldly reality centered exclusively on human history, there is the danger of losing proper perspective on the ultimate meaning of earthly existence and forgetting the eternal life of grace that is humankind's supernatural destiny. Theologians refer to this necessary reminder as the imperative of retaining an "eschatological reservation" regarding worldly affairs. Remembering that humans are citizens of heaven before they are citizens of any earthly society is an indispensable task of Christian identity. This awareness has the beneficial effect of relativizing all secular loyalties and placing into clear perspective all human endeavors, including all efforts at social improvement.

Since the very dawn of Christianity, theologians have addressed with great care the complex relationship between human history and God's Kingdom. Today, we join those who have gone before us in asking questions such as these: Is the Kingdom already somehow present among us, as Jesus proclaimed? If so, can our efforts do anything to bring the Kingdom closer, or does such talk somehow amount to blasphemy or idolatry? Does our work for social justice have any bearing on the unfolding of salvation history, the process of human redemption and ultimate reconciliation with God?

Many approaches to these mysteries have been proposed, but the best responses are those in which the dual nature of the human person remains always prominent. Each human person is simultaneously a body and a soul; the material and spiritual aspects of every individual are inseparable and are united in a mysterious and holy way. Accordingly, human beings can never be reduced to mere bodies, nor can they be adequately understood as disembodied souls. Any responsible theology must consider, with the utmost seriousness, both aspects of our reality. To truly respect people is to demonstrate concern for their earthly well-being as well as their heavenly destiny. Care must be exercised to avoid straying into either extreme: the exclusively this-worldly approach or the exclusively otherworldly approach. Responsible evangelization will always display these two faces, balancing them carefully so that neither human dimension is denigrated. Church activity must always include social action to make life on earth more humane, but it must never become so politicized that we lose sight of our transcendent purpose.

TOGETHER ON PILGRIMAGE

The history of Christianity is full of attempts to address the proper balance between these extremes. Some of these attempts turned out to be false starts or dead ends—theologies that distorted the proper relationship between the material and the spiritual realms and often ended up being recognized as heretical once their shortcomings were exposed. Perhaps the most helpful approach to this bundle of mysteries is summarized in a simple metaphor that has at once consoled and challenged millions of Christians over the centuries: the metaphor of *pilgrimage*. By recognizing themselves as a "pilgrim people," members of the Christian community have developed a useful vocabulary for speaking about the significance of the present world as well as the Kingdom of God—the ultimate destination recognized by believers. The importance of each world is neither exaggerated nor neglected, for pilgrims are concerned about both the end point of their journey and actual conditions along the way.

Like all travelers, pilgrims experience a dual identity. They feel deeply connected to the road they walk even as they feel in their hearts that they belong to the holy place they approach. The twin memberships may cause considerable tension but, at its best, this is a creative tension, one that continually allows pilgrims to experience a true unity of intention and purpose. The light that reaches their eyes from the heavens does not distract them from their earthly journey but, rather, illumines the path they walk toward their destination. With faith in God and goodwill in their hearts, Christian pilgrims have discovered within themselves the energy and motivation to give their full attention to the deliberate action of walking along the way of life. They nurture the hope that, by working together to improve the present age, the ultimate justice of God's Kingdom will be reflected a bit more clearly through the achievement of greater social justice in the world we share.

The wonders of this simple metaphor explain why it has played so prominent a role in Christian reflection on the meaning of earthly existence in many ages. It guided St. Augustine in writing his long work *The City of God*, his fifth-century attempt to explain the significance of Christian faith in the context of the late Roman Empire. The same metaphor was employed by St. Thomas Aquinas and Martin Luther in their distinctive approaches to the challenges of living an authentic Christian life in their own centuries. It also guided the Second Vatican Council as it grappled with the realities of a rapidly changing global society that was developing an uneasy relationship to Christian faith.

This metaphor of pilgrimage forms a helpful backdrop for serious reflection about the social mission of the Church in this new millennium as well. It makes it possible to view the world of politics and secular culture in a new light—not as hostile territory to be conquered or shunned, but rather as a privileged place along the way, perhaps even as a place where people may encounter the God of all longing in the multiple environments of daily life.

QUESTIONS FOR REFLECTION

1. Have you ever felt tension between being a citizen and being a disciple? On what occasions and around what issues did these tensions arise?
2. Do you know anyone whose life is lived, in part or in full, according to the sectarian option? Have you ever had a conversation with others about the difficulty of reconciling modern secular culture with your life of faith? How might such a conversation go?

3. Can you think of additional examples from history when religion played an excessive or exaggerated public role? Were the lessons available from these episodes at all different from the examples (the Crusades, Manifest Destiny, Prohibition) discussed in this chapter?
4. Do you agree that it is important to have a vision of utopia? Why or why not? How does possessing a picture of an ideal order assist someone in participating in the politics of everyday life?
5. Which temptation are you more apt to fall into: an excess of this-worldly aspirations or of otherworldly spirituality? Do you find the Catholic Church's statements leaning too far to either side of this spectrum for your comfort?

TOPICS FOR FURTHER RESEARCH

1. The proper differentiation between religious and political spheres of authority
2. The interpretation of various biblical passages relating church and state authority
3. The history and legacy of the social and political movements mentioned in this chapter (for temperance, peace, abolitionism, civil rights)
4. The sectarian impulse and the philosophy of various sectarian groups
5. The debate over the merits and dangers of Constantinianism and of theocracy
6. The Crusades—their history and rationale
7. Christian and secular works on the theme of utopia (such as the work of Saint Thomas More or the nineteenth-century Utopian Socialists such as Robert Owen, Saint-Simon, and Charles Fourier)
8. Vatican II and its treatment of the role of the laity, the autonomy of the secular order, and the spirituality of everyday life
9. The influence of the doctrine of Manifest Destiny and U.S. civil religion today
10. Successful and unsuccessful attempts to relate human history and God's Kingdom

3

✝

Inheriting the Tradition of Catholic Social Teaching

The previous two chapters explored some of the pressing questions that arise when religious people reflect on the implications of their faith for the way they live in modern society. Left on their own to tackle these questions, individual Christians would have nearly a full-time job discerning the "signs of the times," trying to interpret contemporary events in the light of the Gospel, and attempting to balance all the conflicting messages. This could lead to ceaseless concerns about a number of rather difficult questions: On which key problems of the day should I make a special effort to stay informed? Am I placing too much hope in history, or perhaps not enough, in my approach to social issues? What balance should I, as a disciple and as a citizen, strike between charity and justice on any given issue? Am I guilty of an excessively crusading spirit, or am I perhaps becoming too apathetic about contributing to public dialogue and action to combat injustices? Might my habitual approach to public affairs result in (to use the vocabulary of Tertullian once again) Jerusalem speaking too much, or perhaps too little, to Athens?

This chapter comes as good news for those who might feel weighed down by the burden of grappling with such questions. The message of this chapter is that much of the homework and legwork have already been done on our behalf. Over the past century or so, the Catholic Church has developed a body of social teachings that contains immense wisdom. In a dozen major documents, popes, bishops, and other church leaders share valuable reflections on the intersection between faith and politics. As the following chapters demonstrate, this does not mean that all potential questions and issues are resolved in advance. Catholic social teaching retains a creative open-endedness in both its articulation of principles for social living and in the way those basic principles are applied. While there is much of substance in the content of Catholic social thought, this body of teachings exhibits great sensitivity to the shades of gray in our complex world and to the ways that even universal principles require careful and sensitive application to specific circumstances in various places. It is encouraging to discover how, on the national, regional, and worldwide levels, the Catholic Church is seriously committed to providing leadership and assistance to all believers who seek to develop an authentic faith-based response to changing political, social, and economic conditions.

THE DOCUMENTARY HERITAGE

Table 3.1 contains a list of twelve documents of the universal Catholic Church, texts that first appeared between 1891 and 1991. Ten of these documents were published by various popes who served since the end of the nineteenth century. Most documents in this category are referred to as *encyclicals*, substantial writings (often fifty pages or more) that are presented in the form of letters and are intended to circulate widely among members of the Church. Popes have been writing encyclicals since 1740, when Pope Benedict XIV began to write pastoral letters to issue instructions on church-world relations. Recent popes have published dozens of encyclicals on many topics (Pope John Paul II, for example, wrote fourteen of them), but the list in table 3.1 contains only the ones considered to be *social encyclicals*. While almost any writing signed by a pope has some social implications, these particular encyclicals are primarily concerned with the challenges of political and economic life in the contemporary world.

For the sake of convenience, table 3.1 lists the Latin title of each document and its usual English translation, followed by its year of publication and the name of the pope responsible for it. Encyclicals are usually divided into sections or chapters, and citations from them usually mention the standard paragraph numbers that appear in the original Latin text of each document.

Table 3.1 attempts to situate each document in its historical context by summarizing the key social challenges facing the Church and the world at that moment. Finally, table 3.1 summarizes how each document responded to that challenge by listing the most memorable new message or idea contained in that document. These last two columns, of course, are subject to diverse interpretations, as various readers of each document may well come away with different impressions of the key issues treated and the contributions offered in each instance.

TABLE 3.1. MAJOR DOCUMENTS OF MODERN CATHOLIC SOCIAL TEACHING

Categories correspond to the six lines of each of the twelve entries below:

Latin title
English title
Year of publication
Source
Major challenges it addressed
Major new messages or ideas

Rerum Novarum
The Condition of Labor
1891
Pope Leo XIII
Industrialization, urbanization, poverty
"Family Wage," workers' rights

Quadragesimo Anno
After Forty Years, or The Reconstruction of the Social Order
1931
Pope Pius XI
Great Depression, communism, and fascist dictatorships
Subsidiarity as a guide to government interventions

Mater et Magistra
Christianity and Social Progress
1961
Pope John XXIII
Technological advances
Global justice between rich and poor nations

Pacem in Terris
Peace on Earth
1963
Pope John XXIII
Arms race, the threat of nuclear war
A philosophy of human rights and social responsibilities

Gaudium et Spes
Pastoral Constitution on the Church in the Modern World
1965
Second Vatican Council
Younger generations questioning traditional values
Church must scrutinize external "signs of the times"

(continued)

TABLE 3.1. (*continued*)

Populorum Progressio
The Development of Peoples
1967
Pope Paul VI
Widening gap between rich and poor nations
"Development is a new word for peace."

Octogesima Adveniens
A Call to Action on the 80th Anniversary of Rerum Novarum
1971
Pope Paul VI
Urbanization marginalizing vast multitudes
Lay Catholics must focus on political action to combat injustices.

Justitia in Mundo
Justice in the World
1971
Synod of Bishops
Structural injustices and oppression inspire liberation movements
"Justice . . . is a constitutive dimension of the preaching of the Gospel."

Evangelii Nuntiandi
Evangelization in the Modern World
1975
Pope Paul VI
Cultural problems of atheism, secularism, consumerism
The salvation promised by Jesus offers liberation from all oppression.

Laborem Exercens
On Human Work
1981
Pope John Paul II
Capitalism and communism treat workers as mere instruments of production.
Work is the key to "the social question" and to human dignity.

Sollicitudo Rei Socialis
On Social Concern
1987
Pope John Paul II
Persistent underdevelopment, division of world into blocs
"Structures of sin" are responsible for global injustices.

Centesimus Annus
On the Hundredth Anniversary of Rerum Novarum
1991
Pope John Paul II
Collapse of communism in Eastern Europe
Combat consumeristic greed in new "knowledge economy."

Note that table 3.1 includes two social teaching documents that do not come exclusively from popes. One of them is *Gaudium et Spes*. As we noted in chapter two, this long and wide-ranging document of social teaching was approved in 1965 by the Second Vatican Council, a worldwide church gathering that included cardinals, bishops, and other church officials, along with Pope Paul VI, who presided over the final sessions of the council. Also appearing in table 3.1 is *Justitia in Mundo* ("Justice in the World"), a document from the worldwide Synod of Bishops convened in Rome in 1971. As its title indicates, this document (incidentally, by far the shortest one on this list) deals with the theme of global social justice and certainly belongs among the key social teaching documents. The full texts of all twelve documents (and many other social teaching resources, in English and several other languages as well) are easily available at the website of the Holy See (www.vatican.va). Most people find the Vatican website surprisingly easy to navigate and to search; it really is quite user friendly overall, even for people with limited knowledge of Latin. Further information on locating these texts in print and electronic formats appears in the Annotated List of Resources for Further Study at the end of this book.

When people talk about Catholic social teaching, they are usually referring primarily to these twelve documents. (Plenty of additional encyclicals, such as Pope Benedict XVI's 2006 letter *Deus Caritas Est*, touch at least briefly upon themes of social justice, but without devoting their entirety to this message and usually without adding much to what these dozen documents affirm.) Each of the documents in table 3.1 breaks new ground by introducing original concepts and novel ways of thinking about the economic and political challenges of its day, but there is also a broader interpretation of what counts as Catholic social teaching and where it is located.

A careful observer of Vatican affairs will note the huge number of other occasions when church officials speak out on public issues. For example, whenever a pope gives a speech, sermon, or interview, whether in Rome or while traveling around the globe, there is a built-in opportunity to address social, political, and economic matters. Prominent among these occasions is the annual "Message for the World Day of Peace" presented by the sitting pope around New Year's Day. Just as they have done in formal presentations to the corps of diplomats attached to Vatican City and with addresses to various pontifical academies of scholars, recent popes often use such opportunities to comment on key social principles and their application to contemporary world affairs.

In addition, several Vatican offices, commissions, congregations, and secretariats regularly issue statements that include at least some messages with public import. Particularly influential in this regard is the Vatican Secretariat of State, which represents the Holy See at international conferences (such as at the proceedings of the United Nations and its affiliated organizations) and maintains diplomatic relations with most nations of the world. Another important player is the Pontifical Council for Justice and Peace, a distinguished group of scholars, bishops, and other church officials who are charged with numerous study, research, and writing projects, giving the Church an active presence in international circles of social concern. One recent accomplishment of the Pontifical Council was the production of the 2004 *Compendium of the Social Doctrine of the Church*. In 250 pages of text, this reference book presents a systematic survey of all the theological themes and social principles treated in the long tradition of Catholic social teaching. While the style of writing in that volume may leave something to be desired (catechism-type reference works always struggle with the issue of readability), bringing together all this material in such a compact form is a major achievement.

An additional component of the broader heritage of church social teaching comes not from the Vatican at all but from the 108 regular local gatherings of Catholic bishops in every nation or region of the world. The regular meeting of bishops from a given area is referred to as an *episcopal conference*. In most nations with a significant number of Catholics, the bishops within the nation will convene at least annually to coordinate church activities. This task includes both internal church matters, such as initiatives on new liturgical texts, improving religious education, and the training of clergy, and external social issues on which the Church is called to display its public face and to speak out on important political matters, such as peace, justice, and human rights.

The importance of the contributions of these national or regional meetings was reaffirmed during the 1960s, as a greater appreciation developed for how bishops could share their social teaching mission. That pivotal decade witnessed a sharp increase in the advocacy activities of bishops' conferences around the world, encouraged by Vatican II and several papal pronouncements on the importance of *collegiality*. In this context, the word collegiality is a technical term that describes the growing desire for cooperation among bishops on a level above that of individual dioceses, those territorial entities over which a given bishop presides. To reconfirm this impetus toward coordination and common endeavors on a regional and national basis, the necessity for collaboration among groups of bishops is mentioned often in the New Code of Canon Law, published in 1983, which stands as the most recent updating of official laws and procedures in the Catholic Church.

The bishops of the United States have been meeting in one form or another since the mid-1800s. The American bishops now number over two hundred and include ordinaries (the main bishop who oversees a given diocese) and auxiliary bishops from all fifty states as well as the District of Columbia and a few U.S. territories, such as the U.S. Virgin Islands. They typically gather twice a year, usually in Washington, DC, under the name United States Conference of Catholic Bishops, an organization mentioned in chapter one as a locus for social justice efforts. The cumbersome title is often shortened to the Bishops' Conference or simply abbreviated as USCCB. Assisted by their professional staff in Washington, the bishops divide their work among numerous committees and offices, several of which concentrate on social issues. The most prominent of these is the Office of Social Development and World Peace, which maintains an excellent webpage at http://www.usccb.org/sdwp/.

Over the past few decades, the USCCB has written and approved (usually by nearly unanimous votes) many documents on public affairs. In the context of the life of the Catholic community in the United States, these bishops' statements are rightly considered to be an important part of Catholic social teaching. A careful perusal of pastoral letters from the American bishops reveals a clear overlap with the social concerns of the universal Church centered in Rome. It is accurate to say that the agenda of the U.S. bishops on social issues is to apply the more general principles contained in Roman documents to the specific context of the United States. Most noteworthy among the major pastoral letters of the USCCB are the 1983 letter *The Challenge of Peace: God's Promise and Our Response* and the 1986 statement *Economic Justice for All: Pastoral Letter on Catholic Social Teaching and the U.S. Economy*. Although many such pastoral letters are just a few pages in length (printable in pamphlet format), these highly detailed analyses of the morality of national policies are full-length books in their own right, reflecting years of work by teams of bishops, consultants, and scholars. While the episcopal conferences of many other nations have issued their own outstanding statements on similar topics regarding peace and justice, these are the two most significant letters that have influenced public debate within and beyond the Catholic community in the United States.

These, then, are the sources of official Catholic social teaching: papal encyclicals and apostolic letters; statements of Vatican offices and commissions and worldwide church councils and synods; and pastoral letters from individual bishops, regional groupings of bishops, or entire episcopal conferences. Beyond these, some church observers call attention to several other sources of unofficial (but nonetheless fully authentic) Catholic social teaching. While only popes, bishops, and those they specifically delegate for the task of clarifying doctrine can be said to have formal teaching authority (the Latin word for this is *magisterium*) in the Church, there is a related authority readily observable in upstanding Catholics who interpret and put into practice the words of the magisterium.

Some of these exemplary figures are members of the clergy (that is, priests and deacons), while others are lay men and women. Since so few people actually read lengthy and complex social teaching documents, it naturally happens that the task of spreading the Church's social message falls to people on the local level, figures known more often for their deeds than their words. They are practitioners—people whose activities complement the efforts of theorists of Catholic social teaching. A parish priest preaches an especially passionate sermon on social justice; the lay editor of a diocesan newspaper writes an effective column about moral obligations owed to the poor; a director of religious education for a wealthy parish courageously adopts a curriculum encouraging greater sharing of resources; a deacon commits himself to visiting prisons or city hospitals more often—these are the ways in which Catholic social teaching is spread in everyday life. Theologians, parish-based community organizers, and Catholic labor union advocates also make their own distinctive contributions, often providing service and leadership that bishops and popes cannot accomplish for lack of time, expertise, and local contacts.

Of course, none of these everyday contributions replaces the need for theological reflection, scholarly work on the justice dimensions of contemporary issues, and the publication of documents at the highest levels of the Church. Yet noting the necessity for active grassroots contributions does serve as a needed reminder that there is more to doing justice than merely talking about it and writing learned documents. Surely some of the most courageous advocates of peace and justice in our day have indeed been popes and bishops with formal teaching authority. It is also true, however, that among the most recognizable voices of Catholic social teaching have been several beloved figures—Mother Teresa of Calcutta, Lech Walesa of Poland, and Dorothy Day, the founder of the Catholic Worker movement in New York, among others—who were representatives of unofficial but undoubtedly authentic church-based reflections on social justice. It is wise, then, to maintain the broadest possible interpretation of what constitutes Catholic social thought and to recognize a large number of vehicles by which this message about peace and social justice is legitimately transmitted. Particularly helpful at times is the reminder to look to the prophetic actions of the many, not just to the eloquent words of a few elite leaders. As Saint Francis of Assisi is reported to have said, "Preach the Gospel at all times—if necessary, use words."

A LOOK BACK TO THE NINETEENTH CENTURY

So far this chapter has focused on the *form* that official Catholic social teaching takes. A closer look at the actual *content* of this teaching comes in chapter five, which is dedicated to a thorough examination of its major themes. But to gain an initial appreciation of the change over time in the content of that teaching, it might be helpful to conduct a brief thought experiment. Note that the first modern social encyclical, the first item in table 3.1, was Pope Leo XIII's encyclical letter *Rerum Novarum* ("The Condition of Labor"), published in 1891. The concepts discussed by Pope Leo had developed gradually within the consciousness of church leaders over the previous fifty years or so. Because each of the subsequent documents in table 3.1 gradually brought us closer to where the Church stands today on social, political, and economic issues, it is instructive to conduct a comparison between the social message the official Catholic Church might have professed in, say, the year 1841, precisely fifty years before *Rerum Novarum*, and what we have come to expect it to say today.

Starting with the present, situated in the early years of the new millennium, consider this initial question: If you were told that the current pope has just released a new social encyclical and that a half-page summary of this new teaching letter will appear on the third page of tomorrow morning's newspaper, what would you expect to read when you picked up that paper and turned to page three? Would you not expect several mentions of phrases such as "human rights," "the equal dignity of all peoples," "social justice," and "peace and reconciliation"? Would you not expect any new encyclical to challenge people to promote dialogue and to build bridges toward others, to advance the cause of human freedom, to make sacrifices for the less fortunate, to advocate for social changes that create new opportunities for people of all nations, and to denounce the injustice of extreme inequalities in wealth and income?

These themes have indeed been among the dominant messages in the last several decades of Catholic social teaching and will surely continue to play a prominent role in the Church's social documents as the twenty-first century unfolds. The 1965 Vatican II document *Gaudium et Spes* summarizes these typical concerns of recent social teaching when it boldly declares:

> . . . with respect to the fundamental rights of the person, every type of discrimination, whether social or cultural, whether based on race, sex, color, social condition, language, or religion, is to be overcome or eradicated as contrary to God's intent. (no. 29)

However, it was not always this way. Even turning as far back as *Rerum Novarum* in 1891 would reveal little support among Church leadership for the notion of equality among all people. But let us go back even further, to 1841, to those years before the Church began to wake up to the call to advance social justice (a term rarely used, incidentally, before 1931). In the early decades of the nineteenth century, the Catholic Church was very much a Europe-dominated church, one where Latin was spoken almost exclusively in liturgy and church affairs and where nostalgia for premodern customs was prevalent. There was little sensitivity among Vatican officials, or even among most missionaries, to the riches of non-Western cultures or the needs and vulnerabilities of the less-developed and colonized lands of Africa, Asia, and Latin America. The concerns of church leaders were dominated by the political situation in Europe, a continent that was still recovering from the upheaval of the French Revolution and the turmoil of the Napoleonic wars.

Having been stripped of so much land and so many privileges during the French Revolution and having lost so much prestige in its aftermath, the Catholic Church struck a reactionary posture, deeply suspicious of modernizing political and economic trends and new ways of thought. The Church in the middle of the nineteenth century saw the wealthy elites of Europe, especially the royal and aristocratic families, as its primary allies in a politically dangerous world. It became an outspoken opponent of social change, shunning and even condemning movements that promoted greater freedoms and benefits for workers. Many church leaders yearned for a return to the medieval order, one in which the common people of farms and villages accepted their place at the bottom of a sharply segmented social ladder. In its desire for political security and a stable social order, the Church by and large opposed any secular ideas for scientific progress or social change, such as the impetus toward democratic practices. Its hostility to the new currents of thought ushered in by Enlightenment thinkers such as John Locke, Jean-Jacques Rousseau, and Immanuel Kant made it a rather reactionary force in the world at that time. The religious establishment of the day perceived the new rationalism and liberalism as threats and sought to preserve familiar ways, even when this meant opposition to proposals that would advance what today is known as social justice.

During those early and middle decades of the nineteenth century, church leaders took every opportunity to denounce notions of human rights, human equality, religious toleration, broader freedom of speech, and interfaith dialogue, as well as efforts directed toward the organization of modern labor unions, as dangerous ideas and practices. In 1864, for example, Pope Pius IX published the famous "Syllabus of Errors," a document that warned Catholics against the temptations of a list of eighty errors, including dozens of such modern ideas. As just one illustration of its fearful stance, consider that the Syllabus condemns the opinion that the "Church should be separated from the state, and the state from the Church." Instead, it insists that the "Catholic religion should be treated as the only religion of the state," and it denies that each person "should be free to embrace and profess the religion which he thinks to be true."

Today the majority of humanity not only takes for granted the desirability of most of the ideas once condemned by Pius IX, but the contemporary Catholic Church enthusiastically supports many of these very things in its social teachings. It took a formal Vatican II declaration (called *Dignitatis Humanae*), issued precisely one century later, to reverse the earlier condemnation of freedom of religion and conscience, and it did so in very stark and explicit terms. Although it might be conceded that the reaction of the Church at the time may have been quite understandable given all that had preceded it, most observers today would reach the blunt but honest conclusion that during these decades, the Church found itself squarely on the wrong side of history, at least on a particular range of social issues.

This thought experiment provides two lessons. First is the familiar insight that no one should take for granted certain features of the contemporary world as we encounter it today. Situations that people today consider natural and inevitable, such as the support of church leaders for human rights, freedom, and social equality, could well have turned out otherwise. Indeed, for much of its history, the Catholic Church frankly opposed these ideas as dangers to the divinely ordained social order. It took a long time for religious leaders to imagine a constructive alternative to the sharply hierarchical, almost caste-like division of society that dominated medieval Europe. The second lesson involves an appreciation for what it was that changed in the course of the nineteenth century. What social conditions or theological principles led a pope, specifically Leo XIII, to alter the Church's official stance on political and economic realities so dramatically by the end of that century? What forces set into motion this revolutionary transformation of the Church's entire approach to social relations?

PIONEERS OF SOCIAL CATHOLICISM

The answer to this last question is too complex to develop fully here, but space does allow a brief glance at the work of a few brave pioneers of social justice in the nineteenth century. These are public figures whose efforts sparked profound social movements and eventually created the momentum that led the Church to side boldly with the underprivileged members of society rather than continuing to identify primarily with the nobles and elites of Europe.

When it began to realize the extent of daily suffering that was going on beyond the walls of the Vatican, the official Church gradually changed its social posture. Under the guidance of a few influential pioneers of social concern, the Church's position on economic and political matters evolved from an embattled, reactionary brand of defensiveness to a more progressive, open-minded stance that looked upon the struggles of the least advantaged workers and families with genuine concern. Over time, church leaders even developed an eye for the structural dimensions of advancing the cause of social justice—part of the shift described in chapter one from a "charity alone" to a "justice in addition to charity" orientation.

Who were these nineteenth-century pioneers who influenced modern Catholic social teaching? The following paragraphs offer a very brief look at just a handful of key figures. Perhaps the single most influential person was Archbishop Wilhelm Emmanuel von Ketteler (1811–1877) of Mainz, Germany. In the middle decades of the 1800s, Archbishop von Ketteler was a leader among the *social Catholics* in Europe. This was a group of thinkers, consisting of bishops, clergy, and laity, who recognized quite vividly the great potential for both harm and progress in the new industrial order. With the rise of a factory-based system of mechanized production of goods, the new capitalist order held the promise of bringing immense gains to the masses of workers. Technological advances and greater efficiency might be harnessed to improve the conditions of life for all, especially the millions who were part of a massive influx of population into the great cities of Europe and North America.

But, similar to concerns voiced today that globalization is not distributing its benefits widely enough, nineteenth-century urbanization and industrialization were clearly not benefiting all social classes in an equitable way. The majority of ordinary laborers in factories, mines, and service work were trapped in overcrowded, unsanitary slums and had little or no access to schooling or other means of upward mobility. Wages were low and labor conditions were appalling; twelve-hour workdays, backbreaking toil, arbitrary employment policies, and the ever-present danger of industrial accidents were demoralizing the workers of Europe. The hard-pressed working class desperately needed an advocate, but up until that time the Church had been unresponsive.

Both before and after his appointment as bishop in 1850, Ketteler spearheaded a remarkable movement among Catholics. In words and deeds, through direct involvement in the lives of struggling workers as well as in sermons, speeches, and his many writings, Ketteler inspired others to look at poverty with new eyes. Poverty should not be viewed primarily as a punishment for the supposed laziness, sin, or vice of an individual, he insisted, but rather as a result of systemic injustice that kept wages unconscionably low and cut off the vast majority of people from opportunities to improve their lives. As long as subsistence wages were the rule, even the most hardworking and blameless of families would remain trapped in a cycle of desperate poverty. A large number of social ills, including crime, violence, disease, and family breakup, could be remedied if the root causes of poverty could somehow be addressed.

Archbishop Ketteler was not afraid to identify the Church as a potential and pivotal agent of social change. He encouraged Catholics to organize in labor unions and other church-based lay associations to protect their rights and promote the common good. He drew inspiration from scriptural and theological sources, including the thirteenth-century writings of St. Thomas Aquinas on justice and related virtues. His knowledge of the Catholic tradition convinced Ketteler that it was his duty as a church leader to denounce extreme inequality, cutthroat competition, and misguided notions of unlimited property rights that had the effect of sacrificing the legitimate needs of the community to the interests and ever greater profits of a few super-wealthy captains of industry. He even used the occasion of his election to the Frankfurt national assembly in 1848 (a year of great upheavals and near revolution in Germany) as a springboard for further advocacy on behalf of the poor and outcast of his day.

During these years, other industrializing nations witnessed similar efforts on the part of key Catholic figures who sought to awaken the Church and the wider society to the true character of poverty in the new industrial order. In France, for example, the plight of the working class was championed by diverse figures who, despite a common grounding in the same Catholic faith, occupied all wings of the political spectrum. Among the most prominent was Antoine-Frédéric Ozanam (1813–1853), one of the founders of the St. Vincent de Paul Society, a Catholic charitable organization that is still active in some 300,000 parishes around the world. A learned and affluent layman known for his frequent visits to the squalid homes of the poor of Paris and Lyons, Ozanam was extraordinarily dedicated to performing direct works of charity, even when he found himself seriously ill or preoccupied with the numerous demands of his career. Remarkably, his commitment to acts of charity did not prevent Ozanam from speaking forthrightly about the need also for justice—the necessity for serious changes in social structures to benefit the desperately poor.

Other proponents of liberty and social reform in France during these decades included Charles de Montalembert (1810–1870) and Albert de Mun (1841–1914). Each of these laymen was a talented writer, orator, and politician who moved in the inner circles of power in the turbulent French society of that age. Although they both grew up in aristocratic families, they came to advocate the well-being of the poor as a crucial concern of any authentic agenda of the Catholic Church.

The best representative of nineteenth-century social Catholicism in England was Cardinal Henry Edward Manning (1808–1892). First in his private reflections as a young man and later in his capacity as the Catholic Archbishop of Westminster (London), Manning considered it a serious and ominous omission that so few Catholics were concerned about the problems of exploited factory workers. He was worried that atheistic socialism would begin to appeal to the dockworkers and factory employees he came to know personally. This concern would become even more of a threat if Christian churches continued to be perceived as indifferent to workers' demands for better treatment.

Besides fervently speaking out against social injustices, Cardinal Manning performed many symbolic and substantial deeds to demonstrate his concern for the poor and his desire to awaken affluent Catholics out of their slumber of apathy. In the 1860s, he canceled plans to build a new Westminster cathedral so that the money set aside for construction could be used to open over twenty new schools for children from poor families. Manning looked for creative opportunities to alleviate the plight of those suffering horrendously in the slums of London, weathering hardships chronicled so vividly and poignantly in the novels of Charles Dickens, one of the Cardinal's contemporaries. Manning consistently supported labor unions, workers' rights, and progressive social legislation that would benefit the working class. Parlaying his prominence in British political circles for philanthropic purposes, he corresponded with cabinet ministers and sat on royal commissions in his pursuit of social justice. He joined his voice in coalitions with other Victorian-era reformers who insisted that government agencies should shoulder a greater share of social obligations to assist the destitute.

These examples from the three countries mentioned—Germany, France, and England—could be multiplied many times over, offering a fuller picture of the social reform impulse of these pivotal decades. All of the leaders of social Catholicism in Europe played a role, directly or indirectly, in the birth of modern Catholic social teaching. They prepared the way for the definitive moment when the official Catholic Church would stand up for the rights of workers and issue a formal protest against the starvation wages that threatened the very lives of millions of workers and their families. Today's proponents of the tradition of Catholic social teaching owe a great debt of gratitude to the laity and clergy of previous centuries who, by their words and deeds, nudged the Church closer to the stance of deep concern and social responsibility so often taken for granted today. No one deserves credit for this achievement more than Archbishop Ketteler, who planted so many of the seeds of reform, and Cardinal Manning, who was fortunate to live just long enough to witness the adoption of his proposals for worker justice by Pope Leo XIII when the pontiff issued the first social encyclical, *Rerum Novarum*, in 1891.

THE WRITING OF THE SOCIAL ENCYCLICALS

Each of the twelve major documents of Catholic social teaching deserves careful study and analysis, for each is a unique contribution with a distinctive message. However, it is not possible in these pages to march through the list of all twelve documents to investigate what makes each encyclical special. Entire books have been dedicated to this task, some of which are listed in the Annotated List of Resources for Further Study. Rather than analyzing each document in turn, chapter five devotes its attention to an explication of the content of all of these documents considered as a whole and presents a thematic survey of the messages within these texts. The remainder of this chapter explores some of the central questions regarding what the documents have in common and how best to understand the historical unfolding of the tradition of Catholic social teaching.

One question that naturally arises concerns the timing of new encyclicals. How does a pope decide that the time is ripe for writing and publishing a new document of social teaching? Part of the answer becomes obvious if one looks closely at the list of dates for the documents contained in table 3.1. It is no mere accident that so many of the social encyclicals were published on major anniversaries of *Rerum Novarum*, which appeared in 1891. The fortieth, seventieth, eightieth, ninetieth, and one hundredth anniversaries of Pope Leo XIII's first social encyclical were marked by subsequent popes publishing new documents of social teaching. Indeed, some of the Latin titles of these documents make explicit reference to the anniversary dates. In every year that ends in a one, it is reasonable to expect a new social encyclical to be released, for this pattern held true in 1931, 1961, 1971, 1981, and 1991. Most of these anniversary encyclicals spend several paragraphs in tribute to their predecessors, often explaining at length how the new teaching follows from the basic principles contained in *Rerum Novarum*.

But there is more to the timing of social encyclicals than the sheer momentum of the calendar or force of habit. Each social teaching document represents the Church's response to a specific set of events or social concerns that demanded the attention of political and religious leaders at that specific moment of history. For example, the writing of *Quadragesimo Anno* ("After Forty Years" or "The Reconstruction of the Social Order") in 1931 was prompted by a worldwide economic crisis that crushed the confidence of millions. The sudden stock market crash of 1929 and the shock of startling levels of unemployment in the early years of the Great Depression demanded a substantial response from Pope Pius XI as he agonized over the financial chaos, ruined dreams, and sudden destitution of millions of families in Europe, America, and other regions of the world.

Another dramatic example is Pope John XXIII's 1963 encyclical *Pacem in Terris* ("Peace on Earth"), which included a plea for peace and disarmament just months after the Cuban Missile Crisis of 1962 threatened the world with the specter of nuclear annihilation. Further, even if 1991 had not been the hundredth anniversary of *Rerum Novarum*, Pope John Paul II might well have taken the opportunity to comment on the events of 1989 and 1990 (including the fall of the Berlin Wall, the demise of Soviet Communism, and the breakup of the USSR), as he did in *Centesimus Annus* ("On the Hundredth Anniversary of *Rerum Novarum*").

In a sense, then, each new social encyclical can be interpreted as an occasion for the Church to address the challenges of new events on the world stage. Sometimes these events are dramatic; at other times, however, they reflect more gradual developments. Such was the case with the phasing out of colonialism, which is a major concern of *Populorum Progressio* ("The Development of People") in 1967, or the growth of international trade, treated in *Sollicitudo rei Socialis* ("On Social Concern") in 1987. Whenever we look at a document such as the encyclicals of Catholic social teaching, it is wise to ask the revealing question: To what conditions or events is this author responding? Situating the encyclicals in their historical context is an indispensable first step toward understanding their message and significance.

While it is true that each encyclical constitutes a response to the particular political and economic challenges of its era, another powerful dynamic at play in Catholic social teaching is the way each successive encyclical builds upon the insights of its predecessors. The documents have a wonderful way of combining the new with the old, of building novel structures upon existing foundations. The tradition renews itself by constantly considering the state of secular affairs and holding up this picture of the world to the continuous light of the Gospel and Christian theology. While new times surely call for creative solutions that adjust to changing realities, there is also a set of core principles regarding social justice and moral obligations that should shape human activity in every age.

Scholars who trace the development of Catholic social teaching have studied the dynamic of continuity and change in the social encyclicals as it is described in the paragraphs just above. Perceptive authors have staked out various positions along a spectrum of opinions about the nature of the encyclicals. At one extreme is the idea that social and theological principles pass in an uninterrupted line, as it were, "from papal mind to papal mind," with a tight, organic connection between everything successive popes might say about political and economic affairs. At the other extreme is the notion that each encyclical captures only the idiosyncratic views of its author and is essentially unrelated to what came before it or will come after it.

Obviously, the truth lies somewhere between these extremes. Undeniably, there exists substantial continuity between the messages of the popes, even when their encyclicals appear decades apart from one another. But the march of time and social progress give each successive encyclical a broader and, it might be argued, a more constructive approach. The most recent documents grapple seriously with certain realities—including the aspirations of women for social equality, the urgency of nuclear disarmament, and the need to address the painful legacies of colonialism—that the earliest documents could scarcely acknowledge. The progress of Catholic social teaching may be summarized as steady growth toward ever-wider circles of social concern, reflecting the increase of awareness within the Church of numerous injustices that demand our attention, commitment, and action.

One development that has without a doubt contributed to the widening of the circle of concern in Catholic social teaching in recent decades is the emergence of the school of thought known as liberation theology. While the themes of authentic freedom and liberation from sin and its effects have been a part of Christianity since its very beginning, it was only in the late 1960s that a distinct school of theological thought rallied around these notions. Led at first by Peruvian priest Gustavo Gutiérrez and other theologians from throughout Latin America, liberation theology grew in influence and came to challenge the Church around the world to take greater notice of oppressive political and economic structures that trap millions in misery.

It is interesting to note that liberation theology exerted considerable influence, especially in the 1970s and 1980s, in two starkly different settings. First, at the very grassroots of Catholic circles in Latin America, it inspired many thousands of *base Christian communities*. These consist of regular gatherings of small groups of church members, often from among the very poorest rural and urban dwellers, who meet at least weekly for scripture study, literacy training, faith-sharing, and mutual support. Second, liberation theology was very influential at the very highest levels of church life. A number of prominent and dedicated bishops and even cardinals, especially in Brazil, Mexico, and the small nations of Central America, citing the theme of liberation as their inspiration, became outspoken advocates of social change on behalf of the desperately poor flocks they were called to shepherd. Perhaps the best known of these is Archbishop Oscar Romero (1917–1980) of El Salvador, a powerful prophet of social justice who died as a martyr for the cause of liberating the poor of his struggling country.

Further, the regional meetings of the Conference of Latin American Bishops (a super-grouping of the whole continent's episcopal conferences that goes by the Spanish acronym CELAM and meets approximately every ten years) have come to reflect the influence of liberation themes such as the *preferential option for the poor*. This was especially true of two consecutive CELAM meetings: the ones held at Medellín, Colombia, in 1968 and at Puebla, Mexico, in 1979. In each instance, deep concern for the poor and marginalized was reflected in the proceedings and in the final documents of the conference. Even long after what is usually recognized as the heyday of liberation theology, this commitment has continued to play a prominent role in CELAM meetings right up to the present (the last such meeting as of this writing was held in May 2007 in Aparecida, Brazil).

While liberation theology continues to provoke stark opposition, and while it is probably true that the original energies of the movement have to some extent dissipated, it is nevertheless an influential force even today. As the examination of the theme of the preferential option for the poor at the end of chapter five will reveal, many of the concerns of liberation theology have trickled up into official documents of universal Catholic social teaching and have even found their way into papal encyclicals.

Libration theology is just one example of the events and developments that have influenced Catholic social thought. There are many similar topics worth considering as one reaches for a more comprehensive analysis of church social teachings. Some are treated in subsequent chapters of this book, while further relevant currents of theological and secular thought may be traced by using the Annotated List of Further Resources. Additional study of the many developments that have influenced Catholic social teaching will surely reveal that church authorities are always responding to world events and secular trends that affect the achievement of justice. Careful investigation of how social teaching documents come to be written and promulgated can only correct any false impressions we might have that the role of popes and bishops is simply to teach, as if in a monologue. Rather, a clearer picture of the history of Catholic social thought suggests how important it has been for church leaders to listen attentively to "the signs of the times" and to dialogue with many diverse voices and alternative sources of information and wisdom. This is one of the central themes of the next chapter, which examines in detail the sources and methods of Catholic social teaching.

One further helpful resource is table 3.2. This table provides a simple timeline of key events that have shaped the documents of Catholic social teaching. Most of these have been mentioned earlier in this chapter, but it might be illuminating to ponder how the course of Catholic social thought might have unfolded differently had these events not occurred.

TABLE 3.2. TIMELINE OF KEY EVENTS SHAPING CATHOLIC SOCIAL TEACHING

Note: Bold entries indicate the publication of documents.

1740	**First modern encyclical issued by Pope Benedict XIV**
1789	Start of the French Revolution
1815	The end of the Napoleonic Wars
1848	Bishop Ketteler advocates for workers at Frankfort National Assembly
1848	Karl Marx and Friedrich Engels publish the *Communist Manifesto*
1864	**"Syllabus of Errors" of Pope Pius IX**
1865	Cardinal Manning becomes Archbishop of Westminster (London)
1870	First Vatican Council
1891	***Rerum Novarum* of Pope Leo XIII**
1914–1918	World War I
1929	Stock Market Crash and beginning of the Great Depression
1931	***Quadragesimo Anno* of Pope Pius XI**
1939–1945	World War II
1961	***Mater et Magistra* of Pope John XXIII**
1962–1965	Second Vatican Council
1962	Cuban Missile Crisis
1963	***Pacem in Terris* of Pope John XXIII**
1965	***Gaudium et Spes* from the Second Vatican Council**
1967	***Populorum Progressio* of Pope Paul VI**
1968	Medellín (Colombia) Conference of Latin American Bishops
1971	***Octogesima Adveniens* of Pope Paul VI**
1971	***Justitia in Mundo* from the worldwide Synod of Bishops**
1975	***Evangelii Nuntiandi* of Pope Paul VI**
1979	Puebla (Mexico) Conference of Latin American Bishops
1981	***Laborem Exercens* of Pope John Paul II**
1987	***Sollicitudo Rei Socialis* of Pope John Paul II**
1989	Fall of the Berlin Wall, collapse of Soviet Communism
1991	***Centesimus Annus* of Pope John Paul II**
2001	Terrorist attacks of September 11
2003	Start of the War in Iraq
2004	***Compendium of Catholic Social Doctrine* from the Pontifical Council for Justice and Peace**
2006	***Deus Caritas Est* of Pope Benedict XVI**

QUESTIONS FOR REFLECTION

1. How familiar are you with the work of the United States Conference of Catholic Bishops and other national episcopal conferences? Can you list some of their functions and contributions? Are there any initiatives that you would like to know more about or that you wish they would undertake?

2. If you had lived in the years before *Rerum Novarum* was published in 1891, would you likely have joined the effort of the early pioneers of social Catholicism? Would you have found these projects attractive? Why or why not?

3. Do you see any similarities between the crisis of industrialization that the world experienced in the 1800s and the economic situations facing workers today, including the reality of globalization? If so, can you recommend any messages that might be contained in a new encyclical written today that would courageously address this new phase of industrial woes, as *Rerum Novarum* did in 1891?

4. This chapter's treatment of social Catholicism and of lay leaders in social justice efforts might suggest that social teaching is as much a trickle-up phenomenon (in which grassroots experience affects the positions of official leaders) as it is a top-down phenomenon (in which official teachings come to be promulgated at local levels). How do you judge the relative weight of these two dynamics? Is there a historic trend in which one model is eclipsing the other?

5. It has been remarked that the role played by prominent proponents of Social Catholicism in the nineteenth century is now being supplied by strictly nonreligious voices, such as the network of international non-governmental organizations (NGO's) that steer clear of religious discourse in their advocacy efforts for justice. Do you judge this to be true, or are you aware of enough faith-based advocacy for causes such as human rights, economic development, and the relief of poverty that you would dispute this claim?

TOPICS FOR FURTHER RESEARCH

1. The operation of periodic Synods of Bishops such as the influential Roman gathering in 1971 that produced the document *Justice in the World*

2. Pope Benedict XVI's first encyclical letter *Deus Caritas Est*—its main messages regarding social justice and the relationship between charity and justice

3. The work of the Pontifical Council for Justice and Peace (Latin: *Justitia et Pax*)
4. The tradition of papal messages for the World Day of Peace (January 1 each year)
5. An analysis of the 2004 *Compendium of the Social Doctrine of the Church*
6. The work of episcopal conferences such as the United States Conference of Catholic Bishops (USCCB)
7. The Vatican II Declaration on Religious Liberty (Latin: *Dignitatis Humanae*)
8. The effects of the Enlightenment and the French Revolution on the Church
9. Other figures prominent in European social Catholicism of the nineteenth century or similar U.S. circles in the twentieth century , especially Msgr. John A. Ryan (1865–1945) who for many years directed social justice efforts for the U.S. bishops
10. Liberation theology and the way its message overlaps with official teachings or is distinct from them

4

+

The Sources and Methods of Catholic Social Teaching

Catholic social teaching is just one example of a tradition of ethics. Throughout human history, people all over the world have developed and shared a wide variety of ethical traditions that have shed light on how best to plan their lives and to allocate limited resources in cooperation with their neighbors. Members of human society inherit this wisdom from previous generations as well as finding it in their own new experiences, both individually and collectively. No matter what system of thought they espouse, people tend to look for new sources of wisdom that might help them shape their actions and adapt to an ever-changing world.

Ethics almost always involves making generalizations, including drawing up laws, agreeing upon moral principles, and following a variety of other behavioral guidelines. If a group discovers a beneficial pattern of behavior or a set of useful reflections about appropriate human activity, members of the group may record it in written form or find some other way of sharing it with contemporaries and future generations. At the dawn of human history, codes of virtuous behavior were passed down orally; some of the earliest surviving written documents were codes of laws inscribed on stone tablets in the ancient Near East. Today, people might look to law libraries and online legal journals for constantly updated interpretations of what constitutes legal and illegal activity. Both religious ethicists and secular legal systems produce bodies of scholarly commentary on morality and jurisprudence in this constructive way. This is how ethical traditions take root and grow over time.

It is important to remember that ethics is a field that is always evolving, even after a law or principle is agreed upon and recorded in some authoritative way. Subsequent reflection and commentary upon laws and principles make valuable contributions to discerning how best to understand and apply standards of human behavior. This process includes making provisions for commonsense exceptions to general laws, for enforcing laws when they are violated, and even for incorporating creative suggestions for motivating people to observe a given law or ethical principle. For example, society benefits not only from district attorneys aggressively prosecuting corporate fraud and insider trading of securities, but also from efforts to actively discourage conflicts of interest that might lead to this type of white-collar crime. Similarly, it is one thing for police to ticket a speeding motorist or to arrest a drunk driver, but a better course of action would be to prevent reckless driving through public service announcements and publicity campaigns. Most people respond favorably to sincere efforts to assist them in forming their consciences, so such educational efforts about socially responsible behavior are promising directions for enhancing sensitivity to moral obligations.

These examples underline some of the broad concerns of Catholic social teaching and the wider discipline of social ethics to which it seeks to contribute. These teachings address the whole person, in all his or her aspects as a member of society, not narrowly as a disembodied subject of fixed and inflexible civil laws. The field of social ethics concerns itself with broader questions than merely who violated the law and how violators will pay for their crimes. It also seeks to form people who are sensitive to the well-being of their neighbors, beyond the strictures of the letter of the law.

THE FOUR SOURCES OF CHRISTIAN ETHICS

As one particular tradition of moral reflection, Christian ethics has witnessed distinctive features and patterns of growth over the past two thousand years. When members of the Christian community turn their energies toward the task of "doing ethics," they seek to discover the behavioral implications of their faith in God. They fervently desire to cultivate a healthy relationship with their Lord and Creator, acknowledging certain solemn obligations toward God. Some of these are summarized in the First, Second, and Third Commandments of the Decalogue: the call to worship and praise God, to observe the Sabbath in appropriate ways, to respect the name of the Lord, and to be mindful of all that is holy.

Simultaneously, Christians recognize certain moral duties to other creatures, for loving one's neighbor follows closely from loving the God who created all that exists. People of faith consequently desire to respect life in all its forms, to preserve the beauty of the natural environment, and to avoid all actions (such as stealing, lying, adultery, and murder) that harm other people. Many of these obligations are contained in the Fourth through Tenth Commandments. The dual obligations toward God and toward others are really part of a unified call to be loving people filled with all the virtues of generous and faithful disciples of Jesus. However convenient it may be to draw a distinction between duties to God and duties to others, the devout Christian recognizes these obligations as cut from the same cloth, as part of a seamless response to a God whose boundless love is reflected in the goodness of all created things. There is an indivisible unity in the web of relationships that leads Christians to pursue love and justice toward all.

The Ten Commandments have served for thousands of years as an excellent summary of collective moral wisdom for communities of faith around the world, first for the Jewish people and then for Christians as well; their usefulness has never diminished. In a complex and rapidly changing world, however, it has become desirable to supplement them with other types of moral wisdom, particularly with guidelines concerning our large-scale social relations. Catholic social teaching is one such attempt to provide ethical counsel regarding just relationships in political and economic life—levels of our everyday activity that are barely mentioned in the Ten Commandments. As new church documents are issued and as local faith communities attempt to apply the insights of Catholic social teaching to their particular situations, the tradition of Christian ethics continues to grow and mature. Each generation of Christians experiences the opportunity to renew its commitment to the Gospel by improving its understanding of what actions and attitudes are required by the call to be loving and faithful disciples.

The growth and development of Catholic social teaching is a creative process, then, but it is governed by certain standard approaches and tendencies. This chapter describes the pattern by which certain sources (sometimes called "fonts") of wisdom contribute to Catholic social teaching. As is the case in all of Christian ethics, whether Catholic, Protestant, or Orthodox, the social teachings of the Church draw upon four major sources of insight that contribute to their authority and shape their conclusions: (1) revelation, (2) reason, (3) tradition, and (4) experience. The remainder of this chapter explores how each of these sources serves as a resource for the development of Catholic social teaching.

1. Revelation: The Role of Scripture

The word *revelation* refers to the ways God shows God's self to people. The Judeo-Christian tradition has never rejected the possibility that certain individuals might at any time experience profound revelations from the Almighty and even receive specific messages from God in the form of mystical visions. While it is probably wise to retain an initial stance of skepticism about any particular claim regarding a private revelation (for example, a Marian apparition or someone hearing the voice of Jesus in a direct way), it would be presumptuous to turn one's back entirely on the possibility of such authentic experiences. But the standard way of speaking about revelation as a source of theology is to emphasize the guidance offered to all believers in the more public and accessible form of the scriptures. The Bible has always been the starting point for Christian ethics. Even while they tend to understand the significance of scripture in slightly different ways, Christian thinkers invariably agree that the biblical record of God's revelation must play an important role in what Christians say about the morality of human behavior.

There have always been differences of opinion about the precise nature of the Bible and how it should be used. Those who lean toward biblical fundamentalism view scripture as an accurate, indeed inerrant, record of events and commands that come directly from God. Others recognize the human and historical dimensions of scripture, recalling that both the Hebrew scriptures and the New Testament are products of human communities, however true it is that God may be considered the ultimate author. For centuries, theologians have speculated about the relationship between the divine and human origins of the canon (or accepted body) of scripture, and no clear consensus has yet emerged. To this day, there are serious differences of opinion regarding notions of the authorship of these writings, and a variety of contending models have been proposed for describing how best to portray the divine inspiration of scripture.

In fact, it is misleading even to refer to the Bible as a single book, for it is really a collection of dozens of writings assembled over hundreds of years that only gradually won recognition as an authoritative source of religious wisdom. The official Roman Catholic version of the Bible today recognizes 46 books of the Old Testament and 27 books of the New Testament, and the variety of styles and genres of literature contained in scripture is dizzying. While there is without doubt a certain unity to all these writings, it is crucial to avoid the mistake of assuming a single viewpoint in this vastly diverse literature. While they may find themselves bound neatly together in a single volume, the prophetic, poetic, historical, and theological literature contained in the Bible displays a great variety of forms and messages that would take a lifetime of study to untangle and to relate to each other in a systematic way.

For present purposes, it suffices merely to note that morality in general, and social ethics in particular, are only a small part of the overall concerns of scripture. It would be misleading to think of the Bible as a book of detailed rules to regulate our behavior. Even in those few passages where scripture does offer firm moral laws, significant efforts at interpretation are required before anyone could apply their precise prescriptions to contemporary moral life. For the most part, scripture is a record of God's gracious ways of dealing with fallen humanity, offering successive covenants that contain the promise of redemption and salvation. When various books of the Bible address the morality of specific human behaviors, it is always in the context of an overriding concern to build a faithful relationship with God and others.

One of the key terms that apply to this picture of the universe is the notion of justice, the controlling concept in all of our reflections on social ethics. Justice is a virtue of people who are committed to fidelity to the demands of a relationship, whether with God, with other individuals, or with large groups and categories of other people. It becomes a complex task to trace notions of justice through the Bible, since the various original Hebrew and Greek words for justice have associated meanings that are broader than what we today might mean by "legal justice" or "social justice." Sometimes the original biblical terms for justice (the Hebrew *mišpāt* and *sĕdāqāh*, the Greek *dikaiosynē*) are rightly translated into English terms such as "loving-kindness," "mercy," "steadfast love," "fidelity," and "righteousness"—words that indicate multiple nuances in texts that one might have hoped would offer specific guidance on contemporary economic and political matters. Those seeking to walk the path of biblical justice soon find it converging with other paths in the faith life of Israel and in the spirituality of early Christian communities. Efforts to derive practical social principles for the modern world directly from the fragmentary treatments of justice in scriptural sources usually meet with frustration.

There are several places in scripture, however, where our search for guidance on the topic of social justice is most likely to be fruitful. One is in the books of the Hebrew prophets. Figures such as Isaiah, Jeremiah, Amos, Hosea, Micah, and Ezekiel frequently denounce violent and fraudulent practices that, in their lifetimes, were harming the weakest members of Israelite society—widows, orphans, the poor, the outcast. Several prophets uttered stirring words that appealed for the establishment of a new order of social concern and harmony. Of course, these prophets often met stiff resistance to their stern reminders that all Israelites should heed God's call to practice social justice, share the wealth more broadly, and respect the delicate web of communal relations. The Psalms and the Book of Proverbs also offer vivid portrayals of the two sides of justice: the harmony that accompanies the fulfillment of justice and the turmoil associated with its violation.

The New Testament contains the Christian scriptures that witness to the revelation of God in the person of Jesus Christ. Many of the stories about

Jesus in the four gospels offer us glimpses of a vision of justice that is bound up with the Kingdom of God, also translated as the Reign of God. One of the remarkable things about this Kingdom as Jesus describes it (often by means of parables) is that its establishment is not portrayed as merely a future event. Rather, it is also somehow already present among us in some mysterious way. The Kingdom is the power of God active in the present world, and the mercy and miraculous deeds of Jesus reveal God's love and justice. In his acts of healing, feeding, resuscitation, and exorcism, Jesus time and time again reaches out to those estranged from the social mainstream and in danger of falling through the cracks of respectable society. His is a ministry of justice, which includes reconciliation and restoration of right relationship. While nothing in the teaching and ministry of Jesus offers a crystal clear definition of social justice, at least not in the abstract, readers of the gospels readily recognize Jesus as fearless in confronting the major injustices of his day. A distinctive feature of his itinerant ministry is the way he flouts social conventions to extend the hand of fellowship in extraordinary ways to establish solidarity with the ostracized, the stigmatized, and other victims of inequities.

Justice is also an important concept in the letters of St. Paul. Among Paul's central concerns is the formation of communities of covenant people; for Paul, proper relations within Christian communities are governed by justice as well as charity. He repeatedly urges the fledgling churches in many parts of the Mediterranean world of his day to share resources of talent and money so that none experience dire want and so that all might thrive. Although some of Paul's practical advice seems dated and less than helpful today (he accepted the institution of slavery and rather sharply subordinated women to men in the life of the church), his treatment of justice and related themes such as freedom and reconciliation are immensely insightful and inspiring.

How do the documents of Catholic social teaching make use of scripture? On many occasions, passages of scripture are cited directly in the texts of encyclicals to borrow an insight or to justify a judgment. For example, in paragraph 137 of the 1931 encyclical *Quadragesimo Anno*, Pope Pius XI quotes a verse from Paul's first letter to the Corinthians to urge readers to develop bonds of solidarity, since, as Paul writes, "if [one] part suffers, all the parts suffer with it" (12:26). In other instances, biblical materials are used more indirectly to evoke a sense of urgency or obligation. For example, when Pope John Paul II (in paragraph 33 of the 1987 letter *Sollicitudo rei Socialis*) wishes to inspire greater sharing of resources between rich and poor nations, he alludes to the familiar parable of the beggar Lazarus and the rich man who excluded him from his banquet table (see Luke 16:19–31). Although (on the surface at least) the original words of Jesus were about individual acts of charity and hospitality, this encyclical extends their significance to apply the principle of mercy to the complex world of global politics. Behind such applications of scripture lies a confident assumption within Catholic social teaching that the Word of God revealed many centuries ago still finds relevance today, even in new situations that open up entire worlds far beyond the original context of divine revelation.

Ultimately, scripture shapes Catholic thought and practice in ways that go well beyond the occasional quote or reference in official documents such as encyclicals. The biblical witness to God's saving love permeates all church activities, including worship and service work as well as doctrine. Indeed, a strong case may be made that the greatest contribution of scripture to moral theology and social ethics is not in specific biblical injunctions or commands, as important as they might be, but rather in the overall shape of the narrative of God's relationship to the faithful. A responsible approach to interpreting scripture, then, is to look to these holy writings not so much for detailed moral guidance regarding specific choices that might confront someone today, but rather for a general but reliable picture of reality, including the working out of salvation history. This is an insight captured in the often quoted motto, "The Bible is to be interpreted as *revealed reality*, not so much as *revealed morality*." In utilizing scripture in ethics, the wise interpreter does not expect a blueprint for every detail of moral decision making, but rather an overall portrayal of what values and goals to pursue in shaping a praiseworthy moral life.

By no means does this last point mean that particular teachings in the various books of the Bible are to be discarded or completely relativized. There are many valuable kernels of social wisdom contained in discrete scriptural verses and passages. To offer a flavor for some of the most influential scriptural material within the tradition of Catholic social teaching, table 4.1 lists a representative sampling of 41 scriptural passages that are especially important for social ethics. Each entry contains insights into the obligation to pursue social justice and right human relations in every age. Communities of disciples particularly dedicated to the pursuit of peace and justice have found rich inspiration in each of the passages included in this list.

2. Reason: The Natural Law

Already noted in chapter two is the Catholic tradition's tendency to favor a both-and position on many issues. Catholic theology seeks to combine concerns for both body and spirit, both heaven and earth, both natural and supernatural life, both grace and nature. Another pair of terms to be synthesized is *reason* and *revelation*. All Christians acknowledge that the revealed Word of God in scripture is a special and privileged place to

TABLE 4.1.   A SAMPLING OF SCRIPTURAL TEXTS INFLUENTIAL IN PEACE AND JUSTICE COMMUNITIES

Old Testament (14)

Exodus 3:7–8
"Then the Lord said: 'I have witnessed the affliction of my people in Egypt and have heard their cry of complaint against their slave drivers, so I know well what they are suffering. Therefore I have come down to rescue them from the hands of the Egyptians.'"

Leviticus 25:8–50
Description of the "Year of Jubilee" and the principles of periodic debt forgiveness and the redemption of alienated property.

Deuteronomy 15:1–11
"You shall have a relaxation of debts. . . . There shall be no one of you in need . . . . I command you to open your hand to the poor and needy."

Deuteronomy 24:14
"You shall not defraud a poor and needy hired servant . . . . You shall pay him each day's wages before sundown on the day itself."

Psalm 41:1
"Happy is he who has regard for the lowly and the poor."

Psalm 72:2, 7
"He shall govern your people with righteousness . . . . Justice shall flower in his day, and profound peace . . . ."

Proverbs 21:13
"He who shuts his ears to the cry of the poor will himself also call and not be heard."

Proverbs 31:9
"Open your mouth, decree what is just, defend the needy and the poor!"

Isaiah 1:16
"Make justice your aim: redress the wronged, hear the orphan's plea, defend the widow."

Isaiah 2:4 (also Micah 4:3)
". . . they shall beat their swords into plowshares . . . ."

Isaiah 32:17
"Justice will bring about peace; right will produce calm and security."

Jeremiah 22:13
"Woe to him who builds his house on wrong, his terraces on injustice; who works his neighbor without pay, and gives him no wages."

Amos 5:24
"Let justice surge like water and goodness like an unfailing stream."

Micah 6:8
"What the Lord requires of you: only to do the right and to love goodness and to walk humbly with your God."

New Testament (27)

Matthew 6:24
"No one can serve two masters . . . . You cannot give yourself to God and money."

Matthew 20:1–16
Jesus offers the parable of the laborers in the vineyard. The workers receive equal pay despite their different efforts, demonstrating the mysterious justice of God.

Matthew 22:21 (also Luke 20:25)
"Give to Caesar what is Caesar's, but give to God what is God's."

Matthew 25:31–46
The parable of the last judgment. Whatever we do to the least of our neighbors, we do to Christ.

Mark 10:43
"Anyone among you who aspires to greatness . . . must serve the needs of all."

Mark 12:28–34
The "Great Commandment" links love of God and love of neighbor.

Luke 1:46–55
The Magnificat of Mary. God raises up the poor and lowers the rich.

Luke 4:16–30
Jesus announces his mission, "to bring good news to the poor; to proclaim liberty to captives."

Luke 6:20–26
The Beatitudes of Jesus begin with "Blest are you poor . . . ."

Luke 6:27–31
Jesus' teaching on non-violence: "Love your enemies . . . turn the other cheek."

Luke 10:25–37
The parable of the good Samaritan. A call to love all neighbors.

Luke 12:15–21
The parable of the rich landowner. One's worth is not determined by possessions.

Luke 16:19–31
The parable of "the rich man and Lazarus the beggar."

John 13:3–17
The humble Jesus, the servant of all, washes the feet of the apostles and invites all to do the same.

Acts 2:43–47 and 4:32–35
The early Christians shared all goods in common.

Romans 12:4–8 (also I Corinthians 12:4–11)
All God's gifts are meant for service.

Romans 12:21
Overcome evil with good.

I Corinthians 12:12–26
Analogy of the body. If one suffers, all the members suffer with it.

(continued)

TABLE 4.1. (*continued*)

2 Corinthians 8–9
St. Paul urges generous sharing of offerings and resources among communities to meet the needs of the poor.

Galatians 3:28 (also Colossians 3:11)
Human distinctions are unimportant. "All are one in Christ Jesus."

Galatians 5
A message of Christian liberty and hope. Use well the freedom Christ won for all. Live in accord with the Spirit and avoid all vices.

I Timothy 6:10
"The love of money is the root of all evil."

I Timothy 6:17–19
Advice to the rich to be generous and ready to share.

James 1:22
Appeal for good works. Be doers, not just hearers of the word.

James 2:26
"Faith without works is as dead as a body without life."

James 5:1–6
Harsh warnings to the rich. "Here crying aloud are the wages you withheld from the farmhands who harvested your fields. . . . You lived in wanton luxury on the earth; you fattened yourself for the day of slaughter."

I John 4:20–21
"Whoever loves God must also love his brother."

encounter God and to discern God's intentions for the world. But Catholic theologians are especially eager to combine what they learn in the Bible with insights gained by other means of human knowledge, specifically through human reason.

This optimism about the operations of the human mind stands in contrast to fundamentalist Christians, whose stated policy is to follow the Bible alone, inerrant as they profess it to be. It even sets Catholics apart from many mainstream Protestants whose roots in the theology of the Reformation (primarily from the sixteenth-century reformers Martin Luther and John Calvin) lead them to be more distrustful of the operations of the human mind. This classic Protestant position emphasizes that human faculties are likely to be corrupted by the sinful tendencies unleashed by the fall of Adam, which, they often assert, "darkened the mind and weakened the will."

What effect does this typical Catholic confidence in reason have on Catholic social teaching? In general, modern social encyclicals exhibit a marked tendency to trust solutions and strategies that are derived through careful application of rational analysis to complex problems. While it is never excluded from these Catholic texts, scripture plays a far less central role here than it does in documents from parallel Protestant sources, such as the social teachings of the World Council of Churches (a Geneva, Switzerland-based association of primarily Protestant religious communities) or individual Protestant denominations.

One specific way of using reason in theological writings is to employ a form of argumentation called *natural law reasoning*. Although its influence on the documents of Catholic social teaching has been diminishing somewhat over time, natural law is still important for students of Catholic ethics to understand and appreciate. Explanations of natural law have a tendency to become very technical, but the basic pattern of thought behind natural law is not so complicated. The fundamental belief of a natural law approach to ethics is that God structured the universe with certain purposes in mind. God also created humans with enough intelligence that they can use their reason to observe the natural world and to make reliable judgments about God's purposes. Humans are fully capable of figuring out how their behavior may cooperate with God's plans; they can also conspire to frustrate the clear purposes of their Creator. Indeed, all humans experience a moral obligation to make good use of their minds to discern God's intentions and to muster the courage to act on these convictions in daily life. To ignore the law of nature, which is mysteriously inscribed in human hearts and minds (see Romans 2:14–15 for St. Paul's description of this point), is to sin by disobeying God's will.

Normally, Christians think of God's will as coming to them through scripture, such as in the contents of the Ten Commandments. A key claim of natural law theory is that nature is another path by which people may learn God's will, albeit in a less direct way than through revelation. By closely observing the structures of nature, including their own bodies and the healthy instincts and inclinations built into their minds, human beings gain reliable knowledge of the natural order God intends. For example, our innate desire to preserve our lives suggests the divine prohibition against suicide and, by extension, murder and even wanton destruction of wildlife. The natural human desire to live peacefully in society is cited as evidence to support all the rules of social order (to avoid stealing, lying, adultery, and other social trangressions) that contribute to social stability and harmony. Indeed, it might even be argued that in this way a majority of the Ten Commandments could be derived from human inclinations on the basis of natural law reasoning. These observations do not displace the need for scriptural revelation, of course, but they do suggest a felicitous overlap between revelation and reason.

Enthusiasm for natural law reasoning is often tempered by sober assessments of what it cannot realistically accomplish and also by imagining its potential abuses. It remains difficult, in the end, to build an airtight case for any specific proposal using natural law reasoning alone. Further, invoking the laws of nature to support a pet agenda has also been misused on occasion, either to discriminate against innocent people or to mount absurd arguments. An extremist might use natural law to argue, in effect, that biology is destiny and that no one may ever interfere with any bodily process (including perhaps even the spread of preventable diseases) without frustrating God's purposes. Key to sorting out such claims and predictable counterclaims is a clear definition of just what makes something "natural" or not, and whether some things that are rightly labeled artificial are actually fully reconcilable with the will of God. Judgments about the morality of the entire field of medical technology hinge on such definitions of terms.

Such misinterpretations as the simplest versions of the "biology is destiny" argument overlook an additional gift of God to every person: the endowment of intelligence and creativity that all people should use to improve their lives and achieve their full potential, always within the limits of the moral law. At best, natural law assists the process of moral reflection by limiting the field of allowable activities and reminding people not to frustrate the intentions that God encoded in nature. Natural law helps to direct human freedom in moral matters, but it does not completely determine the course of action anyone will necessarily choose. Natural law reasoning may instruct people in certain reliable principles (such as "preserve human life whenever possible" or "spread knowledge to the next generation"), but the hard work of sorting out the relationship between means and ends still remains to be accomplished. Not to be overlooked is the vital and indispensable role to be played by the virtue of prudence, which allows individuals to apply principles in good conscience, according to their best judgment.

This is why natural law has sometimes been called a "skeleton law." In order to make sound moral decisions about practical matters, people need to know far more than the few hints that natural law reasoning can offer regarding divine purposes for the universe. In fact, one of the major objections to the use of natural law is that theologians too often attempt to use this pattern of thought to make overly specific judgments concerning worldly matters (especially regarding science and economics) about which they know little. This serious error treats ethics as if it is more a science than an art, as if moral truths can be deduced with precision in the same way that mathematical formulas and geometric proofs are derived from timeless principles of logic. It also treats natural law in a faulty way, as if it were law in the sense of a codified body of precepts rather than what it really is—a more modest achievement of reason that discloses a limited set of standards for moral behavior.

The potential for these misuses of natural law ethics should not prevent anyone from employing natural law in appropriate and constructive ways. At its best, natural law is a tradition of reason that sheds much light on how people may use their divinely granted gift of intelligence to discern proper courses of action. It is also a wonderful resource in the fight against ethical relativism, a school of thought that categorically dismisses all claims that there exist objective rights and wrongs in the universe. It is one thing, of course, to agree that there are certain absolute truths and quite another thing to reach agreement on precisely what those truths are. Because natural law is merely a tool for interpreting the universe, people will continue to use natural law in their own preferred ways—and will without doubt continue to reach conflicting conclusions. The final interpretation that emerges in any given case, of course, will depend on who is using that tool.

How has natural law been used in Catholic social teaching? In the earliest social encyclicals in particular, popes used natural law reasoning as the basis for criticizing unjust arrangements of property and wages. Leo XIII and Pius XI both noticed a huge gap between God's intentions for the world (that all people should share resources so that God's gifts support human flourishing) and the actual state of affairs in the modern industrial world (millions starving while only a few enjoyed luxuries). In an era before the widespread adoption of minimum wages and similar regulations to tame labor markets, both popes reached the conclusion that this violation of human dignity runs contrary to natural law.

Although both these popes were basically conservative in temperament, their employment of natural law compelled them to advocate for sweeping changes in the capitalist order. They urged governments in industrialized nations to implement legal protections for workers, and they called upon employers to change the way wages were determined, thus giving families a chance to lift themselves up out of conditions of near starvation. Although the actual civil laws of most countries at that time did not require better treatment of workers, the natural law, as these popes interpreted it, mandated reforms. Change was necessary because God's higher law, which stands above humanly created civil laws, demanded the preservation of life and greater respect for the aspirations of working families to live in dignity. In a similar way, natural law reasoning is a potentially powerful tool in the hand of anyone seeking reforms that will bring conditions in the actual world into closer conformity with the order of justice God intends for all people.

3. Tradition: Theological Reflection in Church Life

A third source of Christian ethics is a bit harder to pin down, but its contribution to Catholic social teaching is still important. The word *tradition* as it is used here refers to all the previous reflection on social issues that has gone on within Christian theology. This serves as a reminder that what is known today as modern Catholic social teaching is only the latest in a long line of thinking within the Church about the meaning of peace and justice. Although no social encyclicals were written or published before 1891, voices within the Church have always been active in commenting on issues of life in society, including its political and economic dimensions.

Unfortunately, many valuable contributions of priests, bishops, members of religious orders, and active laity over the ages have been lost because they were not written down and preserved. Low levels of literacy and inattention to record keeping in the early centuries of Christianity prevent today's observers from acquiring even a partially satisfying view of all the events of the ancient, medieval, and even the early modern era. How interesting it would be to have a complete record of the many occasions when sermons on responsible social living were preached by clergy, when religious sisters discoursed on justice and charity within or beyond their convent walls, or when lay advisors to kings cited faith-based reasons to recommend one policy over another. In seeking to consult the Christian tradition, we are more or less limited to those few sources that happen to have been written down at the time, items such as published sermons, political treatises, and letters arguing for Christian responses to particular social challenges.

One easy way to trace the source of previous reflections on social issues is simply to check the footnotes of the twelve major social teaching documents listed in table 3.1. Most of the encyclicals contain numerous references to earlier theologians and other church figures who wrote and preached about justice and related social issues. Several of the most influential figures in this regard lived during the earliest centuries of the Church. Collectively, they are referred to as the Fathers of the Church. From the Latin root word for "father" is derived the term *patristic*, which describes the era in which these men lived. Among the major patristic figures are Clement of Alexandria, Tertullian, Origen, Athanasius, Basil the Great, John Chrysostom, Ambrose of Milan, Augustine of Hippo, and Jerome.

Most of these men have been recognized as saints or doctors (in the sense of "great teachers") of the Church. Writing and preaching between the second and sixth centuries of the Christian era, these theologians addressed numerous matters of church doctrine and contributed greatly to the Church's understanding of the Holy Trinity, the identity of Jesus Christ, the sacraments, scripture, and the very mission of the Church. Part of this mission is for people of faith to play an active role in the life of the wider society. The many writings left behind by the Church Fathers contain much insightful advice for Christians trying to live a life of faith amidst the challenges of a politically and economically divided world.

Perusing patristic literature might leave the contemporary reader rather dissatisfied with some of the positions staked out on social issues. They may seem at first blush to be overly simplified and, therefore, largely irrelevant to the complexities of the modern world. For example, on the issue of private property, several of the Church Fathers wrote angry denunciations of greed and selfishness but did not pay sufficient attention to detailed arguments supporting the continued recognition of private ownership of property. Basil the Great, for example, preached a famous sermon in which he boldly stated that all our surplus wealth belongs directly to the needy and should be distributed to the poor immediately. John Chrysostom went so far as to advocate a form of primitive communism when he wrote:

> For "mine" and "thine"—those chilly words which introduce innumerable wars into the world—should be eliminated . . . . The poor would not envy the rich, because there would be no rich. Neither would the poor be despised by the rich, for there would be no poor. All things would be in common.

Here as elsewhere, the Fathers brilliantly advance our understanding of the social implications of the faith that come to us from scripture, but do not succeed as well in offering practical steps to improve society. That is why their social messages are cited by popes in recent social encyclicals primarily as reminders of basic religious virtues such as generosity and selflessness, but not as offering complete and fully sufficient blueprints for life in society.

The task of better bringing together the ideals of our faith with the practical demands of the everyday world fell to a later group of Christian theologians who wrote extensively on social issues—the Scholastics (literally, the "school men") of medieval Europe. The towering figure among all the Scholastics was St. Thomas Aquinas (1225–1274), a thirteenth-century Dominican priest and scholar who is quoted frequently in the modern social encyclicals. Aquinas had an extraordinary eye for finding ways to merge and reconcile many traditions of thought into a unified whole, or synthesis. His works, such as the masterful multi-volume *Summa Theologica*, build upon the traditions of ancient Greek and Roman scholars as well as scripture and the writings of the patristic era and the intervening centuries.

Aquinas had quite a knack for summarizing the major arguments on controversial issues and applying carefully drawn principles to reach clear and moderate conclusions grounded in logic and reason.

For example, on the issue of private ownership of property, Aquinas affirms the wisdom of the insights cited above from Basil and Chrysostom, but he uses a natural law argument to moderate the force of these patristic insights. He first recognizes that God fully intends humans to share equitably in the common gifts of creation. Concern for the common good, therefore, demands a broad distribution of resources so that no one is cut off from access to social participation and the means to a decent livelihood. But Aquinas also recognizes the fallen nature of humanity, a condition that makes a total sharing of resources unlikely to work out for practical reasons. As a keen observer of human nature (and as a member of a religious order in which he had to share overcrowded rooms, precious books, and scarce tools held in common), Aquinas knew that problems such as laziness, jealousy, the human tendency to shirk unpleasant work, and the likelihood of disputes over shared property justify some division of goods.

While common use of all things is a laudable goal and perhaps indeed the original intention of the Creator, for Aquinas the institution of private ownership of goods is a necessary social principle in a fallen world. As a great forger of compromises, Aquinas does not so much refute the patristic sources he cites; rather, he judiciously concedes that their insights about sharing apply to the *use* of the goods that all people need, not to their actual *ownership*. This distinction (Scholastics loved to make distinctions) between the use and the ownership of material goods has found its way into several of the documents of modern Catholic social teaching that take up the question of justifying private ownership of property.

Besides property, another illuminating case study in the growth of traditions of Christian social thought involves the use of deadly force. Most New Testament references to violence contain blanket prohibitions against harming others for any reason whatsoever. Jesus clearly ruled out violence as an appropriate response to any situation, even on the occasion when he was about to be unjustly arrested and led away to execution. In fact, it was common practice for the earliest Christian communities to be strictly pacifist, avoiding military service as a matter of principle and even refusing to defend themselves when captured or attacked during the Roman persecutions. By the fifth century, a few patristic voices distanced themselves from this uncompromising position on nonresistance to evil. Most notable was St. Augustine of Hippo (354–430), a great scholar who supported a policy of using military force when absolutely necessary to preserve social order. On a number of occasions, Augustine cited arguments to justify armed interventions for good causes, including the suppression of several dangerous heresies that threatened the local church in North Africa where he served as bishop.

By making carefully reasoned arguments for the limited use of force, Augustine became a founder of the tradition of *just war theory*. Later Christian authors such as Aquinas and the Jesuit theologian Francisco Suárez (1548–1617) expanded the reflections of Augustine and derived a list of several strict conditions that defensive wars must meet in order to be considered fully justified. This list of appropriate criteria, despite having no clear basis in scripture, has become an accepted part of modern Catholic social teaching. Chapter five describes the categories that comprise the just war theory and includes a listing of the justifying conditions most often cited in the tradition (see table 5.2). Just war theory is mentioned in several of the papal social encyclicals and is treated at length in the U.S. bishops' 1983 pastoral letter *The Challenge of Peace*. Debates in recent years about the appropriate response to terrorism and the morality of waging war in Iraq have often revolved around conflicting interpretations of the just war theory, in both its religious and its more secular versions. The ongoing relevance of just war theory in ethical discourse underlines the fascinating ways that traditions of Christian reflection continue to grow and to find resonance in arenas far beyond the boundaries of the Church itself.

Because Scripture has always served as the starting point for Christian theological reflection, there is an especially intimate connection between scripture and tradition, the first and third sources of Christian ethics treated in this chapter. The Vatican II document *Dei Verbum* ("Dogmatic Constitution on Divine Revelation") speaks movingly of the close relationship between these two fonts of Catholic theology. This document points out that:

> . . . both of them [scripture and tradition], flowing from the same divine wellspring, in a certain way merge into a unity and toward the same end. (no. 9)

Scripture and tradition cannot be separated. As key sources of Christian ethics, they work together to help believers know and interpret the Word of God as it addresses the contemporary world.

4. Experience: Engaging in Social Analysis

The last of the four sources is in a sense already contained in each of the first three. It would be impossible to talk about revelation, reason, or tradition without presuming an important role for human experience. Every idea a given person talks about, writes down, and hands on to the next generation first passes through his or her five senses and should be considered part of human experience. Even scripture, which at first glance might seem far removed from this category, amounts to a record of human experience—in this special case, the human witness to distinctive revelations of God. In the world of social ethics, however, the word experience has come to mean something quite specific, namely a method by which contemporary people seeking to form moral judgments take into account what they observe and learn from worldly events. The brief section below describes the process of social analysis as it contributes to the *experience* dimension of Catholic social teaching.

Part of the task of Catholic social teaching is to help people of faith read and interpret "the signs of the times." This is a phrase that appears in the Gospel of Matthew (16:3) as well as in paragraph 4 of the Vatican II document *Gaudium et Spes*. But just how does this "reading" take place? The shortest answer to this question is to observe a common pattern that effective people follow when they meet a new situation. First, they take a careful look at the situation; next, they make an accurate judgment about what is going on and how best to respond to it; and finally, they act vigorously upon what they have learned. Anyone eager to keep a favorite houseplant alive, for example, is familiar with this simple pattern of activity. Even if he is no expert in botany, such a person keeps an eye out for signs of a thirsty plant (brown leaves, parched soil), makes a judgment call about the right time for a watering, and follows through by reaching for the watering jug. Having a green thumb turns out to entail little more than reading the signs of the times and overcoming natural human laziness. Successful plant care is often more about maintaining attentiveness and rousing a bit of energy than it is about any innate skills or technical knowledge of horticulture. Many further examples might illustrate this commonsense insight.

This three-step process, abbreviated as *see–judge–act*, has long been found useful in church circles, not only in large-scale social matters but also in the spiritual discernment of individuals and small groups, as people seek to harvest the fruits of both contemplation and action in their lives. By noting the implicit rhythm of action and reflection, people attentive to these three steps have frequently gained insight into the necessity of the type of social engagement that preserves a place for periodic meditative withdrawal from the bustle of social ministries and other work activities, in order to ponder new realities and interpretations of worldly events. Carving out time for observation and ongoing judgment not only ensures more effective analysis of programs and efforts, but often provides needed respite for the renewal of burdened personnel, who easily fall into burnout and overwork. In fact, the three steps of see-judge-act have proven so helpful in church circles that they are described in some detail in paragraphs 236 through 241 of *Mater et Magistra* ("Christianity and Social Progress"), Pope John XXIII's 1961 social encyclical. A slightly more elaborate version of this same process is outlined in a four-step schema that is usually called the *pastoral circle*. Because theologians have a fondness for fancy labels, the terms *circle of praxis* and *hermeneutical circle* have also been used to describe this method of understanding and acting on worldly realities. Whatever name it goes by, this process emphasizes the crucial two-way relationship between action and reflection and includes these four steps: (1) experience, (2) social analysis, (3) theological reflection, and (4) pastoral planning. Although the phrase "social analysis" often gets the most attention, each of these steps is a necessary part of engaging in church-based efforts for social justice. A brief look at each stage, or "moment" of the circle follows below.

1. *Experience*: The first step involves the initial gaining of experience itself. This requires insertion into a local situation to gather data about social problems and their effects. It goes without saying that a certain amount of courage is necessary to get involved in controversial issues and perhaps even to find oneself in unfamiliar or dangerous places. But there is no substitute for leaving our armchairs and getting our hands dirty in the real-life situations that affect the lives of so many. To refuse to venture out of one's comfortable cocoon is to deprive oneself of the very experience upon which the pastoral circle is based. Further, it does not require any rare or special powers of observation in order to gather the basic data required to jump-start the pastoral circle. Very often, people use this as an excuse to exempt themselves from volunteer projects or service-learning activities. In the end, most people find that simply keeping their eyes open in the midst of new experiences or unfamiliar cultures provides plenty of information for further reflection.

2. *Social analysis*: The second step is the least obvious but perhaps the most crucial part of the circle, for only when observers undertake serious social analysis can they understand all the factors behind a given social situation. Social analysis entails asking hard questions about the causes of injustices and the connections between issues in pursuit of reliable hypotheses about who is really responsible behind the scenes for social problems. The purpose of social analysis is to unveil the systems or patterns of activity that perpetuate injustices. This second step may require the assistance of outside experts who can apply their specialized knowledge in fields such as sociology, anthropology, economics, political science, and even psychology. It often becomes helpful to probe the historical roots of current injustice, tracing them back to causes that may not seem obvious at first. A

good piece of advice at this stage is to retain a healthy sense of skepticism about much of conventional wisdom, since preferred ways of seeing the world often depart significantly from the underlying truth. The wisest course of action is to insist on hearing all sides of the story before drawing any firm conclusions. It is extremely important to draw independent and critical judgments, because the whole process could be defeated by giving in to a misleading interpretation at this stage.

3. *Theological reflection*: This step accompanies social analysis and, in tandem with it, provides the tools to make proper judgments about social realities. Acknowledging this third stage serves as a reminder that the experiences gained in the first step and the data collected in the second step must also be viewed in the light of the living faith, as the Word of God and the theological tradition is brought to bear on contemporary situations. It is here that the documents of Catholic social teaching may be most useful, as they open up new insights and raise new questions that may otherwise be overlooked. While the other three stages of the circle emphasize our own initiatives as active participants, this stage invites us to combine our own creative thinking with a solid commitment to consult established sources of Christian social wisdom, such as the riches of scripture, reason, and tradition described earlier in this chapter. This third step is the most distinctively religious part of the circle of praxis and the one that takes most explicit advantage of the inheritance of theology and social ethics.

4. *Pastoral planning*: This step involves determining the appropriate response to the new knowledge gained in the previous steps. Here participants in the process chart a course of action to guide them in preparing for the future. This is where the hard work of the earlier three stages pays off, for all that precedes this final step contributes to the reaching of sound decisions and the choice of effective strategies. The goal is to design programs of action that, by taking advantage of previous experience and reflection upon the lessons of the past, will be more helpful in meeting upcoming challenges. The pastoral circle is completed when participants are able to return to the experience, or insertion, phase equipped with what they have learned from the journey so far.

The experience dimension of social ethics makes an even greater contribution when this process is envisioned as not merely a one-time episode but as an ongoing process of learning more and more about the world and seeking to act ever more effectively based on increasing knowledge. Ideally, the fruitfulness of all future social efforts will benefit from past and present learnings. Emphasizing the increasing possibilities of this process aids the recognition that, when it succeeds, the pastoral circle is not a mere circle at all but a spiral ascending upward. At the end of each project, participants do not really return to where they started but, rather, find themselves at a higher location, better informed about their social context and better prepared to take effective action in the next round of involvement.

UNIVERSAL PRINCIPLES AND LOCAL APPLICATIONS

In the 1971 Catholic social teaching document *Octogesima Adveniens* ("A Call to Action on the 80th Anniversary of *Rerum Novarum*"), Pope Paul VI offers important advice about how best to make use of the Church's reflections on justice, peace, and life in society:

> In the face of such widely varying situations, it is difficult for us to utter a unified message and to put forward a solution which has universal validity. Such is not our ambition, nor is it our mission. It is up to the Christian communities to analyze with objectivity the situation which is proper to their own country, to shed on it the light of the Gospel's unalterable words and to draw principles of reflection, norms of judgment and directives for action from the social teaching of the Church. (no. 4)

Those three sentences contain much wisdom, and the message of this chapter provides a context for understanding and benefiting from the words of Pope Paul VI. This chapter has introduced the major sources and methods that contribute to the documents of Catholic social teaching. The remaining questions to consider here are: (1) How does one combine the four sources of Christian ethics in responding to the social issues of the day? and (2) How does one apply to local circumstances the rich insights of Catholic social teaching that come from Vatican documents?

When he upholds the role of local Christian communities in social action in the above quotation, Pope Paul VI demonstrates a solid appreciation for the division of labor portrayed in the pastoral circle. After all, three of the four moments of the circle describe activities that unfold almost exclusively on the local level. When a parish, diocese, or other religious organization undertakes a new community involvement, reflects on its effectiveness, and updates its program planning, very little conscious attention to the documents of Catholic social teaching is likely. No pope or Vatican commission can spare the time to serve as a consultant to a local Catholic school, soup kitchen, or counseling center, even if given the opportunity to contribute through active participation. The great bulk of the work, in both the reflection and the action phases, must be done on the grassroots level.

This is the same insight contained in Pope Paul VI's words. The center of gravity in social ministries must lie with the local communities of Christians who find themselves facing a great variety of challenging social conditions. They are the ones who most often engage in the threefold task of seeing, judging, and acting. The seeing and acting will certainly never be able to move forward on a worldwide level. As Pope Paul VI affirmed, it is difficult for any Vatican voice to address the diverse social problems of all corners of the world simultaneously by proposing detailed solutions that aspire to have universal validity. However, it is in that middle stage of judging where Catholic social teaching makes its great contribution.

How is this so? Recall that the four-part pastoral circle suggests that judging includes two components: (1) social analysis, which relies on secular fields of study such as sociology and economics; and (2) theological reflection, which relies on tools provided by the Christian tradition, such as Catholic social teaching. There are, of course, some things church documents can never accomplish. For example, they cannot substitute for the wisdom of many years of life experience, nor replace vigorous local efforts to forge the best possible analysis of a particular social situation. This is why Pope Paul VI reminds us that universal messages from Rome cannot supply all the wisdom a Christian community might need to meet its specific local challenges.

But the teachings of the universal church do have an indispensable role to play in offering general principles regarding the attainment of justice and peace. Vatican social encyclicals do much of the necessary homework for their readers in advance. Their descriptions of the meaning of common good, solidarity, freedom, and other social virtues inspire people everywhere to strive for improvement in the life of their own local communities. Reading these documents connects us to scripture and church tradition, giving us many important tools to guide our own judgments and to apply God's summons to live justly in our daily lives. The next chapter examines nine of the major themes treated in the Church's social teaching documents.

QUESTIONS FOR REFLECTION

1. Of the four sources of Christian ethics, is there one you particularly favor or disfavor? What are the reasons for your enthusiasm or reservations?

2. In describing how the four sources are sometimes combined, this chapter examines two examples of social teaching topics: ownership of private property and the just war theory. List some other social issues on which the Church has spoken, and discuss the relative weight that has been given or should be given to each of the four sources in developing this teaching.

3. How useful is the Bible for contemporary morality? Are there certain topics or ethical issues where scripture provides particularly strong or particularly inadequate guidance? How is it possible to recognize scripture as divinely inspired, but still not a fully complete rulebook for modern living? Discuss the best model for applying biblical materials to contemporary moral issues.

4. Have you ever engaged in a project that, knowingly or not, followed the pastoral circle? Describe the steps you went through, whether consciously at the time or not. At the end of the process, did you feel that you were back where you started, or was there a sense of spiraling upward toward greater knowledge and more effective involvement?

5. The section of this chapter on experience included a short description of social analysis, which always includes an effort to discover the causes of social problems and the linkages among social issues. Construct a "user's guide" for social analysis, one that seeks to anticipate problems that may arise in this process. How may the discernment go astray? Pay specific attention to two items: first, the particularly urgent questions that should be asked at the start of any inquiry into the various dimensions (historical, economic, social, political, cultural) of any given social problem; and second, the things that can go wrong in any such inquiry, such as the intrusion of biases and warped judgments that might skew the findings and mislead an observer.

6. How would you summarize the proper relationship between universal principles (such as the ones we find in the documents of Vatican social teaching) and local applications (as when smaller groups use the pastoral circle)? Are the more universal statements merely good background resources for one or two stages of local decision making, or should we think of them as basic starting points?

TOPICS FOR FURTHER RESEARCH

1. Principles of jurisprudence regarding the patterns of legal interpretation over the ages

2. The various schools of hermeneutics, the science of literary and biblical interpretation

3. Scriptural guidance on social justice beyond that offered in table 4.1
4. The history of natural law reasoning from the Stoics through the Christian era
5. Key figures in patristic theology: their dominant concerns and messages
6. The innovations, contributions, and shortcomings of Scholastic theology
7. The reinterpretation of theories of private property throughout various Christian eras
8. The just war theory, its history and disputes over its correct application
9. The pastoral circle (or circle of praxis) and how social analysis proceeds
10. The relationship between universal teaching and grassroots-level projects

5

+

Nine Key Themes of Catholic Social Teaching

The previous four chapters examined many important questions regarding the significance and context of Catholic social teaching. The material covered so far provides necessary background regarding such topics as the rationale for social action on the part of the Christian community, the historical development of the Church's social teaching, and the scriptural and theological sources of the documents that contain that teaching. In fact, it seems that we have accomplished almost everything except what many readers probably most desire: a detailed exploration of the content of the teaching that we have heard so much about.

It is time to reward the reader's patience. This chapter is the payoff, as it investigates the actual messages contained in the social encyclicals. Recall that each section of table 3.1 provides brief summaries of the challenges and new messages of each of the twelve Vatican social teaching documents. This chapter offers a greatly expanded account of the central topics and arguments of these documents. The analysis offered here will proceed primarily in a thematic way, rather than in a historical fashion. Instead of marching through the encyclicals in chronological order, this chapter treats nine themes that form the heart of Catholic social teaching as it has developed over the course of more than one hundred years.

There is nothing magical about the number nine in this context and nothing definitive about this particular listing of themes. Similar lists of various lengths have been compiled by other observers of this tradition. The Annotated List of Resources for Further Study at the end of this book includes several sources that contain such lists. Although these lists rarely match perfectly, there is general agreement about the basic items that belong on any list of the core Catholic social teaching principles. Table 5.1 offers a handy at-a-glance listing of these nine themes along with three of the most important texts in the documents of Catholic social teaching that treat each theme.

1. THE DIGNITY OF EVERY PERSON AND HUMAN RIGHTS

The claim that people have great worth and dignity is certainly a familiar assertion. In fact, it would be hard to think of a culture or religion that did not in some way affirm the value of human life. But the Catholic Church

Table 5.1. Key Texts for Nine Themes in Catholic Social Teaching

Theme	Most Important Texts
1. The Dignity of Every Person and Human Rights	*Pacem in Terris* 8–38 *Gaudium et Spes* 12–19 *Centesimus Annus* 6–11
2. Solidarity, Common Good, and Participation	*Pacem in Terris* 98–108 *Gaudium et Spes* 26–32, 68–75 *Sollicitudo rei Socialis* 35–40
3. Family Life	*Gaudium et Spes* 47–52 *Octogesima Adveniens* 13 *Laborem Exercens* 10, 19
4. Subsidiarity and the Proper Role of Government	*Quadragesimo Anno* 76–87 *Mater et Magistra* 51–77, 122–77 *Pacem in Terris* 140–41
5. Property Ownership in Modern Society: Rights and Responsibilities	*Quadragesimo Anno* 44–52 *Mater et Magistra* 51–67,104–21 *Centesimus Annus* 30–43
6. The Dignity of Work, Rights of Workers, and Support for Labor Unions	*Rerum Novarum* 1–3, 20–21, 31–38 *Mater et Magistra* 68–81 *Laborem Exercens* 1–27
7. Colonialism and Economic Development	*Mater et Magistra* 157–211 *Pacem in Terris* 121–25 *Populorum Progressio* 1–87
8. Peace and Disarmament	*Pacem in Terris* 109–119 *Gaudium et Spes* 77–90 U.S. Bishops' *The Challenge of Peace*
9. Option for the Poor and Vulnerable	*Gaudium et Spes* 1 *Octogesima Adveniens* 23 *Centesimus Annus* 11

addresses the topic of human dignity in a special way that leads to some particularly firm conclusions about what is permissible both in individual moral choices and in the ethical practices of entire societies. The positions staked out by Catholic social teaching on a wide range of issues are solidly grounded in a complete view of the origin, nature, and destiny of all people.

One key foundation of this picture of human life is that all humans are made in the image and likeness of God. This idea appears in the story of creation that is portrayed in mythical language in the opening chapters of the Book of Genesis. Because all humans somehow reflect the image of God in their rational minds and in their physical bodies, they are all entitled to be treated with the greatest of respect and dignity. Because we are intelligent and free beings, God intends us to be immune from all slavery, manipulation, or exploitation. At all stages of our lives—from the moment of conception through the vulnerable years of childhood and old age to the very moment of natural death—we deserve the care and attention that belong to beings of inestimable worth. Indeed, according to this doctrine, there is nothing a person can do or undergo that leads to the forfeiture of this lofty status. Even those who commit heinous crimes, who acquire debilitating diseases, or who find themselves separated from their homelands or from gainful employment retain immense worth and are to be accorded the greatest of human dignity. All people—whether they are languishing on death row in a prison, receiving treatment at an AIDS clinic in a hospital, or living in a refugee camp in the most remote corner of the world—deserve to be treated with inalienable respect as children of God.

This insistence on the sanctity and immeasurable value of each human life has led the Catholic Church to uncompromising opposition to various threats to human dignity, including abortion, euthanasia, and capital punishment. In its moral teachings, the Church has courageously held fast to a pro-life position on numerous controversial issues, advocating respect for all human life, especially that of the vulnerable and outcast. Perhaps the most articulate spokesman on these matters among American Catholics was the late Cardinal Joseph Bernardin (1928–1996) of Chicago. In the last decades of his life, this prominent church leader wrote and spoke frequently about the topic of "a consistent ethic of life." In advocating an attitude of profound respect for the sanctity of life at every moment of its duration, from conception to natural death, Cardinal Bernardin often used the biblical metaphor of the seamless garment (see John 19:23). This comparison suggests that any attack against innocent life is an offense and potential threat to all human life. Bernardin appealed not just to believers but to all people of good will to recognize the worth of all people and to do all in their power to protect the vulnerable.

One important aspect of human dignity is the notion of equality. The Catholic tradition interprets the key moments of the drama of human life in a way that treats all people equally. From God's original bestowal of life (in the act of creation), to the sending of God's Son into the world to save all people from sin (in the Incarnation), to the expectation of a final invitation into God's Kingdom (in the Resurrection of the Dead), Catholic doctrine testifies to a fundamental equality in God's gracious activity. When Catholic social teaching calls for a more equal sharing of political power, social status, and economic resources, it is merely extending the Christian theological doctrine of equal human dignity to the concrete realm of social existence. There are certain things that all children of God deserve, and when vast inequalities prevent people from attaining what they need to preserve their lives and develop their potential, people of faith must speak out against these injustices.

Of course, human life in actual societies has always been filled with many types of inequality. Nothing could be more obvious than the basic social fact that some people enjoy vast holdings of wealth and resources while others struggle for mere survival. While it is surely true that many affluent people deserve the possessions they accumulate through hard work and effort, the sheer luck of being born into the right family or a particularly thriving homeland also accounts for a major share of such disparities in life chances and measurable outcomes. The race for income, wealth, and status does not take place on a level playing field, as opportunities for education and social mobility are never evenly distributed, either within or between societies.

Bridging the gap between the ideals of the Christian principle of equal dignity, on one hand, and the blatant perennial differences of wealth and privilege that divide people into distinct social classes, on the other hand, is a major challenge. No one expects rapid progress toward the goal of universal recognition of fundamental equalities. It is a safe bet to wager that future generations will witness the same glaring disparities in wealth, income, and power that continue to trap millions in destitution and deprive them of their full dignity today. However, the realization of greater equality, at least in guaranteeing all people life and access to the basic goods necessary for a dignified livelihood, remains a noble aspiration and a worthy focus for faith-based advocacy as well as other forms of social activism.

The twentieth century witnessed a remarkable movement toward a worldwide consensus regarding human rights. International covenants (such as the Universal Declaration of Human Rights approved by the United Nations General Assembly in 1948) often base their arguments on the centuries-old concept of human rights. Beginning especially with *Pacem in Terris* in 1963, the documents of Catholic social teaching also use the language of human rights as one way of expressing what is owed to all human beings by virtue of their dignity. Pope John XXIII included in *Pacem in Terris* a full listing of the many types of human rights, calling these rights "universal, inviolable, and inalienable." This groundbreaking encyclical treated various types of rights (including social, cultural, religious, economic, political, and civil rights) and correlated them closely with duties to be observed and fulfilled within society. Because it was the first strong statement of a human rights position from the Church, *Pacem in Terris* earned the nickname "the Catholic charter of human rights." Pope John's encyclical letter echoes similar documents from other religious communities around the world that offer parallel calls for the recognition of a full range of human rights. The convergence of worldwide opinion, both religious and secular in nature, around human rights is an encouraging sign for the prospect of greater cooperation and further improvement in the social conditions facing people of all nations and creeds.

But it is helpful to note that the Catholic view of human rights is distinctive because it is grounded on a complete theological framework in which God is the ultimate source of our rights. The Catholic tradition of reflection on human rights is also special in that it always situates rights within human communities. In comparison, purely secular doctrines of rights have no similar foundation in a compelling portrayal of human nature and its origin. In this sense, they are "thin" doctrines, lacking a solid theory or cosmology behind them. This is perhaps a necessary concession on the part of international human rights advocates to the great pluralism of world opinion, a condition that makes agreement on all but the most general principles very difficult to sustain, but it remains a troublesome shortcoming. Such secular rights theories are susceptible to the weighty charge that rights just seem to float around, adhering to people without any satisfying justification behind their passing claims and sweeping assertions. Because of the resulting inability to link rights claims with corresponding obligations that specific parties must discharge to the benefit of others, rights within such theories tend to remain vague and merely hortatory in nature.

While secular rights theories are certainly useful in speaking boldly about our immunity from being harmed by others, the claims they make have the shortcoming of not fitting into a shared comprehensive view of the universe. Because they remain quite thin, such theories can offer little guidance on difficult questions such as how to resolve seemingly interminable conflicts of rights. The treatment of rights in Catholic social teaching reflects most of these same positive concerns and goals, but has the additional advantage of situating talk about human rights within a more satisfying and complete picture of the world. Because it is grounded in reverence for the sanctity of creation and its Creator, the Catholic approach to human rights can consider the entire web of relationships that connect God, the natural environment, persons, governments, and local communities. Although relatively recent, Catholic human rights theory is a particularly strong contribution within church social teaching.

2. SOLIDARITY, COMMON GOOD, AND PARTICIPATION

This second theme serves as an important counterbalance to the first and helps to prevent a rampant and destructive individualism. Rights should always be placed in the context of solidarity and concern for the well-being of the wider community. To consider only the dignity and infinite worth of the individual in isolation risks neglecting the insight that rights come paired with duties. All the things that persons have rightful claims to are necessarily matched with the things these same persons are expected to give back to others who depend upon them. The Catholic social encyclicals teach that to be human is to experience not only rights but also obligations to others.

Solidarity is a single word that captures a complex of meanings. It calls attention to the easily observable and indisputable fact that people are interdependent; they rely upon each other for almost all their biological and emotional needs. The complex fabric of social life, including human achievements such as language, art, culture, and education, testifies to the many ways in which people depend on shared efforts in all fields of human endeavors. To employ the term solidarity entails recognizing human interdependence not only as a necessary *fact* but also as a positive *value* in our lives. We cannot realize our full potential or appreciate the full meaning of our dignity unless we share our lives with others and cooperate on projects that hold the promise of mutual benefit.

In his three social encyclicals, namely *Laborem Exercens, Sollicitudo rei Socialis,* and *Centesimus Annus,* Pope John Paul II repeatedly lauded solidarity as an essential virtue of social life. He argued that God not only allows people to depend upon each other, but absolutely wills that humans share themselves in the context of intimate as well as larger groupings of our neighbors. To be human is to be a social being, one whose very life is and should be bound up with those in close proximity and even distant strangers.

Solidarity begins as an inner attitude and, when it has fully taken root within a person, expresses itself through numerous external activities that demonstrate a person's commitment to the well-being of others. Just as children naturally reach out to their peers to find playmates and to build friendships, all humans display a natural propensity to form and nourish many social relationships. Catholic social teaching portrays each person as naturally fitting into the larger society. Except in unusual situations, such as becoming a consecrated hermit or finding oneself shipwrecked on a desert island, human flourishing is always communal and social. The full range of features that constitute human nature and dignity come to maturity only in the context of community life, where many relationships develop and ripen. Developing the virtue of solidarity is thus the perfect antidote to any temptations toward an egoistic individualism that neglects social obligations or subordinates the needs of others to personal and possibly narcissistic agendas.

Two especially important aspects of social life are summarized by a pair of terms frequently linked together in Catholic social teaching: *common good* and *participation*. To speak of the common good is to recognize that there are numerous proper goals in life beyond our own private benefits. Responsible people look for opportunities to contribute to worthy causes and to improve society in many ways, even when the benefits of this progress will go primarily to others. In *Mater et Magistra*, Pope John XXIII defines the common good as "the sum total of those conditions of social living whereby men are enabled more fully and more readily to achieve their own perfection" (no. 65). Everyone has an obligation to promote the common good by making whatever contributions are necessary to improve the lives of others.

Consider one example that illustrates the obligation of all people to promote the common good. One of the key conditions for human flourishing in society is the education and maturation of youth. Since this is often an expensive task, and since everyone ultimately has a stake in quality schools, it falls to every member of society to support education. It is not far-fetched to imagine an elderly, childless couple launching an argument to explain why they should be exempt from paying taxes to support education for future generations. Perhaps this couple would base such claims on the argument that they themselves will not benefit from costly improvements in public schools, as neither they nor any members of their immediate family will be attending schools. At first blush, based solely on the logic of self-interest, such an argument seems to make a certain amount of sense. However, an understanding of common good that is consistent with Catholic social teaching would point to the obligation of all citizens, however indirect one's stake, to make significant sacrifices for such improvements that will bring broad benefits to society, including future generations. The importance of such contributions transcends the expected benefits to any given individual; people pay their share of social dues simply because they are members of society.

Perhaps the most compelling example of an urgent common good issue today involves the natural environment. Every creature on earth depends upon a healthy ecosystem for its continued existence. Human mishandling of the environment has led to crises such as global warming, resource depletion, endangered species, and pollution in all its forms. Everyone has an obligation to contribute to conditions that will serve life better and provide ecological sustainability to benefit future generations. Because this huge and important topic appears only quite recently and belatedly in official documents of the Church, coverage of environmental issues will be taken up in chapter seven, where the future of Catholic social teaching is treated in some detail. The common good will emerge in that context as a pivotal concept in sparking concern and activism for ecological justice and as the single most important lens through which to view future efforts to preserve environmental integrity.

The other related term is participation. As the tradition of Catholic social teaching has unfolded in its full appreciation of the equality of all members of society, the theme of equal participation has come to play a more and more important role in its documents. Every person has at once a right and a duty to participate in the full range of activities and institutions of social life. To be excluded from playing a significant role in the life of society is a serious injustice, for it frustrates the legitimate aspirations of all people to express their human freedom. Anything that blocks full political participation (such as unreasonable restrictions on voting rights for minorities) or economic participation (such as racial or gender discrimination in educational or employment opportunities) counts as a serious offense against human rights. A sincere regard for the common good will inspire concerned members of society to oppose such injustices and encourage full participation for all, regardless of differences of race, gender, or creed. Calls for full and fair participation in all sectors of society punctuate the documents of the Catholic social tradition.

These moral imperatives apply to both *economic* and *political* life in human society. The ordinary way that people participate in the economy is through their labor. A close look at Catholic social teaching on questions of work and employment will accompany the examination of item six on this list of nine themes. The ordinary way for people to participate in the political life of society is through democratic activity that allows them to determine the basic structures of their government and to exert considerable influence on its ongoing operations. When it is fulfilling its proper role, government is the instrument of a people, not something that drains their resources or threatens to control them. Government earns its legitimacy when it assists the people's efforts to pursue a happy, prosperous, and meaningful life without undue interference with their God-given liberties, including freedom of religion and conscience.

Catholic social teaching portrays government as the privileged agent of the common good and as a natural part of a well-ordered human community. The God who intends people to live together in society also enlightens their minds as they seek to organize their large-scale social cooperation. Citizens naturally turn to the assistance of properly selected public authorities whose policies supplement private efforts to order society justly. These government officials are entrusted with the task of safeguarding the rights of all and carrying out the full range of duties to other members of society. Without government as an expression of human solidarity, individuals could do little to ensure peace and advance the cause of social justice. Further commentary on how the tradition of Catholic social thought treats the role of government, including prudent limits to state intervention in society, appears below in this chapter's section on the principle of subsidiarity.

3. FAMILY LIFE

It makes good sense to follow the treatment of solidarity, which describes that aspect of human identity pertaining to membership in the wider society, with a complementary treatment of the most basic unit of society: the family. The family occupies a special place in Catholic social teaching. It is the most intimate sphere in which people cooperate and the first place where children learn about themselves, their individual identities, and their vocations within the wider social world. Church documents sometimes refer to the family as the "domestic church" because it is also where young people first encounter God, form their consciences, and learn moral virtues. Elsewhere it is referred to as the "first cell of society," for no institution can substitute for the important social roles played by families. The responses of justice and charity that are called for in the social encyclicals depend upon decisions made along with loved ones in the context of family life and on the fundamental level of the individual household.

The well-being of the entire society absolutely depends upon healthy families, committed marriages, and responsible parenthood. Family life is where people learn and practice the virtues of love and compassion that allow them to imagine alternatives to the ruthless competition and selfish individualism witnessed all too often in the business world and in today's market-based society. Outside of family life, it is rare to witness a spirit of profound self-sacrifice and generous giving to others that does not count the cost to oneself. But within our families, no one is surprised by (and indeed we almost expect) habitual acts of forgiveness and self-emptying love on the part of spouses, parents, and children. In a world of bewildering complexity and rapid, unpredictable change, the stable relationships of family and home life are like a safe port in a fierce storm. Families are the place where the unconditional love of God is reflected in everyday human activities, where people gain a glimpse of the unity and communion that they hope to find in the Kingdom of God.

But it is wise also to be on guard against excessive idealism about family life. Real-life families experience serious challenges and numerous problems, from within (stemming from their members, who are rarely saints) and from outside (stemming from the public world beyond the household). To its credit, *Gaudium et Spes*, the 1965 Vatican II document that contains the most extended treatment of family life of any of the twelve Vatican social teaching documents, describes a number of these challenges in a frank and eye-opening way. Several pages of this document are devoted to the problems encountered by families today. *Gaudium et Spes* introduces its survey of these problems with the compassionate observation that:

> . . . serious disturbances are caused in families by modern economic conditions, by influences at once social and psychological, and by the demands of civil society. (no. 47)

Many of these problems come from perennial sources of hardship that vex humanity in every age, such as poverty, illness, materialism, and the irresponsibility and routine inattentiveness of family members. Others come from newer pressures, such as overwork, modern rootlessness, the entry of more women into the paid workforce with a resulting scarcity of reliable daycare, and the adjustments associated with divorce and blended families. Indeed, our thinking about family life itself is constantly challenged by the existence of new family patterns that do not conform to accustomed notions of the nuclear family. The most recent such challenge, of course, is the growing legal recognition accorded to same-sex couples, who in some jurisdictions are now entitled to a range of civil and economic benefits that in some cases are exactly equivalent to what traditional married couples enjoy. Unlike in years past, households form and combine for nontraditional reasons and with new relationships among children and adults drawn from several generations.

In the face of such challenges, wise public policies can make a huge contribution to the health of millions of families. A forward-thinking government will invest prudentially in families through such measures as social welfare programs, subsidies for quality daycare, medical leave provisions, unemployment compensation, and suitable retirement benefits. Pope John Paul II offers a comprehensive list of constructive government policies toward families in his 1981 encyclical *Laborem Exercens*. Some nations, particularly in Western Europe, are far ahead of the United States in adopting such family-friendly economic policies. Corporations and other private institutions are also under obligations to support family life for the benefit of their employees, their customers, and all citizens. Catholic social teaching suggests that any compassionate society will count the health of family life as among the highest priorities on its policy agenda.

4. SUBSIDIARITY AND THE PROPER ROLE OF GOVERNMENT

Of the nine themes on this list, this one features the title that will probably baffle the most people. The term *subsidiarity* comes from the Latin word for assistance, and it refers to the way the various levels of society should relate to each other and assist one another in bringing about the best outcomes for all people. The term was coined by Pope Pius XI who, in the 1931 encyclical *Quadragesimo Anno*, draws a distinction between "higher collectivities" on one hand and "lesser and subordinate bodies" on the other hand.

The Pope's message is about the proper division of labor among human institutions. For example, there are some tasks and goals that should be accomplished on the local level and others that are more appropriate for larger entities, such as national governments. While it is not always immediately clear which level applies best to a given task, the rule of thumb laid out in Catholic social teaching is to rely as much as possible on those solutions that are closest to the people affected and that employ the smallest groupings and mechanisms that are still effective. Abraham Lincoln was thinking of the same delicate balance when he stated:

> The legitimate object of government is to do for a community of people whatever they need to have done, but cannot do at all, or cannot so well do, for themselves—in their separate, and individual capacities.

This wise description of the proper balance to be struck in relying on government action is surely a better guide to real-life situations than the often quoted but overly simplistic motto, "he governs best who governs least." One of the benefits of the principle of subsidiarity is that it respects the natural groupings that people form with their neighbors. For example, if the people of a small village agree on a goal (say, constructing a new road or cleaning up a polluted swamp) and have the means to accomplish it, they should avoid involving any larger bodies in the task. Pope Pius XI specifically mentions not only geographical but also vocational groupings (trade and professional bodies such as labor unions and the medieval occupational guilds they gradually replaced) among those human associations that should exercise rightful autonomy where possible. Their activities should not be subsumed under larger umbrellas unless there are good reasons and some real benefits from this shift.

But Pius XI hastens to add an insight that the common sense of any attentive observer of human affairs might also suggest: there are many occasions when larger bodies can make a real and indispensable contribution to local efforts. In terms of American government, this would refer to the need for state or even federal assistance to supplement the efforts of municipalities and counties. In many projects, such as large-scale public works, regional infrastructure improvements, pollution control, security and air-traffic control, and even police investigations, there is no substitute for government activity on higher levels.

As many episodes in human history demonstrate, large-scale efforts of national governments are often the only effective means of marshaling and mobilizing the resources needed for immense and complex tasks. Without the authority and funding mechanisms of a centralized government, neither national defense, nor a parks system for preserving wildlife, nor many other desirable resources would be possible. This insight is captured in the common expression, "you should have *only* the government you need, but also *all* the government you need." While it will always be necessary to make judgments on a case-by-case basis, a good summary of the wisdom of subsidiarity is, "as small as possible, but big when necessary."

Pope Pius XI lived in an age that was witnessing the growth of totalitarianism, including the threats of fascism and communism. His wise counsel to resist needless centralization echoes to our own day, when so many people also recognize the drawbacks and inefficiencies of an over-reliance on large-scale government. Overly intrusive government reduces incentives for beneficial self-help and may have such unintended consequences as fostering an attitude of learned helplessness. To avoid such pitfalls of what has been called "the nanny state," it is certainly desirable to respect the authority of local institutions, from voluntary associations to families themselves. Nevertheless, it is prudent to remember that national governments are not to be portrayed as our enemies but, rather, as the very instruments by which citizens join their efforts together when necessary to accomplish important goals that could not be addressed on local levels.

Members of the Catholic Church are, of course, not the only ones grappling in recent decades with sincere efforts to strike a healthy balance in attitudes toward central government. A wide variety of political philosophers, public officeholders and other observers have reflected profoundly on how best to recognize the proper circumstances that justify government action. Many such voices have converged around what is sometimes called the "sensible center" of the spectrum of opinions on such questions. Echoing the insights of the principle of subsidiarity, whether or not they actually use the term, such commentators stress the wisdom of avoiding either extreme position, in an effort to be neither addicted nor allergic to state intervention in the life of society. Government is not always the problem, nor is it always the solution to social problems. Wise public policy depends upon a polity's ability to grow beyond mere sloganeering, blanket generalizations, and ideological posturing to come up with constructive discernment regarding what truly advances the common good.

As long as a given society maintains a robust set of medium-sized bodies and voluntary associations that bridge the levels between individuals and their national government, a healthy balance can be established that averts the threat of totalitarian control. People will still have the freedom to join clubs and participate in local affairs without feeling dwarfed by an overactive and intrusive government. Most citizens will discover their richest satisfactions in belonging not just to a nation but also to organizations of like-minded people in groups such as the Knights of Columbus, Rotary, Elks Clubs, the St. Vincent de Paul Society, and numerous leisure associations, from bowling leagues to golf clubs. Through these affiliations, society can progress smoothly, taking advantage of the efficiency of large-scale endeavors at the same time as it respects the rights and prerogatives of individuals and local bodies. Because it is widely recognized that the health of a given society depends upon the vitality of such groups (sometimes called the mediating structures of civil society), sociologists take special care to measure the prevalence and popularity of such nongovernmental and voluntary associations. If people were to cease exercising their right to free assembly (that is, if they suddenly stopped being "joiners"), this would serve as a warning sign that democracy is losing some of its strength and fading in its appeal.

At the heart of the principle of subsidiarity, then, is the crucial distinction between state and society. Catholic social teaching has long been mindful that the strength and vitality of a people goes far beyond its government structures and officials. However useful and necessary government action is, it must never be forgotten that the state is just one small part of the larger society that it is meant to serve, never to control.

5. PROPERTY OWNERSHIP IN MODERN SOCIETY: RIGHTS AND RESPONSIBILITIES

Chapter four noted the wise way in which St. Thomas Aquinas treated the difficult subject of private property. His writings on the subject recognized two competing values: the requirements of the common good, on one hand, and the advantages of individual ownership of property, on the other hand. As seen earlier in this chapter, a true respect for the common good suggests that the material things necessary for a good life should be widely available for use by the whole human community. But the Catholic tradition also testifies to the benefits of individual ownership, which not only encourages the most efficient and orderly of arrangements for material goods but also offers people an incentive to be productive and to care for the goods God has created.

Catholic social teaching has closely followed the path mapped out by Aquinas regarding property and has attempted to apply his principles to new situations in the modern world. From the 1891 encyclical *Rerum Novarum* on, it has consistently defended the basic right to private ownership of property. But it has also adjusted its message to account for new situations and needs that place prudent limits on property holding and therefore has issued stern warnings against unlimited acquisition of wealth. To ignore the needs of our less-fortunate neighbors, whether out of selfish motives or mere neglect, is to frustrate the very purpose of God in creating the material world we share. The Creator intends the common gift of the earth to be used for the nourishment and sustenance of all God's children, not just for the benefit of a few privileged members of society.

A good example of this type of limitation on the holding of property appears in the 1967 encyclical *Populorum Progressio*. In paragraph 23 of that document, Pope Paul VI reminds us that:

> . . . private property does not constitute for anyone an absolute and unconditional right. No one is justified in keeping for his [or her] exclusive use what he [or she] does not need, when others lack necessities.

In the very next paragraph, the pope indicates the contemporary injustice that prompted him to repeat this long-held Christian prohibition against the hoarding of wealth. Those who hold a great deal of property (Paul VI was probably thinking about the wealthy owners of Latin American *latifundia*, or large landed estates) hurt the poor when they allow their plantations to lie fallow for long periods of time while nearby landless peasants are close to starvation. The encyclical reaches the judgment that if these tracts of land are "extensive, unused or poorly used" and if these ownership patterns "bring hardship to peoples or are detrimental to the interests of the country, the common good sometimes demands their expropriation" (no. 24).

To *expropriate* property means to take it from its present owner, a course of action not normally recommended in the documents of Catholic social teaching. The earliest social encyclicals strenuously opposed any attempts to seize property, especially socialist and communist programs to nationalize industrial and agricultural property. According to *Rerum Novarum* (1891) and *Quadragesimo Anno* (1931), this form of socialism is against natural law and constitutes an injustice to all property holders. But by the 1960s, social conditions had changed so much that several recent popes have modified the teaching to reflect new challenges. Even before Pope Paul VI's 1967 argument that some expropriation might be justified in extreme conditions, Pope John XXIII had discussed the need to consider larger shares and new types of property as the common possession of the people of a nation. He presented these arguments in paragraphs 51 to 67 of his 1961 social encyclical *Mater et Magistra*. It will be helpful to examine in some detail what he says in this pivotal passage.

Pope John spends many paragraphs of *Mater et Magistra* surveying recent global developments, such as vast improvements in technology, transportation, and communication. He notes:

> One of the principal characteristics of our time is the multiplication of social relationships, that is, a daily more complex interdependence of citizens. . . . These developments in social living are at once both a symptom and a cause of the growing intervention of public authorities in matters . . . . (nos. 50, 60)

A proper understanding of property must also adjust to these changed circumstances. Because all people are increasingly dependent upon certain types of industrial production (such as electricity, oil, and communications), the companies that make up these industries must be more responsive to the needs of all people.

John XXIII calls this process of guaranteeing greater accountability and social responsibility *socialization*, and he identifies government as its primary agent. Alongside the familiar private obligation upon each person to pursue the common good, the Church had now come to recognize the legitimacy of public and governmental efforts to exercise socially responsible use of property. By no means does this suggest that all property should be collectivized or that all industries should be nationalized. Rather, it implies that the social character of property can be safeguarded when certain key utilities are regulated or perhaps even owned by the entire people as represented by their government. To contemporary observers, this is not really such an unfamiliar idea; many utilities, even in the United States, are considered to be in the public domain or have come to be at least somewhat regulated by various government agencies to prevent harmful monopolistic behavior by private corporations.

The notion of socialization was widely misunderstood when *Mater et Magistra* first appeared. Some people, for example, confused the term with the similar-sounding word socialism. William F. Buckley, a prominent Catholic intellectual and political correspondent, commented: "*Mater si, Magistra no.*" With this Latin phrase, a play on words making playful reference to the title of Pope John's letter, Buckley meant that he would continue to consider the Church his spiritual mother (*mater*) but no longer a reliable teacher (*magistra*) on social issues. Buckley and other free-market conservatives feared that John XXIII was advocating not just the prudent limitation of private ownership of property, but its utter elimination. They did not trust the principle of subsidiarity to guard against a rampant centralization of the functions of government. Nor did they welcome the Vatican II document *Gaudium et Spes*, which, when it appeared four years later in 1965, reaffirmed socialization as an important principle to advance the common good and the rights of the most vulnerable members of modern interdependent societies.

We have already seen Pope Paul VI's treatment in 1967 of the occasional necessity of expropriation of private property. Twenty years after that comment appeared in *Populorum Progressio*, Pope John Paul II introduced yet another way of thinking about limitations upon private property. In paragraph 42 of *Sollicitudo rei Socialis*, he wrote:

> . . . the goods of this world are equally meant for all. The right to private property is valid and necessary, but it does not nullify the value of this principle. Private property, in fact, is under a social mortgage.

Anyone who has ever held a mortgage on a house surely knows what this means. Just as borrowers cannot truthfully say that they fully own a house until the bank mortgage is completely paid off, no one can really claim to be the final owner of the material gifts that come from God. As long as we remain God's handiwork, our holding of property is strictly conditioned on fulfilling our social obligations to the rest of God's creatures. As a matter of fact, this insight has long been incorporated into U.S. law, which recognizes the principle of eminent domain as an exception to the legal system's usual stance of according nearly absolute property rights to holders of title deeds. Under this legal principle, land or other property that is judged especially critical to the public interest may be altered or even seized outright (usually with significant compensation to its previous owner) by public authorities in order to provide for crucial public needs, such as security or infrastructure improvements.

In either its legal or its more thoroughly theological versions, this insight into the fundamental nature of property ownership challenges many assumptions about the relationship between people and their goods. To recognize our property as coming under a social mortgage means that we cannot disregard the needs of the less fortunate, use our property in ways that harm them, or exclude them from full participation in society. No one who affirms the principle that material goods are intended for the benefit of all, a prominent theme of Catholic social teaching, can rest easy with an economic system where ability to pay is the only legitimate claim to vital goods such as food, housing, and health care. John Paul II's words, like those of several of his predecessors who issued social encyclicals, offer much to think about regarding the social dimension of the property that people hold.

6. THE DIGNITY OF WORK, RIGHTS OF WORKERS, AND SUPPORT FOR LABOR UNIONS

As chapter three documented, the historical origin of the tradition of Catholic social teaching is closely bound up with the Church's concern for workers. Social Catholicism in the nineteenth century courageously dedicated itself to improving the conditions of labor wherever possible. In many ways, the Church was ahead of its time in advocating for better treatment of workers. Contemporary observers may take for granted many of the original goals of these early church efforts. Government has become the instrument that now routinely enforces prevailing labor protections, at least in most industrialized nations. These include minimum wage laws, safety and health regulations, pension plans, social insurance, and the rights of workers to organize into labor unions.

The two encyclicals with the most extensive treatment of labor issues are *Rerum Novarum* in 1891 and *Laborem Exercens* in 1981. Although separated by ninety years, they share at least one remarkable feature: both display a tendency to move back and forth rather quickly between abstract theological reflection and practical principles of worker justice. This quick passage from eternal truths to specific measures reflects the great confidence shared by both their authors that the nitty-gritty reforms advocated in these documents are fully congruent with the will of God for the world. Both Leo XIII and John Paul II hold up an ideal of worker justice that demands close attention to the concrete conditions that face workers in the actual workplace and in the labor markets that determine the availability of work and the terms of employment. While both popes respect the fact that the great diversity of conditions complicates the way broad principles of worker justice are applied from place to place, neither is shy about insisting on the importance of concrete measures, such as the institution of "living wages" and reasonable work hours, for the entire workforce.

Of all the positions regarding work staked out within Catholic social teaching, perhaps the most controversial is the Church's abiding and enthusiastic support for labor unions. Workers' rights to organize and enter into collective bargaining are considered an important outgrowth of other human rights, such as the right to free association and the right to participate fully in the economic and political life of society. Of course, it is well known that labor unions have come under substantial criticism on a number of grounds, sometimes with good reason. For example, we often hear them associated with corruption, favoritism, and the threat of disruptive and potentially violent strikes. They also are accused of driving up the cost of doing business and sacrificing the international competitiveness of domestic industries because of the allegedly excessive wage demands they make.

Clearly, there are some problematic aspects of union activity. Yet Catholic social teaching forthrightly contends that a world without labor unions would witness a much less favorable environment for achieving justice and an equitable sharing of the earth's resources. Without the ability to combine their voices through the collective bargaining power of organized labor, workers would be at the mercy of their far more powerful employers who might take advantage of their inferior position. Viewed from this perspective, labor unions are crucial elements in the overall balance of power in the economy, and Catholic social teaching consistently portrays them as playing a constructive role in the pursuit of economic justice. Indeed, it is increasingly a source of concern that in many places unions seem to be on the decline. As unions represent a smaller and smaller percentage of the overall workforce and enjoy a lower profile in economic life, the power of workers to bargain effectively to protect their rights will unfortunately diminish greatly.

It is, of course, not surprising that executives and supervisory personnel of large corporations have frequently opposed and resisted, sometimes with coercive and even blatantly illegal tactics, the unionization of their shops. Management has every incentive to squeeze workers out of higher pay and fringe benefits in order to lower the production costs of their enterprises. The history of labor relations reflects the often conflictual nature of employer-employee interactions, although the historical record also contains much encouraging evidence that mutual respect and constructive cooperation can develop, with or without the presence of labor unions. One recurring problem is that union-free workplaces may easily devolve into exploitative environments, as the persistence of degrading sweatshop conditions in many places attests. A healthy union presence in a given industry may well be the best way to retain adequate checks against potential labor abuses. Those who argue that unions are unnecessary today generally present only one side of these complex issues. The assumption that benefits will eventually trickle down to all workers in a prosperous, competitive industry, even in the absence of vital labor unions, contradicts much of the evidence produced by studies in labor economics.

Alongside its support of labor unions, Catholic social teaching contains many additional messages about work. In these documents labor is portrayed neither as a mere necessary evil nor as a drudgery-filled means to the end of supporting family life; rather, labor is presented as something that is intrinsically good for all people. Through their work, ordinary people regularly discover rich sources of meaning, a renewed sense of purpose, and the opportunity to develop their full potential. Even in the humdrum routine of daily life in the workplace, work is more than a taxing or boring necessity. At its best, engaging in labor opens up new avenues of communication and planning with our colleagues, with whom we toil for common purposes and build up mutual respect.

Of course, by painting this rosy picture of the creative possibilities of work, Catholic social teaching in no way intends to ignore or invalidate the real-life problems that accompany so many jobs. For too many people, the workplace does remain a place of drudgery, conflict, repeated humiliation, and even despair. But at the same time, work represents a positive opportunity to collaborate with others, to develop particular skills, and to contribute distinctive individual talents to the wider society. As long as people work, they will have to look at both sides of the coin of human experience, neglecting neither the positive nor the negative aspects of what it means to labor.

Besides its practical benefits, then, human labor also carries theological significance, as it contains the human response to the God who invites all people to become cocreators of the material world. This is why human work should never be treated as a mere commodity, something to be bought and sold in a cavalier way in impersonal markets. This is also why workers must not be treated as cogs in the huge machine of production—an attitude that offends the dignity of all. These concerns are especially prominent in *Laborem Exercens*, where John Paul II repeatedly insists on the "priority of labor over capital." Through labor, people pursue not only a job or a career, but truly a vocation—a calling in which they are summoned by God to develop their capabilities and to follow the Carpenter from Nazareth on the path of discipleship. Catholic social teaching is a great resource for the increasingly numerous attempts to develop a full-blown theology of work and indeed to discover a spirituality of labor appropriate for our age.

7. COLONIALISM AND ECONOMIC DEVELOPMENT

A major topic of Catholic social teaching in the last half century concerns the legacy of colonialism and the challenge of economic development in the poorest parts of the world. In advocating for reforms to ensure fairer treatment for less-developed nations, the Church is entering into a long and complex debate about the nature of economic justice on the international scene. Understanding what is at stake involves appreciating the historical dimensions of the world economy and its roots in the unfolding events of the past five hundred years or more. Some of the ongoing conversation focuses on formal patterns of colonization, while other observers express concern about less obvious but equally pernicious practices described as neo-colonialism or neo-imperialism.

In the contemporary race for economic progress and higher standards of living, it is obvious that entire regions of the world suffer serious and unfair disadvantages. Competition today does not unfold on a level playing field at all, for the simple reason that centuries of domination and unfair practices have trapped many lands into conditions of economic backwardness and subordination. Even after achieving formal political independence, such nations find themselves deprived of true self-determination, largely because the economies of these lands have been warped by prolonged experiences of dependency and domination. These many faces of injustice are the contemporary legacy of patterns of trade and resource exploitation that began with the age of global exploration in the fifteenth century and included the horrendous African slave trade, the bloody age of the Conquistadors in Latin America, and other brutal episodes on all those continents that fell under the domination of European colonial powers. Because these long-standing patterns of inequity cannot be attributed to any single individual, but rather are rightly blamed on entire social systems that display a certain momentum of their own, the terms *social sin* or *structural evil* have been applied to them in recent Catholic ethical thought. Chapter seven will treat the topic of social sin more thoroughly as part of its investigation into future themes for Catholic social teaching.

Besides the political and economic changes wrought by Europeans arriving in the New World, Africa, and Asia after the time of Columbus, the colonizers also pursued a religious agenda. The ships of European explorers and soldiers also carried priests, preachers, and missionaries seeking to spread Christianity to indigenous peoples around the world. Historians have long debated how best to construe the activities and lasting legacy of that age of exploration and colonization. Critics of Western Christianity are quick to point out that European-controlled churches were, for too long, silent about the abuses of the British, French, Spanish, Dutch, Portuguese, and other empires, for the obvious reason that Catholic and Protestant missionaries often relied on these European colonial regimes as their own base of operations. Accounts of forced baptisms and supposed conversions coerced at gunpoint only add to the sense of shameful behavior on the part of colonizing powers and their religious collaborators. There is much truth in the charge that missionaries of many stripes were complicit in the injustices of the colonial era, although careful historical research reveals that many such preachers and ministers were also bold in denouncing injustices, including the slave trade and horrifying patterns of murderous assaults against indigenous populations.

Everyone agrees that the present economic order features large and disturbing gaps between the world's richest and poorest lands. Most people further agree that the histories of European colonialism and superpower imperialism have played an important role in causing these glaring disparities. The remaining differences of opinion concern how much blame to assign to particular international actors who have contributed to these injustices, as well as the hard task of identifying the wisest strategy to address global poverty and underdevelopment today.

Catholic social teaching weighs in on these complicated topics by offering two sets of ideas. The first is the more consistent part of its message. The Church repeatedly insists that all people have a moral obligation to care deeply about world poverty and to do all they can to address this scourge on our common humanity. Despite the artificial divisions of people into races, religions, and nations, all are members of a single human family. Hunger and disease in any part of the world should be a concern for all people and demands the urgent attention of all. The strenuous efforts of people in the richest nations to combat poverty in the poorest lands, even thousands of miles away, are essential and encouraging expressions of human solidarity.

Repeated calls for "mutual assistance among nations" and "taking into account the interests of others" are sprinkled throughout paragraphs 157 through 211 of Pope John XXIII's 1961 letter *Mater et Magistra*, the first section of any social encyclical to deal extensively with global poverty. The message that believers cannot remain indifferent to any human suffering, no matter how far away it might be, is heard frequently in practically all the social encyclicals since then. If we are indeed to fulfill our role as our brother's keeper, then we must resist the temptations of selfishness and isolationism and truly involve ourselves in advancing the well-being of the very poorest residents of our planet. While we often hear the expressions "First World and Third World" or "North and South," we are called to look beyond these artificial divisions to the common humanity and essential unity of all who share the earth.

The second way Catholic social teaching addresses poverty and underdevelopment is by inviting believers to ponder the causes of these problems and to offer suggestions for improvement. This message is harder to summarize because the advice offered by church leaders has shifted over time. At first, proposals contained in encyclicals remained cautious and halfhearted, as they focused mainly on the level of urging individual moral enlightenment and recommending the practice of virtues such as charity and prudence. This turns out to be quite understandable, since it is much easier to call attention to problems such as world poverty than it is to enter the controversial arena of debate over the precise causes and most effective solutions to these problems. But as the seriousness of global poverty became clearer, the Church felt a new urgency to reach beyond the level of vague recommendations, such as *Mater et Magistra*'s somewhat timid call for "international cooperation." In a postcolonial age, Catholic social teaching needed to become more specific about the changes that were so desperately needed. The time had come to start inquiring about particular solutions: What kind of cooperation? To combat which evils? To change which structures?

Among the church leaders most impatient for sweeping changes were the bishops assembled at the Second Vatican Council, including Pope Paul VI, who presided over the concluding sessions of the Council and led the Church until his death in 1978. Because the bishops at Vatican II were assembled from all over the world and shared close quarters for many months, they had ample opportunity to consult with one another. They talked frequently about the dire conditions facing millions of people who aspired against long odds for a better life. In their many formal as well as informal deliberations, these many hundreds of bishops compared notes about how their efforts to be good pastors were so often frustrated by the desperate poverty that discouraged, disrupted, and even directly threatened millions of lives in their various homelands.

Several inspiring passages in the Vatican II document *Gaudium et Spes* reflect the concern and sincere search for solutions on the part of the world's bishops. An especially stirring section, paragraphs 63 through 72, includes a lament over the state of a world in which, all too often, "luxury and misery rub shoulders." Paul VI, the first modern pope to travel widely outside of Europe, went even further in addressing the Church's concerns about maldistribution. He dedicated major sections of three important social teaching documents (*Populorum Progressio, Octogesima Adveniens*, and *Evangelii Nuntiandi*) to the problem of world poverty. Here and in many other writings and speeches, Pope Paul sincerely wrestled with the urgent puzzle regarding what should be done by the Church, by individual nations, and by international agencies to address global underdevelopment.

The writings of Paul VI ushered the Catholic Church into a new era of reflection and advocacy regarding international economics. After the 1967 encyclical *Populorum Progressio*, there was no turning back to the former timid approach that consisted mostly of hand-wringing and vague moralizing about how the wealthy should find it in their hearts to offer charitable assistance to the destitute. The pope boldly identified the vast inequalities separating rich and poor nations as unjust results of sinful greed and of evil structures within world trade and finance that shut the majority of the world's population out of opportunities for self-improvement. While some of the blame might be placed on past generations and the inheritance of European colonialism from previous centuries, the continuation of these imbalances must be confronted and condemned.

Pope Paul VI contended that economies must be restructured to serve true and deep human needs, not primarily the mere wants of the most affluent. He advocated such measures as: (1) land reform in the Third World; (2) an end to export-maximizing policies that warped local economies by favoring the production of goods that would be most profitable for a few, not most useful for the many; and (3) more generous international aid to support micro-development and to increase the availability of credit to farmers and townspeople in Africa, Asia, and Latin America. Measures such as these are designed to place more of the tools necessary for self-improvement in the hands of those who currently have no access to these critical resources.

Sometimes in discussions on development issues, the word *tools* is used metaphorically, standing for educational and employment opportunities or other abstract categories of resources. In other instances, it is access to tools in the literal sense that participants find themselves debating. Micro-development projects that supply sewing machines to women's cooperatives in Africa or farm implements to villagers in Central America are the practical forms of assistance that produce quite tangible results to improve the lives of the most vulnerable. Often what is required is not necessarily an outright gift but, rather, access to credit and marketing arrangements that make possible certain modest income-generating enterprises such as handcrafts and fish farming. To its considerable credit, the Church has sponsored numerous projects such as these through Catholic Relief Services, Caritas International, and similar faith-based organizations, but of course far more remains to be done through international agencies, religious and secular alike. Of particular concern are the economic prospects of millions of displaced people around the world—refugees living in semi-permanent camps, asylum seekers fleeing political persecution, and other marginalized people separated from their homelands and normal sources of livelihood. If global solidarity is to have real meaning beyond pleasant-sounding phrases, then Christians and all others must commit themselves to concrete measures to restructure the world economy and provide opportunities to the disinherited, even where these measures may entail considerable sacrifices on the part of the affluent.

The path taken by Paul VI was continued by John Paul II, whose three social encyclicals also emphasize the structural dimensions of global injustice and maldistribution of resources. Especially in his 1987 encyclical

Sollicitudo rei Socialis, John Paul bemoans the growing gap between rich and poor nations, frequently contrasting the superabundance enjoyed by a few with the desperate struggle for survival experienced by so many. He condemns the excesses of wasteful consumerism and materialism as evidence of a distortion he calls "super-development."

Elsewhere in *Sollicitudo rei Socialis,* Pope John Paul II identifies a number of "structures of evil," including the crushing burden of international debt, the arms race, and a form of economic domination often termed neocolonialism. Drawing upon his observations from numerous trips throughout the world, the most well-traveled pope in all of history denounces these harmful trends and patterns, which are responsible for the worsening plight of the poorest as they suffer from the effects of unemployment, housing crises, illiteracy, and other obstacles to their full human development. In prophetic words in paragraph 37 of that encyclical, John Paul attributes many of these global problems to two basic social sins: the "all-consuming desire for profit" and the "thirst for power." These evils have come to resemble idolatries in the modern world. As mentioned just above, the relatively new notions of social sin and structures of evil will be treated more fully in chapter seven, as will the concept of globalization, which bears obvious and close relation to the issues of economic development and the legacy of colonialism.

Stepping back now from the details of these types of international economic issues, questions of personal perspective often come into play when such large and sweeping topics are broached. It may be hard for average Christians to know how to respond to the Church's challenging message about worldwide economic development. Most middle-class churchgoers in the affluent nations of the North may have a vague sense of guilt about living in a society that somehow benefits from the cheap labor and resources extracted from less-developed nations, but they probably struggle to come up with practical suggestions for making immediate improvements. After all, when Paul VI called for a "civilization of love" or John Paul II urged a "more authentic development," they had in mind a thorough restructuring of worldwide patterns of trade, production, and finance that would spread the benefits of economic progress more fairly and widely. Although Catholic social teaching seeks to energize people of good will to attack these problems, the staggering dimensions of the challenges ahead can easily be experienced as paralyzing in the extreme.

Because no individual in isolation has sufficient power to change the large economic and political structures that determine present conditions, the model of change adopted will have to be one of gradual and modest action, with each person pitching in as he or she is able. But even if progress is measured in baby steps rather than giant leaps, it is impossible in good conscience to ignore the call to all Christians to contribute in some ways to alleviate the suffering of the poorest inhabitants of the world. Besides calling individuals to be generous with the goods they might personally control, Catholic social teaching urges its listeners to discern and discover new expressions of solidarity with the poor. Concerned Christians energized by this prophetic call might join campaigns for worker justice, boycott products that are objectionable because they come from sweatshops, or pressure Congress and the World Bank to forgive more of the staggering global debt owed by less-developed nations.

These and similar action steps of our own design can be creative ways of responding personally to the general call to global responsibility that comes from official voices of the Church. It is understandable, of course, that most of the time our energies and imaginations are focused on the smaller circle of our families, workplaces, and neighborhoods. But this natural tendency to tend most ardently to the familiar world at our doorsteps should not serve as an excuse for shortsightedness or the wearing of blinders. All socially responsible people should take to heart the insightful (if by now somewhat clichéd) bumper-sticker message, to "think globally, act locally."

8. PEACE AND DISARMAMENT

In the documents of Catholic social teaching, the goal of justice is closely linked to the ideal of peace. The proper ordering of God's creation includes not only prosperity and a fair distribution of resources but also the security and stability that is so well summarized in the Hebrew word for peace, *shalom*. Meaning more than just a temporary absence of open hostilities, the ideal of *shalom* calls people to a thorough respect for all their neighbors in relationships that are characterized by an ever-deeper trust and a commitment to providing mutual assistance.

Of course, history teaches many hard lessons that lead perceptive observers to expect anything but the full and immediate attainment of the ideals of *shalom*. Every human age has witnessed wars, bloody civil strife, genocide, and violent ethnic conflict of greatly disturbing proportions. The shame of "man's inhumanity to man" (to cite Robert Burns' mournful sentiment, expressed as far back as 1785) has been sparked by greed, petty jealousies, and sometimes even explicitly religious motivations. Christian responses to war and violence must go beyond vague feelings of distress and regret to genuine and effective strategies of peacemaking and conflict transformation. Of all the possible approaches to the task of building peace, the two dominant Christian approaches to peace are *pacifism* and the *just war theory*.

Chapter four noted the development of the just war theory as one Christian response to the conflicting values present in the real world of human sin and division. For a handy summary of the criteria that make up the just war theory in its traditional formulation, see table 5.2. It is helpful to keep in mind the specific history of the just war approach, which grew out of the agonizing task of reconciling lofty principles such as love of enemies and doing no harm to anyone with the imperative to protect innocent and defenseless people endangered by unjust aggression in a fallen world. From the start, Christians rejected the extreme position of the "total war" approach as completely opposed to the teachings of Christ, but after a few centuries, questions began to surface about whether some types of limited warfare might be allowable. Could there exist situations in which the use of the sword might be reconcilable with Christian discipleship? Starting with St. Augustine, Christian thinkers began to justify the use of force against unjust aggressors in certain circumstances as the most appropriate way to respond to the command to demonstrate love for others with all the means at one's disposal.

The Christian presumption against violence thus gave way to the noble desire to protect the innocent from harm. Many believers reached the conclusion that the best anyone can do in these difficult situations is to limit the damage while defending innocent civilians by means of the deadly force one otherwise would choose to avoid. Taking up arms in justified causes such as these came to be referred to as "strange acts of love," undertaken with the same reluctance and even anguish that parents feel when they are forced to discipline their unruly children. Because it insists on employing the absolute minimum of force to achieve the objective of resolving conflicts, the just war theory at its best can never be used to exact disproportionate revenge or to support agendas of militarism or extreme nationalism. The just war theory came to form the mainstream of Christian reflection on violence for many centuries, and the documents of modern Catholic social teaching generally assume this stance in the few places where they treat issues of war and peace in any significant detail.

Recall that chapter four's brief treatment of the just war theory was intended to illustrate how human reason serves as an important source of Catholic social teaching and Christian ethics in general. The point being made there was that theologians reasoned their way to the criteria of the just war theory, rather than discovering this approach in any already existing Christian source. Another of the four sources examined in chapter four is revelation, specifically scripture. Surveying the New Testament, particularly the gospels in their portrayals of the life and teaching of Jesus, discloses no obvious support for the just war theory or for any approach that would permit the use of force, even to defend innocent lives. Jesus did not lift a finger to save his own life and, in fact, rebuked those who drew the sword to defend him. Many of the sayings of Jesus lend credibility to the pacifists' claim that a true follower of Christ follows a strict policy of nonviolence, never resorting to force for self-defense or even in defense of innocent neighbors. If evil is to be overcome, it will be accomplished by means that are in themselves good.

There are many versions and traditions of pacifism. Some of these are directly inspired by the New Testament and are practiced by communities of Christians, such as the Mennonites, Quakers, and similar groups that began as offshoots of the Protestant Reformation of the sixteenth century. Within modern Catholicism, advocates of pacifism have been relatively rare, but some branches of lay movements, such as the Catholic Worker and Sant'Egidio communities, have been outspoken in support of a lifestyle of strict nonviolence, including opposition to capital punishment and all taking of life. The issue of who actually qualifies as a pacifist becomes complicated when we start considering distinctions between related schools of thought, such as those labeled "nonviolence," "nonresistance," and "passive resistance to evil." Despite the complexity of the topic, suffice it to say that, until quite recently, pacifism seldom received much sustained attention in mainstream Catholic circles.

One would look in vain through the twelve major Vatican social teaching documents for a detailed treatment of the relative merits of pacifism and the just war theory. The encyclicals generally assume that a proportionate and carefully ordered use of force, when justified by a serious threat to a nation or to innocent people, can qualify as a socially responsible reaction when other options have been exhausted. Several times in these writings, popes take the opportunity to decry how regrettable the resort to violence is, urging diplomacy and negotiation as attractive alternatives to counterattacks against aggressors. Although several of the documents use phrases such as "never again war!," the basic stance of the encyclical tradition remains in the just war camp. However much they detest and denounce war, popes have been reluctant to deny sovereign states the right they claim to engage in what they might consider to be legitimate defense. The principle that warfare might be justified under certain conditions remains dominant in Catholic social thought.

Especially noteworthy is *Pacem in Terris*, the 1963 encyclical written by John XXIII, one of several recent popes who witnessed firsthand the horrors of modern warfare. John had served in the Italian army during World War I and was terrified by the prospect of further escalating violence, especially if it were directed against civilians. He wrote *Pacem in Terris* in the wake of the Berlin and Cuban Missile Crises, when the superpower rivalry had recklessly placed the world on the brink of nuclear war. His heartfelt plea for peaceful resolution of differences is extremely poignant, especially where he dedicates fifteen paragraphs (nos. 109–119 and

Table 5.2. Categories and Criteria of Just War Theory

Latin Title	English Meaning	Goal	Criteria
Jus ad bellum	Justice in entering a war	Seeks to limit war by ruling out entry into conflicts for inappropriate reasons	Traditional criteria for when war is permissible: 1. Just cause: Establishing that there is a real and certain danger. 2. Competent authority: Must be legitimate and public (not private vigilantism). 3. Comparative justice: One's side must be clearly more right than the adversary. 4. Right intention: Must be for the sake of establishing peace, not for revenge. 5. Last resort: All reasonable peaceful alternatives to war (e.g., diplomacy, economic sanctions) must have been exhausted. 6. Probability of success: Avoid futile resistance for a hopeless cause. 7. Proportionality: The costs incurred by the conflict must be justified by greater expected gains.
Jus in bello	Justice in the conduct of a war	Seeks to limit war by ruling out the use of inappropriate means within conflicts	Traditional criteria for when the conduct of war is allowable: 1. Proportionality: Responses to aggression must not exceed initial harm. Obligation to counter the possibility of escalation to weapons of mass destruction. 2. Discrimination: No direct attacks on noncombatants. Protections for all civilians.

Jus post bellum   Justice after a war   Seeks to limit war by ruling out strategies of withdrawal that inhibit future peace

Proposed criteria for when war planning provides adequately for a transition to peace:

1. Prudent withdrawal: Adequate plans for an exit strategy to end occupations within a reasonable period of time.
2. Immediate security: Guarantees of protection for all parties after the shooting has stopped.
3. Long-term security: Provision for future political stability and regional security.
4. Just accords: Promotion of treaties that deal with all parties fairly, allow for equitable participation, and prevent future hostilities.
5. Physical reconstruction: Commitment to repair material infrastructure, encourage economic revival, and clean up environmental damage and other residual effects of war.
6. Social restoration: Efforts to rebuild social trust, including resolving cases of wartime atrocities and setting up truth and reconciliation commissions as needed.

126–129) to a description of the merits of disarmament and negotiation. Here the anguished pontiff, writing just weeks before his own untimely death, characterizes any nuclear exchange as completely contrary to reason, as it would risk destroying the basis of life for everyone on earth, not only those targeted by detonated nuclear missiles. Pope John even quotes the words of his predecessor, Pius XII, the pope who agonized so long over the bloody course of the Second World War, which swept around his lonely perch in the Vatican: "Nothing is lost by peace; everything may be lost by war."

There are several recent indications that Catholic social teaching is moving toward a position that is somewhat closer to pacifism, as more doubts are cast on how the just war theory is applied in modern circumstances. Obviously, in a nuclear age, it is hard to imagine how the just war criteria (which prohibit disproportionate responses, needless escalation of hostilities, and the targeting of civilians) can justify many of the ways current weapons of mass destruction are likely to be used. In light of the ever-present threat of swift escalation of hostilities from rifles to tanks to nuclear weapons, all responsible observers should be hesitant to justify the use of even conventional weapons, especially in tense regions such as the Middle East and the Indian subcontinent. Further, many voices within and beyond the Church have pointed out how often the just war theory has been misused in cynical efforts to cover up self-interested aggression. Pope John Paul II, in several statements issued during the 1990s (on the occasions of the First Persian Gulf War and later air strikes by the United States and its allies against Iraq and in the Balkans), scolded world powers for a premature resort to force before the full range of peaceful channels had been exhausted.

The war in Iraq that started in 2003 was the occasion for further heated debate over the merits of the just war theory. Critics cited two types of shortcomings that appeared to be on display in new and serious ways in the Iraq conflict: (1) flaws inherent in the traditional framework; and (2) a tendency for that framework to be misused in actual practice. Various serious controversies surrounding the false pretences that contributed to the rush to war in March 2003 led many to conclude that this tradition of reflection was either entirely bankrupt or at least ill-suited to contemporary conditions. When supporters of the U.S. invasion of Iraq claimed that action against Saddam Hussein's Iraq was justified as a preemptive intervention, they were stretching a traditional category beyond recognition, as observers within and beyond religious circles made the case that any threats coming from Iraq were so remote that they did not really fit within the just war theory.

Further, a modern government's ability to produce false evidence such as manipulated intelligence data to support its case for starting a war raises serious doubts about many of the established criteria for justifying the onset of hostilities. These so-called *jus ad bellum* (Latin for "justice in entering a war") criteria include several conditions that must be fulfilled in order to make a credible claim that a given war has been entered into with due cause and following correct procedures. Other new types of complications include uncertainty about how to invoke properly the authority of international institutions like the United Nations and new questions regarding tools like economic sanctions and how they relate to the criterion of using war only as the last resort. These novel issues raise profound doubts about the continued viability of the traditional *jus ad bellum* criteria.

The other category of criteria traditionally used to measure the just use of force is called the *jus in bello* ("justice in the conduct of war") standards, which seek to limit war in specific ways once a given armed conflict has begun. This bundle of concerns includes stern warnings addressed even to parties who can justify their involvement in a defensive and unavoidable war. Armed forces must conduct their operations in such a way that no harm comes to civilians, who enjoy blanket immunity from the lethal damage of war. Combatants must also conduct themselves in such a way that their reactions are considered proportionate to the threats and capability of the enemy and must not needlessly escalate hostilities by introducing battlefield weapons of ever-increasing destructive scale. Here, too, new global realities are raising serious doubts that the just war theory is still capable of offering adequate guidance to military powers. In an age of widespread terrorist threats, where civilians are routinely targeted and even used cynically as either suicide bombers or deliberate shields against enemy responses, the *jus in bello* criteria appear to be terribly outdated. Even military planners who in good faith intend to observe the rules of international law and just war theory find their positions untenable in the face of new conditions that blur boundaries that formerly appeared quite clear.

Interestingly, even as the war in Iraq cast growing doubts on the traditional framework for evaluating the morality of warfare, certain prominent voices have spoken up in an effort to salvage and perhaps to revive just war theory. Even if the theory were renounced overnight, it would need to be reinvented immediately, some argued, since imposing some limits upon warfare is a perennial desire of all who seek peace. Others sought to bolster a fundamental premise of just war theory, namely its presumption against violence, against rather hawkish commentators who increasingly portrayed war as a neutral option that states might choose to employ on a routine basis, as if it were just another instrument in the large tool kit of diplomacy and foreign policy. This latter approach, influenced by the *Realpolitik* school of international relations, seems markedly at odds with the original moral underpinnings of just war theory, grounded as it was in a sincere quest to find ways to practice love of all humankind.

Perhaps the most creative recent development in just war theory is the proposal to add a third category of criteria that must be fulfilled before any war, even a defensive one, may be considered allowable. To the *jus ad bellum* and the *jus in bello* criteria might be added concern for *jus post bellum*—the ensuring of right order after the shooting has stopped. Presumably this would require powerful nations deciding to go to war, even for otherwise justifiable defensive purposes, to draw up adequate plans for the aftermath of the conflict. They would have to provide not only a realistic exit strategy for their own forces on a reasonable timeline, but also more comprehensive arrangements for security, political stability, the resolution of local interparty conflicts, and even environmental cleanup after the cessation of the actual fighting. These items emerge as a solemn responsibility of powerful countries resorting to force and must not be treated as mere afterthoughts for invading parties, no matter how well intentioned they might be.

It is not hard to see how this proposal for the development of *jus post bellum* criteria gained broad appeal as the occupation of Iraq dragged on for years. The swift and successful invasion of Iraq was followed by a disastrous quagmire of unanticipated insurgency activity, which cost many thousands of lives on all sides and reflected a huge failure to plan ahead. Much needless suffering could have been avoided if the United States and its allies had drawn up post-conquest plans in advance, or if they had perhaps considered the difficulty of doing so as a cogent reason for forestalling the invasion. Many public commentators remarked that if the Iraq fiasco is the logical outcome of using the just war theory, then that theory should be replaced immediately by some alternative, perhaps even a version of nonviolence or pacifism. The case for pacifism could be based on a number of weighty reasons. Compared with just war theory, it is more highly principled, possesses an equally long and rich pedigree, and may even turn out to be just as practical under the complex new conditions of international relations.

Perhaps the two most significant indications of a more favorable view of pacifist stances within Catholicism originated not from recent popes but from gatherings of bishops. First, Vatican II's document *Gaudium et Spes* specifically advocates the rights of conscientious objectors or, as it describes them, "those who for reasons of conscience refuse to bear arms" (no. 79). This innovation within Catholic social teaching opens the way to seeing this pacifist response to the military draft, at least on the individual level, as a justifiable position worthy of respect. Second, the U.S. bishops' 1983 pastoral letter *The Challenge of Peace* went to great lengths to explain the pacifist position and treated it more sympathetically than perhaps any other major document of the Church. The letter lifted up the contribution of this minority position in taking seriously the universal call to commit ourselves to peacemaking and to begin this task within our own hearts and through the lifestyle choices we make. By returning to the New Testament and paying close attention to the signs of the times in a dangerous world, Catholic social teaching appears to be on the brink of passing a further negative judgment on almost all forms of warfare.

Following the U.S. bishops' call to take seriously the task of peacemaking leads easily to the discovery that this path of *shalom* is already a well-trod route. The Christian tradition contains numerous rich resources beyond official church teachings that feed the hunger of many for knowing and pursuing the way of peace. Spiritual writers such as St. Francis of Assisi and more recent social commentators such as Leo Tolstoy, Gandhi, and Martin Luther King Jr. offer inspiring words that challenge us to imagine a world of true and lasting harmony. Organized groups such as Pax Christi, Plowshares, and Fellowship of Reconciliation extend a variety of opportunities to pursue activism dedicated to building a more peaceful world.

Perhaps the greatest American Catholic witness to peace comes from the Catholic Worker, a lay movement founded in 1933 by Dorothy Day and Peter Maurin. Although best known for publishing a newspaper and sponsoring remarkable houses of hospitality for the needy, members of the Catholic Worker count among their primary goals the building up of a firm witness to peace. The organization's often-reprinted mission statement, "Aims and Means of the Catholic Worker," explains the inspiration and principles of this approach to peacemaking:

> Jesus calls us to fight against violence with the spiritual weapons of prayer, fasting, and noncooperation with evil. Refusal to pay taxes for war, to register for conscription, to comply with any unjust legislation; participation in nonviolent strikes and boycotts, protests, or vigils; withdrawal of support for dominant systems, corporate funding, or usurious practices are all excellent means to establish peace.

Even those who are unable to adopt for themselves all aspects of this approach may affirm the utter dedication of the Catholic Worker movement to offer alternatives and to shape their lives so that peacemaking becomes one of the central concerns of everyday life. A great debt of gratitude is owed to Dorothy Day, Peter Maurin, and their followers for supplying this extraordinary vision for the pursuit of holiness and *shalom* in the modern world.

9. OPTION FOR THE POOR AND VULNERABLE

In one sense, the notion of the *preferential option for the poor* is relatively new to Catholic social teaching, as this phrase appeared in no papal social encyclical until 1987 and in no official church documents at all until 1979. But in another sense, the notion of the preferential option for those who are weak and vulnerable has been present within the Christian tradition from the very start. The ministry of Jesus, in both words and deeds, was deeply wrapped up with this commitment to the well-being of the least fortunate. Making an option for the poor is not just a knee-jerk reaction to give the benefit of the doubt to those considered to be underdogs, but an abiding commitment, grounded in scripture and tradition, to support social justice by placing oneself on the side of the vulnerable and marginalized.

Through the ages, theologians and spiritual writers have reflected on God's special relationship with the poor and disadvantaged. In bold sermons and writings since the earliest years of Christianity, many church leaders have challenged the faithful to discern certain moral obligations suggested in the biblical motif of "the great reversal." This phrase refers to the tendency of scripture to overturn conventional expectations about social order, such as the surprising conclusions contained in the Beatitudes (Matthew 5:3–12 and Luke 6:20–26) and the poetic way that Mary's Magnificat (Luke 1:46–55) praises God for lifting up the lowly. Prophetic voices of the Church have called especially upon the privileged to reverse the usual logic of the secular world, where unbridled and selfish accumulation of wealth is expected and rewarded, and to imitate God as best they can in exercising special care for the poor. Without using the precise phrase "preferential option for the poor," the Church has long practiced this option in many ways, formal and informal, as it has placed concern for the most vulnerable members of society among its top priorities.

Echoes of the preferential option for the poor ring strongly in the stirring opening sentence of the Vatican II document *Gaudium et Spes*:

> The joys and the hopes, the griefs and the anxieties of the [people] of this age, especially those who are poor or in any way afflicted, these too are the joys and hopes, the griefs and anxieties of the followers of Christ. (no. 1)

In identifying itself with the concerns of the poor, the Church is here interpreting its entire mission as one of service to those in need. Bringing the Gospel to people in the fullest sense means caring simultaneously for their many needs, both spiritual and material. The Church is most faithful to its identity when it is acting on the imperative to meet the urgent needs of the most vulnerable—the ones Jesus Christ so loves. All such expressions of solidarity and resulting efforts for social change are grounded on the insight that the good news Jesus heralded was above all good news for the poor.

The worldwide church inherits the precise phrase "preferential option for the poor" from documents of the 1979 meeting of CELAM, the abbreviation for the Spanish words (*Consejo Episcopal Latinoamericano*) translated as the Bishops' Conference of Latin America. At that meeting in Puebla, Mexico, as at the previous CELAM meeting in Medellín, Colombia, in 1968, the bishops of those lands, sharply divided as they are between extremes of rich and poor, boldly identified the Church with the struggles of the poor. This decisive shift was not meant to exclude anyone from the life or concerns of the Church and certainly was not an invitation to pass judgments upon certain people simply because their bank accounts or land holdings were too large.

Rather, the significance of this shift lies in the way it reverses a centuries-long pattern that had quite tragically warped the proper understanding of the mission of the Church. As long as the Church was perceived as solidly aligned with the economic interests of wealthy landholders of Latin America, it would remain a hindrance to the full human development of the poor in that region. If the vast majority of people continued to see the Church as a tool in the hands of the upper-class bosses who appeared completely indifferent to their well-being, then this perception would prevent the Church from ever becoming the True Church of the poor Jesus. The initiative of the Latin American church to adopt the option for the poor as central to its mission was a sincere local attempt to fulfill a mandate of Pope John XXIII. In a 1962 address explaining his hopes for the upcoming Second Vatican Council, Pope John charted this anticipated course: "In the face of the undeveloped countries, the church is, and wants to be, the church of all, and especially the church of the poor."

Clearly, the significance of this sudden about-face in the Church's self-understanding was hard to explain outside of Latin America. To observers from other continents where social class divisions were never as sharp, it hardly made sense. They may have feared that church leaders were embracing uncritically a polarizing Marxist concept of class struggle or entirely excluding the affluent from the ambit of Christian concern in an ill-advised way. The Church has, of course, received a mission to be an evenhanded agent of reconciliation between all people, so it would be distressing to think of the Church as taking sides between social groups in some crass way. It is best to understand the renewed embrace of the option of the poor as an act of correcting an equilibrium that had over the centuries swung sharply out of balance. The forceful restatement of the Church's mission had become particularly necessary in Latin America because of the need to offset that continent's long history of clerical abuse and warped priorities.

Vatican social teaching itself had never gotten off on such a wrong track. From its very beginning, when nineteenth-century European social Catholicism started to notice and address the plight of hard-pressed working families, this tradition of social concern had consistently expressed the Church's mission to act as Jesus had acted in befriending the poor of his time. In fact, the 1991 encyclical *Centesimus Annus* contains a passage in which Pope John Paul II interprets *Rerum Novarum's* call, a full century earlier, to improve the conditions of workers as a manifestation of the preferential option for the poor long before the phrase was coined. John Paul points to the similarity between the Church's role as advocate of the poor in 1891 and 1991 as evidence of the "church's constant concern for and dedication to categories of people who are especially beloved to the Lord Jesus" (no. 11). Indeed, throughout his long pontificate, John Paul II made frequent reference to this concept, phrased in various ways, as part of his trademark call to universal solidarity. Though by no means an uncritical proponent of liberation theology, the movement that originated the phrase "preferential option for the poor," Pope John Paul II often raised up in his addresses and writings this social priority of working for the benefit of the least-advantaged members of society. As noted earlier in this chapter, many of his famous travels abroad, especially early in his reign as pope, featured visits to desperately impoverished neighborhoods where he publicized the need for greater solidarity between rich and poor around the world.

The imperative to make an option for the poor takes on distinctive features, of course, in the social context of the world's most affluent nations. Consider, for example, the significance of such an option within the United States, one of the richest societies in the history of the world. Although tens of millions of Americans actually live below the federally defined poverty line, the extent and depth of poverty in the U.S. is not nearly as serious as in Latin America and similar parts of the developing world. Distressing social divisions are not nearly as profound in a society that is dominated by a middle-class ethos and where upward mobility, while never easy, is at least imaginably within the reach of citizens of quite modest means. Opportunities for advancement into the mainstream and even upper echelons of American society exist beyond the dreams of the vast majority of people living in other countries, who find most doors to a materially better life shut firmly against them.

What does it mean, then, in U.S. society, to make a preferential option for the poor? There are no easy answers, of course, as each individual must discern an appropriate personal response to this universal but imprecise call. Interestingly, in the course of their 1986 pastoral letter *Economic Justice for All*, the U.S. Catholic bishops speak frequently of the option for the poor, mentioning the phrase explicitly nine times. Concern for the poor pervades the entire letter, however, and the document urges lawmakers, citizens, consumers, and all others to measure all their decisions by the likely effects they will exert upon the least-advantaged members of society. To make a preferential option for the poor in a relatively affluent society may not entail an agenda of drastic social change to right a history of deep offenses against solidarity, but it does probably mean much greater sensitivity to the impact one's actions exert upon the vulnerable and marginalized. In a largely middle-class society like America, making a sincere preferential option for the poor will lead people to revise their lifestyle choices and numerous personal decisions, as well as to advocate for public policies to advance social justice.

The entire tradition of Catholic social teaching, including all nine themes surveyed in this chapter, can be interpreted as a unified effort on the part of church leaders to advocate for a more humane society where the most vulnerable members are better protected from harm. With its limited financial resources, the Church itself can do only so much to advance the lives of the poor. However, popes and bishops, as the official voices of the Church, have exerted great efforts to speak publicly about political, economic, and social issues that have profound impact upon the prospects of our neediest neighbors. The rationale for all the Church's efforts in this regard may be summarized precisely as the desire to make a preferential option for the poor.

If these church efforts really do bear fruit, then what would the results look like? If the message of justice and peace within Catholic social teaching takes root in the hearts of many believers, these disciples would work energetically for a better world, a world characterized by not only acts of individual *charity* but also structures of *justice* and equity for all people. Racial discrimination and unfair barriers to progress would be eliminated. True human development would be fostered by wider access to property and by socially responsible policies of businesses and governments throughout the world. All social institutions, from schools to corporations to social clubs, would come to be measured by how they treat all members of society, especially the poorest. Priorities would be altered so that more of the benefits of this abundantly blessed world would find their way to those who currently possess the least. In a prosperous age like the present one, no one should be excluded from enjoying an ample set of opportunities or be left to experience the disturbing fear of permanent powerlessness and deprivation.

Catholic social teaching includes a call for involvement in collaborative efforts to invite all people into the social mainstream; it is not an ethic for apathetic or complacent people. To adopt the principles of Catholic social thought is to concur that all people need to make sincere and vigorous efforts so that full participation is extended to all, without favoritism or discrimination. We all have something to contribute to the common good, and all may benefit from the gifts that we bring to the common table of human community and solidarity.

Although it surveys most of the ground covered in the documents of Catholic social teaching, the list of nine themes in this chapter is far from complete. Several of the most obvious omissions will be treated in chapter seven, which peers into the likely future of this tradition. Among the topics noted there are globalization and environmental concern, which, as noted above, richly overlap the already well-articulated concerns regarding the common good, economic development, and other elements of Catholic social thought.

QUESTIONS FOR REFLECTION

1. Which of these nine themes of Catholic social teaching do you consider most important? Are certain ones more foundational than others that may appear more peripheral and that build upon the more basic ones? Do any of them challenge your previously held belief systems or opinions regarding the role of institutions such as government, property labor unions, or family life?
2. How would you explain the principle of subsidiarity to a child, using the simplest possible language? Do you think that this technical-sounding idea is at root a commonsense principle that almost anyone can understand if it is explained properly?
3. How good are the tools offered by recent Catholic social teaching on private property? Do you think this teaching strikes the proper balance between the individual and social functions of property when it speaks of (1) socialization, (2) the social mortgage on property, and even (3) the possibility of a justified expropriation of some means of production?
4. Besides the positions mentioned in section 6 of this chapter, such as support for organized labor and basic worker rights, what else could the Church be doing to foster a sense of the dignity of all human labor? Can you think of concrete measures for spiritual enrichment, theological education, or outreach programs that would demonstrate greater church commitment to improving the lives of all who work?
5. Many readers might feel that the Church's treatment of families (see theme 3 within this chapter) is too sketchy to be of much help. What

more should the Church say about family life and the challenges facing all families today? Which further details would be helpful to provide? Or is it in the end better to offer only general advice and directions?

6. Do you find yourself favoring the approach of just war theory or of pacifism? What are the strengths and weaknesses of each of these Christian approaches to the task of peacemaking? How do recent world developments (the growth of terrorism, the war in Iraq) shed light on your opinions regarding approaches to war and peace?

7. Do you see the preferential option for the poor as a new element of the Church's social message or as a continuation of what came before? How would you defend your opinion? Whether novel or not, in what concrete ways may the option for the poor be practiced by affluent citizens today?

TOPICS FOR FURTHER RESEARCH

1. Cardinal Joseph Bernardin and his advocacy of the "seamless garment of life"

2. The development of human rights theory and various instruments to protect rights

3. The history of overcoming racial and gender discrimination and other barriers to full participation of struggling and minority groups in politics and the economy

4. The variety of church documents, besides social encyclicals, on family issues

5. The notion of civil society and the major threats to its vitality

6. Distribution patterns of wealth and the growth of inequality in recent decades

7. The history of the U.S. labor movement and its relationship to religious communities

8. The major schools of developmental economics and postcolonial theory

9. Various schools of pacifism and nonviolence; the anti-war and disarmament movements in recent U.S. history

10. The successive meetings of the Conference of Latin American Bishops (CELAM)

6

✝

The Role of Catholic Social Teaching Today

Chapter five examined nine of the major themes treated in the documents of Catholic social teaching. Although the survey of themes in that one chapter could only scratch the surface of this tradition, it is already easy to detect the great richness, complexity, and sensitivity to diverse modern conditions present in these teachings. Many aspects of political and economic life in society are treated in the pages of the social encyclicals, which stake out careful positions on the justice dimensions of politics and economics in the modern world.

The task of this chapter is to answer some of the most obvious questions that arise once we have digested the basic content of these teachings about the relationship between faith and justice: How does one go about the task of applying the messages of Catholic social teaching? Should the Church's message be interpreted as supporting some already existing economic system, or is it equally critical of all current alternatives, such as capitalism and socialism? Is it a complete blueprint for an ideal society, or are its challenges more of a modest, scattershot attempt to address serious injustices? Do the judgments reached by church officials in any way threaten to interfere with the political and economic orders about which bishops and popes clearly lack experience and expertise? What is the purpose of writing and publishing all these documents, anyway?

A BLUEPRINT? AN IDEOLOGY? A "THIRD WAY"?

Ever since the beginning of the modern tradition of social encyclicals over one hundred years ago, controversy has surrounded the Church's attempt to offer advice about the structure of society. Many scholars, politicians, and journalists have criticized the entire endeavor, on occasion insisting that the Church has no business interfering in secular matters beyond its expertise, even if the conclusions remain on the level of general principles. Several of these church documents contain long sections that address these voices, attempt to answer such objections, and clarify the purpose of Catholic social teaching. The next few paragraphs allow a few of these encyclicals to speak for themselves in defining the legitimate role of Catholic social teaching in the mission of the Church.

One important statement on this topic appears in paragraph 76 of the Vatican II social teaching document *Gaudium et Spes*. Here, the Council summarizes the twin concerns expressed by several previous popes in order to set the record straight about the proper role of Catholic social teaching. First, the Council fathers issue a reminder that the Church's intention in speaking out on social issues is a modest one of offering helpful advice and proposing useful moral principles. Only those who entirely misconstrue the Church's motives would attribute to church leaders such overly ambitious agendas as somehow attempting to bully or replace governments, or perhaps allying the Church itself with particular political parties in opposition to others. *Gaudium et Spes* asserts:

> The role and competence of the Church being what it is, she must in no way be confused with the political community, nor bound to any political system.

In other words, the world of politics has its own legitimate logic and operations, and the Church has no intention of dictating its preferred policies or intruding into areas where it has no particular competence. Religious voices should always be vigilant against the temptation to say too much about secular matters, to address temporal issues with a level of detail that turns out to be inappropriate for spiritual leaders to venture.

A few sentences later in paragraph 76, this 1965 document speaks about a second concern, an anxiety that amounts to the flip side of the first: the danger that a timid Church might say entirely too little about worldly affairs and thereby surrender part of its own rightful mission of spreading the Gospel and assisting people in their attempts to flourish. The words of *Gaudium et Spes* here remind us that the Church, as a community of people concerned about both the spiritual and material well-being of all people,

> . . . has the right to pass moral judgments, even on matters touching the political order, whenever basic personal rights or the salvation of souls make such judgments necessary.

Without this qualification, readers might conclude that the Church had chosen to withdraw from the world and hold its tongue even when it witnesses grave injustices and abuses in political and economic matters. Quite the contrary, the Catholic Church in the decade of the 1960s found itself increasingly outspoken about social issues. Church leaders summoned up great courage to challenge the intolerable conditions they discovered once the Church rededicated itself to "reading the signs of the times."

But even after these twin concerns were so clearly articulated, some confusion persisted. Commentators from the right, left, and even the center of the political spectrum repeatedly misunderstood the purpose and proper role of Catholic social teaching. Sometimes they selected just a few isolated sentences from the encyclicals and twisted the words to support their favorite system, whether capitalist or socialist in nature. Others disputed the Church's right to say anything at all about social issues, insisting on a sharp split between religion and politics. It fell to John Paul II, the pope who is remembered fondly for his courageous public stance in support of the Polish labor union *Solidarnosc* (Solidarity) and its leader Lech Walesa, to issue the most complete clarification of the Church's stance: the encyclical *Sollicitudo rei Socialis*.

Published in 1987, just two years before the fall of the Berlin Wall and the end of the Cold War, *Sollicitudo rei Socialis* contains John Paul's reflections on the Church's contribution to a world of greater peace and justice. Permit the citation of this long quotation from paragraph 41, a key section where John Paul states his hopes and expectations for a constructive type of church advocacy:

> The Church does not have technical solutions to offer . . . . For the Church does not propose economic and political systems or programs, nor does she show preference for one or the other, provided that human dignity is properly respected and promoted. . . . But the Church is an "expert in humanity," and this leads her necessarily to extend her religious mission to the various fields in which men and women expend their efforts in search of the always relative happiness which is possible in this world, in line with their dignity as persons . . . . [W]hatever affects the dignity of individuals and peoples, such as authentic development, cannot be reduced to a "technical problem." . . . This is why the Church has something to say today . . . about the nature, condition, requirements and aims of authentic development, and also about the obstacles which stand in its way. In doing so the church fulfills her mission to evangelize . . . . The Church's social doctrine is not a "third way" between liberal capitalism and Marxist collectivism, nor even a possible alternative to other

solutions less radically opposed to one another; rather, it constitutes a category of its own. Nor is it an ideology . . . but belongs to the field . . . of moral theology.

This passage is rich in meaning and complexity, but a few key points stand out and deserve to be underlined. First, the opening and closing sentences point out the difference between the "technical" (relating to detailed nuts and bolts of policy decisions) and the "moral" (relating strictly to the level of values in society). There are, of course, many technical political and economic questions about which the Church has chosen to remain silent. Precisely how should Congressional district boundaries be drawn? What is the proper rate for sales taxes or for interest rates on federal education loans? Should nations recognize international waters as beginning at two, twelve, or a full two hundred miles off the coast of a country for purposes of fishing and mineral rights?

On one hand, the Church is unlikely to have much of anything substantial to add to the analysis of secular experts about any of these questions. On the other hand, it would be unwise to rule out the possibility that any given public policy question might have moral dimensions about which the Church rightfully has much to say and to the discussion of which the Church could potentially make a valuable contribution. A bad decision on any of these questions (resulting, for example, in extremely high food taxes that squeeze the poor, or election laws that underrepresent neighborhoods with more minority presence, or international laws that unduly punish landlocked countries) could provoke a justified appeal to the lessons of Catholic social teaching. When people notice these moral dimensions, it is helpful to turn to religious voices as partners in a sincere dialogue about ethical aspects of public policy. The social ethics of Christianity, and indeed of all the religions of the world, can make a truly constructive contribution to the moral and social analysis that informs political and economic decisions.

A second item worth exploring in the above quote regards the ideological competition that raged at the time between capitalism and socialism. When John Paul II wrote *Sollicitudo rei Socialis*, this rivalry was still intense, and certain supporters of each side were eager to claim the Catholic Church as an ally against their sworn enemies. Now that the communist bloc has disintegrated, the controversies of earlier decades may appear irrelevant, perhaps even absurd, to contemporary observers, but they still shed helpful light on the proper understanding of Catholic social teaching by revealing vital elements of the historical context out of which it grew.

The goal of the Church's statements on social issues has never been to ally the Church with a specific party or ideological movement, whether Marxist communism or free-market capitalism or welfare-state democratic socialism. In fact, it is easy to find serious criticisms of all these systems (and others as well) in the encyclicals. Even though certain of the documents have the appearance of leaning a bit toward one side or another of the political spectrum, it is safe to say that Catholic social teaching never gives its unconditional support or approval to any existing economic system.

How, then, should one characterize the role of Catholic social teaching? It is certainly wise to take with the utmost seriousness Pope John Paul II's statement that church teaching is not intended to support any particular ideological system. Nor does it aspire to be an ideology of its own, as if finding a compromise "third way" between communism and capitalism would be the ultimate contribution of this long tradition of reflection on life in society. Instead, this body of teachings must always be considered above all as a *religious* contribution to human society. From its vantage point of theological principles, Catholic social teaching peers down upon the full spectrum of political and economic options and seeks to measure them according to the Church's distinctive view of what contributes to human flourishing.

The yardstick the Church uses to make these measurements has more to do with human dignity and spiritual values (such as the virtues of solidarity and compassion for the poor) than with material goals (such as greater efficiency and increased consumer choice). For that reason, it has never been easy for those who identify themselves primarily as politicians, economists, or practitioners of other strictly secular pursuits to understand fully the principled positions of Catholic social thought. Indeed, at times it infuriates potential coalition partners to learn that the same bishops, clergy, and lay Catholics who applaud their initiatives on certain measures (such as investment in education or health care reform) wind up staunchly opposing them on other issues (for example, sterilization for population control, abortion, capital punishment, and protections for the family farm). Because its key loyalties go beyond partisan politics or quantifiable economic goals to include deeper theological principles and human values, Catholic social teaching can never be placed on the same level as Marxist communism or free-market capitalism, as if it were just another system of ideological thought that competes for dominance and influence.

Recall the nine major themes of Catholic social teaching examined in chapter five. The items making up that list suggest a series of important questions that people guided by the Church's social thought might use to evaluate any particular economic policy or political program. Equipped with this set of concerns, certain critical questions arise: Will this proposal promote respect for human dignity? Does it protect the rights of workers? Will it result in wider participation, or will it further marginalize those who are already poor and vulnerable? Is it likely to foster a more peaceful world, or will it serve to divide peoples and fray the fragile relationships that exist between nations?

How, then, may we summarize the role of Catholic social teaching in the modern world? The best brief answer to this question is one that emphasizes how it aspires to be neither an ideology, nor a "third way" compromise between existing ideologies of left or right, nor a comprehensive blueprint for a perfect society. Catholic social teaching at its best makes no attempt to impose any models of how to organize social life, but it is bold enough to propose a core set of values that should guide powerful decision makers, whether they are Catholics, adherents of other faiths, or members of no religious community at all. These human values, many of them covered in chapter five, are key criteria for measuring good decisions and policies. The Church in every land seeks to remain a faithful witness to these values, to model responsible behavior, and to offer valuable guidance to all people of conscience regarding the benefits of practicing social justice.

Of course, a national leader, legislator, or corporate executive need not agree with the entire Catholic vision of God, the universe, and humanity's place within the cosmos in order to agree with these core values and criteria. Many of the moral principles contained in Catholic social teaching are, in this sense, somewhat detachable from their underpinnings in a distinctively Catholic theology. But a picture of human flourishing that includes such principles as human rights, the necessity of peacemaking, the exercise of social responsibility in the use of property, broad participation in political life, and a special concern for the poorest members of society— this is a promising basis around which to build bridges between many diverse people in the modern world. It is, further, an encouraging foundation upon which to form a consensus regarding which government policies, corporate practices, social customs, and private lifestyle choices might foster a better life for all people.

Perhaps this is the reason why all of the popes since John XXIII have addressed their social encyclicals "to all people of good will," not merely to the world's Catholics. As a worldwide community of social concern, the Catholic Church is always eager to join in coalitions with like-minded people who seek to work together to promote peace, solidarity, and social justice. It is not necessary for coalition partners to agree on every point of theological doctrine in order to engage in effective joint efforts in pursuit of social change. This path of cooperation is a most encouraging direction for putting Catholic social teaching into action.

As seen just above, it is helpful to think of Catholic social teaching as offering a yardstick that is useful in measuring the achievements or shortcomings of existing economic systems. This is a complex process, of course, and to do it thoroughly would involve amassing a huge amount of information about production techniques, efficiency gains, distributive patterns, and social conditions facing people who live under a given system. For example, before anyone could hope to draw firm conclusions about whether a specific nation's economy is making an adequate option for the poor, it would be necessary to collect extensive data on employment opportunities, poverty statistics, demographic profiles, and social indicators such as infant mortality rates and life expectancy. Doing this type of homework is a daunting assignment, but it is by no means an impossible task. Indeed, achieving this level of detailed research is a great service that will hopefully be performed by savvy social scientists with increasing accuracy and ease in coming decades.

The task of using Catholic social teaching to measure the adequacy of economic systems is much easier in the abstract than in concrete settings. It is always simpler to speak about general models or economic schemas than it is to gather detailed information on their actual operations in specific contexts. There is, of course, no space here to review the data on the actual achievements and outcomes of, say, capitalism in the United States during the 1920s or communism in the Soviet Union during the 1970s, but it is possible to review briefly the basic commitments and value orientations of the general models of economic life contained in capitalism and communism. The next two sections of this chapter offer a simplified picture of each of these systems and draw a few preliminary judgments about the merits and defects of each system as viewed from the perspective of Catholic social teaching. The conclusions reached will be modest and surely open to further debate but might well shed some welcome light on the contribution of church positions to the great economic debates of recent decades. This exercise will demonstrate how it is that Catholic social thought can readily be applied as a yardstick to measure the moral achievements and ethical deficits of any economic system.

One preliminary precaution should be noted. Anyone who employs broad terms such as "communism" and "capitalism" is necessarily making sweeping generalizations about many actual practices that have unfolded over centuries. Each of these isms has been practiced in numerous distinctive ways in a variety of contexts and places. To be truly accurate, each term would have to be specified with modifiers such as "early Maoist Communism" or "pre-New Deal laissez-faire capitalism," or hybrids such as "1970s Swedish welfare-state democratic socialism." While the documents of Catholic social teaching occasionally contain statements that seem to address a few of these specific contexts, we would have to read between the lines in extremely creative ways before we could accurately claim that we were matching the judgments of any of these documents to their intended audiences. Instead, it is preferable simply to admit from the outset that we are making broad-stroked applications of a few principles to the simplest models of communist and capitalist world-views. Still, even this modest project can yield some useful insights about the strengths and inadequacies of these two rival systems from the perspective of Catholic social thought.

THE CATHOLIC CRITIQUE OF COMMUNISM

First, let us examine the core principles of communism. As it proceeds from the lineage of Karl Marx, Friedrich Engels, Vladimir Lenin, and Josef Stalin, Soviet-style communism develops from a core commitment to end the alienation that traps most workers in oppression. The dominance of a privileged class of wealthy owners of capital (the bourgeoisie) prevents the class of common laborers (the proletariat) from reaping a fair share of the benefits of their work. When people are thus robbed of the fruits of their labor, they become estranged from the work process, from themselves, and from the whole human race. What is required to reverse this process, as the argument runs, is an abrupt and complete revolution. The proletariat rises up to defeat the ruling bourgeoisie, repaying its cruelty and oppression with a dose of violence that is fully justified in the eyes of the revolutionaries. Social structures are overturned to establish universal equality, not only of opportunities but also of outcomes. This new order is portrayed by doctrinaire communists as a perfect world of harmony, where each person contributes according to his or her ability and receives according to his or her needs.

There are indeed a few praiseworthy aspects of communism evident in this brief and simple description. Employing the principles of Catholic social teaching, we can applaud its high regard for the dignity of work and the call to protect the weakest members of society. There is a laudable sense of urgency about reversing the oppression and alienation that renders a majority of the world's population disinherited and without hope. Further, the communist worldview portrays people as deeply connected to one another by the bonds of solidarity. It also takes seriously the necessity of recognizing the social responsibility that applies to property and the ways it is used. In communism, we find a serious and noble commitment to empower the poor and to end the exploitation of the poor by the rich until greater equality is achieved. Thus, we can easily approve of its ultimate vision of a world where all can participate fully in social life and where material goods are shared so that all urgent human needs are satisfied.

But communism, as it was theorized by Karl Marx and later spread by Soviet armies, contains many features that are objectionable from the standpoint of Catholic social teaching. Three of the most obvious features deserve mention here. First, there is no place for God in this system of thought. The writings of Marx and Engels, in fact, have hostile things to say about the role of religion as a regressive force in exacerbating the oppression of the proletariat. The communist regimes established in the twentieth century were not only officially atheistic; they aggressively persecuted millions of Christians, Jews, and others whose attempts to practice their religion were declared counterrevolutionary. The tendency toward totalitarianism in communist regimes was fed by an insistence on the elimination of religious loyalties that were feared as a challenge to the complete and ultimate authority of the state.

A second set of objections concerns the way communism interprets the necessity of conflict in human history. Because it has a strong streak of determinism, orthodox communism asserts that we have no choice but to resolve the bitter divisions among social classes through a violent revolution in which the bourgeoisie is crushed. It despairs of reaching harmonious social agreement in which the rights of all are respected and in which compromises that benefit both workers and capitalists can be reached. There is no place for reconciliation between people divided by class boundaries or for "loving the sinner" even as we strive to eliminate the structures of sin that cause oppression.

As a result of this harsh view of social relations, communist leaders demonstrated a willingness to use any means, including systematic deception, torture, and mass murder of innocents, to advance the revolution. The atrocities that occurred at the time of the Russian Revolution (its high point was the Bolshevik seizure of power in October 1917) and during later purges carried out under Stalin may be attributed to the vices of particular statesmen and military officers as well as to the inner logic of the communist system of thought. As the decades of oppression behind the Iron Curtain wore on, hardly anyone recalled Marx's original hope that eventually the state, once it had been cleansed of the poison of its former bourgeois masters, would wither away and leave all people with unprecedented freedom. The high ideals of the Revolution had been betrayed. Violent repression and stifling control over captive populations grew from its initial status as a temporary means for attaining an idealistic vision to an end in itself and, eventually, to a brutal habit no communist regime could ever break.

A third set of objections concerns the economic policies carried out by Soviet, Maoist, and most other versions of the communist creed. After any communist takeover, whether in Eastern Europe or Asia, industry was collectivized and all land and productive property became nationalized, usually without reasonable compensation to their former owners. Those entrusted with managing the new state monopolies were seldom sensitive to the true needs of the vast majority of the population. The well-being of the people as workers and consumers was largely ignored, and their freedom of choice in careers and consumer products was rarely a priority for the managers and bureaucrats who ran the corrupt systems. As antagonism between people and their governments grew, dissenters were branded enemies of the state and persecuted mercilessly with no regard for due process of law.

Clearly, anyone whose reflections are guided by the lessons of Catholic social teaching can in no way approve of these aspects of communism. Its disregard of human rights, its squelching of freedom of religion and conscience, and its promotion of violent solutions in the name of a starkly materialistic revolution disqualify it as an acceptable approach to healthy life in society. However much one might be attracted to Marx's original vision of a utopia of universal worker solidarity in a world freed from alienation and exploitation, the inescapable conclusion is that communism was among the most monumental failures in all of human history. The seven decades of communist rule in the former Soviet Union alone cost tens of millions of lives and unleashed upon the world the horrors of a nuclear arms race during both the Cold War and several hot wars as well.

Still, it is wise to pinpoint exactly which are the dangerous elements in the theories of Marx and his followers. This knowledge leaves the observer in a position to salvage any useful elements that might be found there. As a matter of fact, Catholic social teaching is quite careful to distinguish between the objectionable and potentially useful insights of early socialists like Marx. In approaching this task, of course, much hinges upon how we view the relationship between socialism (as a general theory of desirable social relations) and communism (just one concrete political movement that grew out of the early socialist theorists, many of whom were dedicated Christians).

This ambiguity is reflected in *Quadragesimo Anno*, the 1931 encyclical in which Pope Pius XI says, on one hand, that socialism "is opposed to true Christianity" but, on the other hand, that "like all errors, socialism contains a certain element of truth" (no. 120). Four decades later, Paul VI would devote paragraph 33 of *Octogesima Adveniens* to a careful spelling out of four distinct levels of Marxism as he understood it. While the pope urges caution about the clearly unsuitable features of socialism, he also issues a helpful reminder that, like any ideology or system of thought, it is a complex reality. He recognizes that some uses of socialist thought (especially as "a rigorous method of examining social and political reality") could be appropriate for Christians to adopt in their own social analysis. These cautions, coming as they do from within the documents of Catholic social teaching, should be interpreted as valuable reminders to look beyond mere labels to the real content of a political system, to seek to discover how people are actually treated by large social structures and the ideas behind them.

THE CATHOLIC CRITIQUE OF CAPITALISM

The task of using Catholic social teaching principles to evaluate capitalism involves a more nuanced picture. The dreams of capitalism are neither so noble nor its failures so obvious as those of its longtime communist rival. In its purest form, capitalism includes the principle of free enterprise (where there are minimal barriers to starting and running one's own business) and free-market exchange (private trading without government regulation or interference). Capitalism places a high value on the freedom of the individual to pursue his or her own self-interest and is averse to restrictions upon free choice. The favorite economic instrument of capitalist theory, of course, is the market, a mechanism that determines the price and quantity of goods and services in the most decentralized way possible. In a pure free market with perfectly free competition, millions of private decisions about the value of goods and services bid up or down their prices, so that no one person or group controls the buying and selling of goods.

To most people, this brief sketch describes an extremely familiar reality, for we live in an age that takes markets for granted. But it would be an exaggeration to say that this is the only natural way for economic life to proceed. In many cultures and societies throughout human history, economic production, trade, and distribution were carefully regulated by central authorities. Even in medieval Europe, the dominant belief (supported by church officials and most theologians) was that justice required rigidly fixed prices and wages so that economic and social stability could be maintained. Only as the economy became modernized in recent centuries did fluctuating prices, as well as the practice of lending money at interest, become widely accepted. Our modern system of free-market capitalism and liberal international trade practices grew out of a long evolution of the trading and production system through numerous phases. These include state-sponsored mercantilism, colonialism and neo-imperialism with high tariff regimes, the Industrial Revolution with its Fordist and Taylorist production innovations, and, finally, the contemporary mass-consumption economy with its thorough globalization.

Another face of capitalism worth mentioning here is welfare-state capitalism. In the early 1900s, workers and their advocates won major victories in the U.S. and Europe in support of increased government regulation of the economy. Social movements such as the Progressive coalition in the

U.S. campaigned successfully for such measures as shorter workdays and antitrust laws that curtailed monopolies and secretive price-fixing on the part of the aggressive captains of industry, often dubbed "robber barons." These pioneering efforts to use government policy to pursue social justice constituted the birth of the modern welfare state whose protections are still broadly enjoyed in industrialized nations. The U.S. eventually followed the lead of most European governments in expanding the role of public authorities in protecting workers from the dire poverty that so often accompanied industrial accidents, illness, retirement, or unemployment. As popular support for poverty relief and other income security measures grew during the Great Depression, the Social Security Act of 1935 committed the federal government to providing survivors' benefits, pension plans, health insurance, and public assistance programs. Other protections for workers that are part of welfare-state efforts include minimum wage laws, safety and health regulations, legal recognition for labor unions, and subsidies for family nutrition, job training, and education.

Even though recent decades have witnessed the scaling back of these programs in most Western nations as costs mounted and public support for them evaporated, the phrase "welfare-state capitalism" is still an accurate description of most industrialized economies. But the remaining protections do have their vocal critics who want to see the economic system move ever closer to a style of free-market capitalism with a much smaller role for government. Behind these proposals is an entire philosophy of economic life that is called libertarianism, or sometimes neoliberalism. The next several paragraphs offer a brief examination of the underlying principles behind this version of capitalism and then evaluate a libertarian style of capitalism in light of the principles of Catholic social teaching.

A libertarian worldview begins with the idea that personal freedom should be the highest value pursued in society. People are seen first of all as sovereign individuals, ultimately responsible only to themselves. All larger social groupings, such as families, municipalities, or nations, are merely artificial collections of individuals and, therefore, make no legitimate claims upon people unless they consent voluntarily. The best form of government, it is argued, is the type that by and large stays out of the way and allows people to use their individual resources and property as desired. The free market is the supreme natural mechanism for securing natural liberties, and any interference in these markets for capital, labor, or consumer products is judged obtrusive and unwelcome.

The contrast between this sketch of human social life and the worldview of Catholic social teaching is sharp indeed. The libertarian perspective leaves no room for the virtue of solidarity, for the recognition that people really do belong to one another and that natural human social groupings create more than just voluntary or accidental bonds. Catholic social teaching portrays government not as an unwelcome intruder upon basic freedoms, but as the very means by which citizens collectively and rightly act for social betterment and discharge their obligations to their neighbors in need. While libertarians seem confident that the natural order that arises spontaneously from the operation of free markets will be beneficial for all, any genuinely religious perspective would call attention to the imperative to build in some protections for the vulnerable. As markets tend to produce extreme winners and extreme losers, what will happen to those who cannot compete successfully for jobs and goods? Are their needs to be disregarded entirely, since free markets provide goods (even vital goods such as food and health care) only to those able to pay? Libertarians demonstrate a remarkable aversion to considering these questions at any level of seriousness, and this constitutes their ethical blind spot, the Achilles heel of their otherwise elegantly crafted positions.

These objections ultimately boil down to a question of how one comprehends the basic characteristics of the human person. Is each person to be understood primarily as a consuming individual, as merely a bundle of selfish and infinite desires? Is the deepest identity of the modern person wrapped up in becoming a fierce competitor in the game of the modern economy? If so, social arrangements descend quickly into a destructive type of social Darwinism, where the principle of survival of the fittest divides the weak from the strong and relegates some people to the margins of existence, if not eliminating them altogether. The Catholic social principles of common good, participation, and solidarity are ignored when people, no matter how well intentioned, adopt social standards that place the value of liberty too high above the value of basic equality. Balancing liberty and equality is a perennial goal of social theories, and it appears that libertarianism produces a lopsided view of this equilibrium—one that turns out to be unacceptable to a Christian worldview.

Libertarians often defend their free-market positions as necessary conditions for achieving certain social goals they deem crucial: creating the maximum amount of wealth; maintaining economic incentives for people to work hard; and promoting the value of efficiency so that all resources are employed in the most productive ways. Because it so emphasizes the efficiency that it claims can come only from free markets, this extreme version of capitalism sharply opposes any type of planning that might reduce incentives for self-reliance or reserve some share of resources for the poor, such as income supports or health care entitlements. The fear of a centralized system that controls all economic life is so strong among libertarians that commonsense measures to provide for the common good, such as publicly coordinated industrial policies and infrastructure improvements, are spurned as dangerous departures from a free economy.

All too often, libertarians dismiss these objections by means of the one-dimensional argument that all necessary social functions can be achieved by the operation of free markets alone. Solutions that require deliberative civic action, formal democratic procedures, and government legislation, they argue, simply invite inefficiencies and inconveniences into the wondrous market mechanism.

Even many of those who praise the market would admit, at least in moments of frank honesty, that if markets are left unchecked by government regulation, numerous desirable activities would indeed remain altogether undone. The list of such market failures and public goods includes pollution control, the maintenance of parks and roads, the checking of monopolies, regional planning, the alleviation of poverty, and other regulative tasks that contribute to good public order. In a strictly libertarian world, practically nothing would ever happen that is not motivated by the thirst for profits. Guided by Catholic social teaching, we can easily identify numerous social necessities that require a more well-rounded approach to social life.

It turns out, not altogether surprisingly, that a majority of those who call themselves libertarians are the very people who benefit most from free markets. They are, for the most part, the winners in a competition that is made fiercer by means of increased reliance on unregulated markets. Imagine, for example, a Wall Street trader whose chief skill is to manipulate the financial markets every day in pursuit of the winning formula for investing capital in the most profitable corporations and business ventures. Of course, many play this high-stakes game and lose disastrously, but imagine for a moment one of the "stock market whizzes" who consistently makes fortunes (for himself and perhaps for some deep-pocketed backers as well). He vehemently defends the huge personal rewards he reaps as fair payment for the skills he has developed and the service he provides to investors and entrepreneurs. Whenever he hears suggestions that financial markets should be more closely regulated, he opposes such ideas as dangerous interference with the natural order of the universe.

Occasionally our imaginary trader will find himself encountering, as all people do from time to time, others whose life experiences lead them to different conclusions about what is desirable in the fields of economics and public policy. A chance encounter with someone of another social class might well challenge his libertarian worldview. Maybe it will be a street person, one of the many thousands whom the unregulated housing market has priced out of his last home and thrown into a horribly uncertain future. Maybe it will be the low-paid janitor at his office building or a suddenly unemployed and financially strapped cousin he meets at a family reunion. Such an encounter could unfold in any setting and on any occasion when casual conversations reveal how the unfair structure of educational and work opportunities exclude so many from the comfortable mainstream of society.

Allow your imagination to fill in the details of these conversations between people who have received very different treatments at the hands of markets. What topics might come up regarding the fairness of economic structures, realistic prospects for achieving a good life, and huge gaps in social status? Would one of the privileged "winners" be able to defend in a credible way the reasons why the system has favored his skills over the labors of the hardworking blue-collar employee? How might the topics of efficiency, incentive, the distribution of economic opportunity, and fair returns for effort be debated in this conversation?

Of course, there is nothing conclusive about this example, but it may be a helpful thought experiment to reveal the real-life implications of the most radical defenses of free-market capitalism. While the ideas of "cowboy capitalism" and unhindered competition seem to have growing appeal in society today, the luster of the ideal of free markets is tarnished as soon as one considers the plight of the losers. How will society make adequate provisions for those whose contribution of skill and effort is not highly valued in labor markets? What concerns for human values and social justice should check the otherwise unreflective enthusiasm for uninhibited financial freedom?

These drawbacks of the extreme form of libertarianism should by no means lead to a blanket rejection of all forms of capitalism. More moderate versions (such as welfare-state capitalism) that include some regulation of markets to ensure that they serve human priorities are quite constructive and generally deserving of much support. That this support is always conditional, depending upon many local factors, is a point reiterated by Pope John Paul II in his 1991 encyclical *Centesimus Annus*:

> The Church has no models to present; models that are real and truly effective can only arise within the framework of different historical situations through the efforts of all those who responsibly confront concrete problems in all their social, economic, political and cultural aspects . . . . For such a task, the Church offers her social teaching as an indispensable and ideal orientation, a teaching which, as already mentioned, recognizes the positive value of the market and of enterprise, but which at the same time points out that these need to be oriented toward the common good. (no. 43)

As in John Paul II's opinion, this chapter's assessment of capitalism is a mixed bag. It is of course easy to approve of capitalism's high regard for human liberty and resistance to any form of totalitarianism. Yet any sincere observer must remain concerned about how easily capitalism slides into indifference to the needs of the least successful participants in market competition. As has often been said, the market is a fine servant but a bad master. Insofar as they spark human creativity and allow people to contribute to the good life in society without undue interference, market systems measure up quite well to most of the principles of Catholic social teaching. But when extreme versions of free-market capitalist ideology are used to justify crass materialism, unmitigated selfishness, and utter indifference to the plight of weaker members of society, it is then necessary to express objections to some of its features. John Paul II offered wise counsel indeed when he reminded the readers of *Centesimus Annus* that any embrace of capitalism on the part of the Church must always remain a qualified endorsement, one that depends entirely on how markets for goods and labor treat all people, especially the most vulnerable.

APPLYING CATHOLIC SOCIAL TEACHING IN THE REAL WORLD

This chapter has probed some of the complexities that arise in evaluating the two most important isms that dominated life in society over the past century. It has utilized Catholic social teaching as an alternative worldview that provides insight into the positive and negative features of communism and capitalism in their pure forms. But, as is blatantly obvious, the real world of actual economic life is even more complicated than these pure abstract models might suggest. Each nation and region has a mix of various ideologies as well as many distinctive institutions that it has inherited from previous generations. Even those who agree on the principles of Catholic social teaching (or any set of values and principles, for that matter) must constantly update their judgments about how well any given economic or political system measures up to the standards and values it recommends.

An additional challenge is to recognize the simple fact that dominant systems are slow to change. Because one should not expect the basic structure of the economy in a given country to be altered overnight, Catholic social teaching is perhaps most often helpful when used as a guide for advocating gradual changes in the existing system. It is a tool that allows its users to expose and correct injustices, whether dramatic or ordinary in their occurrence. People of faith can use the Church's social teaching as a starting point for dialogue about how to make the economy more humane so that it better reflects the values and principles of peace, justice, and compassion. At most, this tradition of reflection offers the broad outlines of a picture of proper order for the world. Using this picture as a guide, one can then challenge governments, corporations, and individuals to reflect these values in their laws, practices, and choices. There will inevitably be disagreements about precisely which goals to adopt and which strategies to utilize, but a solid commitment to this quest is something that all people are called to live out.

It is revealing to note that even people who share similar sets of beliefs and values may reach quite different conclusions about specific social issues. Table 6.1 illustrates this point by presenting three steps that any moral decision in social ethics must navigate on the way to a conclusion. Investigating the three columns of this table sheds much light on the method by which ethical decisions are reached. It also helps to explain sources of inevitable disagreement about policy judgments. The next few paragraphs unpack the significance of table 6.1. The briefest versions of the message contained in table 6.1 are these two statements: (1) all three columns or stages are necessary in the determination of a moral decision; and (2) disagreements may arise at any of the three stages.

Located in the first column (on the left side of the table) are the basic commitments, values, and ideals that form the moral vision of any given observer of social reality. Drawing upon basic accepted sources of social wisdom (such as scripture and tradition, two major sources of Christian moral approaches described in chapter four), someone faced with a decision usually asks certain basic questions: What is the proper motivation for a good decision in this case? What values should I aspire to accomplish? Either explicitly or in some implicit way, a person faced with a decision usually seeks to promote the core ideals and values of whatever inherited traditions of thought have shaped his or her moral imagination. While there is always room for departures from tradition and distinctive personal appropriations of what is inherited, it is safe to expect a solid measure of continuity with what is familiar. Consulting one's own internal repertoire of ideals and values that are worth preserving is often the starting point for moral decision making.

Table 6.1.   A Model of Moral Methodology Useful in Social Issues

| Step One
Basic Commitments | Step Two
Social Ethic | Step Three
Practical Applications |
|---|---|---|
| Identify values | Articulate norms | Decide policy |
| Establish ideals | Establish structures | Establish procedures |
| Provide vision | Select principles | Make decisions |
| Love | Justice | Prudential judgments |
| Why? | What to do? | How to do? |
| Motivation | Practical reasoning | Calculation |
| What to aspire to? | What to justify? | What to do at the moment? |
| Deal with sources | Deal with power, sin | Deal with cases (casuistry) |
| Pure | Messy, complicated | Indeterminate |
| Expect continuity | Expect variety | Expect change |

But these deep background considerations are only the beginning of the process by which ethical courses of action are reached. While identifying and adopting values is certainly important as a first step, the actual state of the world has a way of constraining our choices when we seek to put them into practice. Column two of table 6.1 seeks to capture the messy process by which the purest and most commendable values find themselves challenged and even compromised by the rough-and-tumble of the real world. The sorting out process that abstract ideals inevitably undergo when confronted with social realities is often referred to as a *social ethic*. This is the general approach that a given person or group adopts under less than ideal circumstances, such as when the effects of sinfulness, power imbalances, or simply ordinary conditions of scarcity force compromises.

Under such conditions, any realistic person will ask a series of questions: How much of the content of my highest ideals may be achieved under these complicated circumstances? Which departures from my deepest values am I willing to justify and tolerate as I seek to navigate these turbulent waters of ethical decision making? In such a situation, most people try to come up with some reliable ethical principles or norms, or even to establish certain structures and procedures for guiding their moral discernment. The complex relationship between love (an ideal that belongs solidly in column one) and justice (a construct that captures the essence of column two) is bound up with the distinction between these two stages of moral reflection.

The progression from column one to column two of table 6.1 may be illustrated by some familiar examples. Within the ambit of column one, a naturally sociable and outgoing young person may find within his or her ethnic or religious tradition a high regard for the values of generosity and hospitality and so may dedicate much energy to practicing those virtues in everyday life. However, experience may soon teach this young person that certain limits should be imposed upon how much trust and goodwill it is wise to display in the public arena. Those who spontaneously invite complete strangers into their homes, lend money very freely to casual acquaintances, or hitchhike frequently soon discover that in the real world of contemporary social relations, trusts are often betrayed and many people will take advantage of a seemingly naïve host. It often proves not only foolish but possibly quite dangerous to trust too many people on too many occasions. Even this simple example about commonsense behavioral principles introduces key points about the progression within table 6.1 from column one to column two. A basic and laudable value such as hospitality soon comes to be modified, though not completely abrogated, by a social ethic that provides certain wise checks on indiscriminate generosity.

A chief element of a workable social ethic is a systematic and adequate rationale for determining what behavior is justified and therefore what courses of action constitute justice—that is, giving people what they truly deserve. In the above example, it might be argued that every passerby one might encounter on a city street deserves a warm smile, but not all such random acquaintances deserve the offer of a loan of bus fare, a ride to their next appointment, or free overnight lodging on one's living room sofa. Of course, in a perfect world, each person would possess the bottomless resources to help every stranger in need, but in the actual world, which is characterized by scarcity and frequent betrayals of trust, finite goods and limited time mean that we must frequently make hard choices as we struggle to live out our highest standards and values. The hard work of forming reliable generalizations about what treatment people deserve from us is the task of constructing a social ethic adequate to our fallen world.

A less trivial example involves a perennial and tragic social issue that was treated in both chapters four and five: the use of force in international politics. In a perfect world, sovereign nations would never need to resort to deadly force and would be free to live out the ideal of nonviolence—a decidedly column one orientation. But the fallen nature of the world means that certain international actors (not only nations, but also terrorist groups and other nonstate actors) abuse the power that they possess and may require coercive force to control. By no means does this entail the conclusion that routine decisions to wage deadly war are self-evidently justified. However, this observation does at least open up the possibility of adopting a social ethic that includes a just war theory as a provision for forging socially responsible behavior.

Even if one is unenthusiastic about the prospect of preparing for war and taking up arms, certain versions of a social ethic may justify resort to the use of force to control greater evils. Whenever deviating from the practice of nonviolence, care must of course be exercised to articulate norms and principles that will prevent abuses and violations of reasonable standards of behavior. The just war theory has been developed over centuries to accomplish precisely the goals described in column two of table 6.1 While it is far from perfect (no one has ever instituted a reliable structure, for example, to ensure against its abuse in the actual world of diplomacy), the theory at its best displays a sense of modesty about its role as one element of a larger social ethic that makes necessary concessions to the fallen nature of human affairs, including the perils of international conflicts.

The final entry in column two of table 6.1 issues a reminder to expect variety among the social ethics espoused by different parties. This may be the single most important item in that column and perhaps also the most obvious in contemporary society. The lack of a clear consensus on so many issues today may be attributed to numerous factors, including the dizzying pluralism of contemporary societies, the wide variety of systems of thought, and the sheer magnitude of print and electronic media now available for the dissemination of opinions. It seems as if there is some organized group or commentator to represent every conceivable viewpoint on every imaginable social issue—religious, political, economic, or cultural in nature. When it comes to social issues such as the topics featured in Catholic social teaching, there does emerge one recurring pattern that provides guidance in sorting out the variety of opinions commonly heard. On so many issues, the most frequently expressed opinions may be arranged on a spectrum that spans the ground from highly idealistic and principled, at one extreme, to highly realistic and practical, at the other extreme. The key item separating these types of opinions is the willingness of a given observer to engage in what is commonly called moral compromise.

Indeed, the issue of compromise is among the most profound sources of moral disagreement in society today. A marked aversion to compromise characterizes holders of many opinions who seek sincerely to cling as tightly as possible to the ideals discussed above and appearing in column one of table 6.1. One frequently hears laudatory as well as less flattering labels for holders of this type of approach, including "people of high principle," absolutists, purists, and naïve idealists. A marked eagerness to enter into ethical compromises, on the other hand, characterizes the other end of the spectrum just described. Whether they are called practical, pragmatic, realistic, or even Machiavellian and cynical, such people feel quite comfortable forging compromises that preserve even a small fraction of relevant ideals as long as the result is a workable solution that accounts for the give-and-take of real-world conditions and conflicts.

It is probably impossible to say definitively what in the end separates these two types of people. Perhaps a psychologist would be able to sort out the variety of ways in which people process experiences, consult authoritative sources, employ reason to analyze given situations, and reach conclusions about what is desirable and what is necessary given inevitable constraints. The important thing is not to place people in artificial boxes in such matters but simply to recognize that there does indeed exist a range of proclivities on moral decision making. Ethicists, for their part, can at least take comfort that the majority of people locate themselves at neither extreme but somewhere in between—eager to hold on to ideals, but also willing to accommodate necessary compromises and concessions to an imperfect world when necessary. If constructing a social ethic involves the use of what is commonly called tough love, it is safe to say that a majority of people have indeed developed a solid appreciation of this reality. While some may shy away from the toughness aspect, and others may be tempted on occasion to lose the sense of still practicing love of neighbor in making difficult decisions, a commonsense perspective on the issue of moral compromise is not so hard to find in society today.

Column three of table 6.1 requires the least explanation, for it is here that the schema of moral methodology leaves behind the realm of theory and enters the concrete order of actual applications. Regardless of what values might be received in column one or which social ethic might be adopted in column two, those with the authority to make decisions inevitably arrive at column three, where concrete decisions must be made, often under the pressure of inflexible deadlines. The final stage of deciding policy is, of course, yet another place where ethical disagreement may be encountered, whether or not divergent views have arisen in the previous two stages. It is a perennial fact of human nature that people can ponder the same decision, consider identical data, and come up with strong recommendations that clash on every point. It should come as no surprise that even people of good will can reach sharply divergent conclusions based on even slightly different perspectives and concerns.

One word worth noticing in column three of table 6.1 is the term *casuistry*. It comes from the familiar word "case," as in the related terms "case study" or "case law." For centuries ethicists and moral theologians have developed the detailed art (some even call it a science) of applying laws or norms to concrete cases. For many decades before a recent revival of this notion, casuistry suffered from a bad reputation, mostly due to its being perceived as an overly calculating procedure that had lost touch with the actual needs of the people and real-life situations that it was meant to serve. The practice of casuistry is at its best when the proper level of flexibility is observed, so that established laws are neither so rigid as to prove unbendable and therefore unreasonable and unworkable, nor so malleable as to be infinitely pliable and therefore too easily overturned for comfort. In the practical sphere that column three addresses, the guidance of norms and properly understood legal restrictions is highly valuable.

The decision maker turns to column three hoping to determine sets of policies at least for the short run and maybe even with permanent significance. In this context, policy can refer to government policy, but it also means corporate policies, church policies, and even the rules of thumb that individuals rely on routinely. Every organization needs to establish procedures and set directions for the future. The people authorized to make final decisions of this nature engage in informed calculations and make their best prudential judgments based on the information available. Because every situation is unique and unrepeatable, all such decisions display a certain uniqueness unto themselves. The natural human inclination to question and gainsay the current or past decisions of others is nicely framed by the folk wisdom that, before criticizing another, it is best to walk a mile in his or her shoes.

The schema of moral methodology just described sheds considerable helpful light on the role of Catholic social teaching in the contemporary world. The task of the Church's social message is to draw in a reflective way upon the sources and ethical values that are already present in the Christian tradition, that is, the ideals and entire vision of human and divine life that are described in column one of table 6.1. Properly speaking, the principles articulated in Catholic social teaching documents provide guidance for people (both private citizens and public officials) seeking to develop a responsible social ethic, the concern of column two of table 6.1. The documents from popes and gatherings of bishops outline social priorities, describe paths of justice, and in general help their readers to sort out conflicting claims about how society should function. Each of the nine themes treated in chapter five—from the sanctity of life to protections of the common good to justice aspects of property, labor, and peace-building issues—is part of an attractive vision of human flourishing that includes a distinctive social ethic. Because Catholic social teaching does not aspire to be a comprehensive blueprint for every imaginable policy decision or social situation that might come up over time, it can be said to provide guidance, but never to completely determine the types of policy applications captured in column three of table 6.1.

COMMITMENTS TO SOCIAL JUSTICE: HEROIC AND ORDINARY

Perhaps, in the end, this chapter produces more questions than answers. If there is no blueprint to follow in the search for justice, how are we to discover the proper course of action? What does it look like in concrete reality? Ultimate answers to these profound questions are not only elusive, but are bound to remain forever just beyond our grasp. This is inevitable because Catholic social teaching is not so much a set of preprogrammed answers that anticipate all of life's challenges, but rather a remarkably flexible and open-ended set of tools. These principles and social priorities may be employed in any number of situations, but the conclusions they suggest still require the active engagement of anyone seeking wisdom in this tradition. The fullest application of Catholic social teaching includes a personal commitment to ongoing discernment that transcends any set of formulas or prefabricated answers to the riddles of social justice.

Applying Catholic social teaching to the real world can touch our lives in many ways beyond reflecting on the big isms (including capitalism and communism as treated in this chapter) that usually play out on levels far above the heads of most people. More basically, it is a matter of pursing a lifestyle of promoting peace, of doing justice, and of exercising social responsibility on the most local of levels. What naturally comes to mind most immediately are extremely heroic actions for justice, often performed by famous and admirable leaders: prophets, missionaries, politicians, and others who speak out for justice and witness boldly for urgent causes. Society certainly needs these high-profile people to exert their important impact on the world. But progress toward social justice also requires ordinary people, like each of us, to influence the many small corners of the world in positive ways.

Mother Teresa (1910–1997), a hero to millions, was famous for calling her admirers to "find your own Calcutta." By this she meant that it is important, wherever one finds oneself, to take advantage of whatever opportunities arise for social involvement and to work ardently for justice. It so happened that her own journey led her to rather dramatic service: founding the Order of the Missionaries of Charity, advocating for social justice at the highest levels of international society, receiving a Nobel Prize, and, soon after her death, embarking on the path to formal sainthood. It is heartening to see a person who dedicated her life to such humble service, beginning her ministry literally in the gutters of one of the poorest cities on earth, receive such accolades and recognition. But even when the paths of justice that present themselves seem quite ordinary, extremely local, and far from heroic, they may be precisely what God is calling one to do at this moment.

Take, for example, the story of St. Peter Claver (1581–1654), often praised as "the slave of the slaves." He started out as an ordinary Spanish Jesuit priest of his day but, almost by accident, found himself ministering to some of the most oppressed people on earth—thousands of Africans kidnapped and in the process of being sold into slavery in the markets of Cartagena, Colombia. Peter Claver dreamed about single-handedly ending the institution of slavery and dramatically confronting the entire seventeenth-century establishment of colonialism that supported the many cruelties he witnessed. But much to his initial frustration, he found himself sharply limited in what he could realistically do: make simple visits to the slave ships and prisons where he could console, counsel, and offer the sacraments to those deprived of their freedom and dignity. Over his forty years of humble service and ministry, Claver baptized some 300,000 slaves and performed dignified funeral rituals for thousands more who succumbed to the inhumane conditions endured by enslaved Africans. By showing these men, women, and youngsters the respect owed to all children of God, he certainly contributed to the change in attitude that eventually abolished the slave trade. The evil isms of his day were not vulnerable to direct attack by a single person, but eventually they were conquered by the power of love and compassion that issued forth in acts of justice. Claver's life's work represented a wager regarding an insight expressed three hundred years later by Martin Luther King, Jr. At the end of the difficult summer of 1967, Dr. King affirmed with confidence that "the arc of the universe is long, but it bends toward justice."

In the end, living out the message of Catholic social teaching is largely about reexamining and purifying our loyalties. It challenges us to ask hard questions about the things we love and are willing to make sacrifices for. Are these priorities merely self-serving or do they include a wider circle of concern? Do our earthly goals somehow relate to our religious beliefs, or is our awareness of God somehow excluded from the majority of our everyday concerns? Would a fully honest account of my stewardship of talent and resources reveal solid commitment to social justice, or perhaps a disappointing level of apathy? While the answers to these questions are quite personal in nature and may well vary from moment to moment of every life, it is well worth striving to maintain the highest integrity amidst the choices life presents at every stage.

This chapter suggests that the dangers of communism and capitalism, or any humanly created social system for that matter, include a warping of proper values. As a result of these inevitable human flaws, goals such as the pursuit of profits, efficient markets, class-based revolution, or the national interest come to take the place of the things that truly deserve our deepest loyalties. Catholic social teaching contains important reminders that no humanly constructed system will ever completely capture the only objects fully worthy of our ultimate loyalty: the God we love and the people God creates and redeems. This is the wellspring and motivation for all our efforts to create the conditions that will allow people throughout the world to flourish as God intends, through an order of peace and justice that benefits all humankind.

QUESTIONS FOR REFLECTION

1. Imagine you are in a room with three people and each of them is making a different argument about Catholic social teaching. The first supports communist collectivism, since (he argues) socialist measures are the logical outcome of all this talk about the common good. The second claims that Catholic social teaching actually issues a blanket vindication of free-market capitalism. The third claims that Catholic social teaching is a distinctive "third way" between capitalism and communism, one that rejects both alternatives and proposes a complete system of its own. How would you respond to these

three voices? Which is closest to the truth, or are all three equally misguided?

2. In your experience of work and the marketplace, do you find our capitalist system mostly a constructive way of organizing life or mostly in need of change? Do its defects outweigh its advantages? If so, would you recommend gradual reforms or is a drastic about-face required to make the capitalist economy better serve human needs?

3. Use your imagination to construct a dialogue between the imaginary libertarian-minded Wall Street trader mentioned in this chapter and one of his less fortunate neighbors. What topics might come up? Is either one likely to experience a change of mind or heart?

4. How do you interpret the events of 1989 and 1990, when the Berlin Wall fell and the Soviet communist bloc crumbled? Did this revolution indicate the utter failure of all forms of socialism or just one particular type of communist-style socialism? Can people in the capitalist West still learn any valuable lessons from socialist theory?

5. Are you aware of any individuals, organizations, or movements that advocate for economic change in today's capitalist order? Is this person or group generally effective or hopelessly ineffective as an agent of change? Do you admire their work or do you have reservations about their approach?

6. Use table 6.1 to analyze each of the nine themes of Catholic social teaching as described in chapter five and summarized in table 5.1. It may be helpful to follow these three steps: For each theme, try to summarize the core values governing this theme as would be found in column one of table 6.1; identify a position on a contemporary issue that is at the "extremely uncompromising" end of the spectrum and another position that is "very accommodating of compromise" as it might unfold in column two (constructing a social ethic); and consider the factors that might lead to sharply divergent conclusions for policy applications in column three, where even people of good will sharing similar values often find themselves in disagreement.

7. Consider the provision of health care as a case study in the issues raised in this chapter. What principles should govern access to lifesaving treatments and medications? How adequate are markets and private insurance arrangements in providing medical care? What criteria for access besides ability to pay seems fair and ethical to you? Are there specific features of health care services that make the principles governing its distribution different from those governing other goods (e.g., consumer goods like electronics or luxuries such as vacation travel)?

TOPICS FOR FURTHER RESEARCH

1. The history of the Cold War competition between Eastern and Western blocs
2. The role of church and labor leaders (e.g., Lech Walesa in Poland) in challenging communism in various eastern bloc nations in the 1980s
3. The career of Monsignor George Higgins (1916–2002), the "labor priest" who popularized the analogy, used in this chapter, of Catholic social teaching as a yardstick for measuring the attainment of social justice
4. The variety of schools of socialist and communist thought, including Christian socialism, through the last two hundred years
5. Social Darwinism, a school of social philosophy best represented by the English author Herbert Spencer (1820–1903)
6. The strengths and weaknesses of libertarianism as a school of social philosophy, including the work of proponents such as Milton Friedman (1912–2006), Friedrich Hayek (1899–1992), and Robert Nozick (1938–2002)
7. Attempts to create workable hybrids between capitalism and socialism, such as the market-based Mondragón system of worker cooperatives for retail and manufacturing in Northern Spain
8. The moral methodology explicitly or implicitly used by any ethicist or moral theologian (good examples of American ethicists might include James Gustafson, Paul Ramsey, Charles Curran, Richard McCormick, Lisa Cahill)
9. The ethical tradition of casuistry, including the manuals of Catholic moral theology
10. St. Peter Claver, Mother Teresa, and other missionaries who contributed to causes of charity and justice while working with utterly destitute people

7

＋

Future Directions for Catholic Social Teaching

This final chapter ventures some guesses about possible future developments in Catholic social teaching. Of course, it is always hazardous to offer predictions about the future, since unforeseeable occurrences have a way of upsetting any neat expectations. In attempting to chart future directions for Catholic social teaching, it seems safe to predict a mix of change and continuity. This chapter makes an effort to identify the most likely developments in each category in the years ahead.

FOUR CONTINUITIES: FURTHER SHIFTS IN EMPHASIS

Like many traditions of thought, Catholic social teaching has updated itself by undergoing a certain amount of change both in its message and in the style in which this message is presented. This does not mean that the Church has in any way renounced or overturned what it previously taught; rather, it has refined its message to better meet the needs of changing times and to dialogue with new currents of thought. This section presents four ways in which Catholic social teaching has updated itself in recent years. None of the four involves a tale about some completely new principle or idea displacing older teachings. Rather, each represents a shift of emphasis or a new way of talking about familiar concerns as the Church addresses a rapidly changing world. In each of these four areas, there is reason to expect even further refinements in the coming years as the tradition of Catholic social teaching continues to grow and mature.

1. Personalism

The first of these shifts has been toward an approach called *personalism*. It is difficult to define this word in a precise way because the term has been applied to various schools of philosophical and theological thought in different times and places. There have been secular and humanistic versions of personalism as well as Catholic and Protestant ones (most notably, a long tradition centered at Boston University). Interestingly, one of the hotbeds of personalism was the University of Lublin in Poland, in the very department where Karol Wojtyla, the future Pope John Paul II, taught in the 1950s. More than any single figure, John Paul II was responsible for bringing a personalist approach into official Catholic social teaching. Although it could be argued that the major themes of personalism had long been present in the Church's social thought, it was with the three social encyclicals issued by the Polish pontiff that personalism came to be embraced in an explicit way in documents of Catholic social teaching.

At the heart of personalism is a deep concern for the value of the human person, especially when it comes under any type of threat from the large structures (such as government and powerful corporations) through which modern life is organized. To be a personalist is to measure all things—including changes in culture, technology, political practices, and systems of production—by their contribution to the well-being of persons. This attractive vision of human flourishing includes a high regard for human freedom, creativity, spiritual development, and openness to God.

All versions of personalism are eager to resist any false sense of determinism that would limit the understanding of human life to its material dimensions. The messages of many personalist writers include an appeal to renew interest in spirituality and the religious dimension of human life, challenging all people to look beyond the level of strictly material needs and their fulfillment. Thinkers guided by personalism have long protested the tendency of political and economic leaders to allow people to be sacrificed for abstract ideologies and questionable national goals. Personalists have looked on in horror at needless wars and other attacks against true human welfare. One particularly influential figure who fits this description very well was the French theologian Jacques Maritain (1882–1973). In the final decades of his long and eventful life, Maritain split his efforts between writing about his vision of personalism (or "integral humanism" as he preferred to call this approach) and active advocacy for social justice on the international stage.

Notice how closely the features of personalism overlap with several themes of Catholic social teaching, especially its emphasis on human dignity and human rights. In this sense, a personalist flavor has always been present in modern church teachings on life in society. Personalism is fully compatible with rich Christian theological themes such as freedom of the will and the inviolability of the human conscience. However, it is only in recent years, especially since Pope John Paul II started mentioning personalism by name in his social encyclicals, that it has received greater attention in church circles.

Personalism is at its most helpful when it guides contemporary attempts to balance the extremes of a radical individualism (a blind spot to which capitalist systems are prone) and rampant collectivism (one of the errors of communism). Going too far in either of these directions yields an approach to life that is incomplete and potentially harmful to oneself and others. This is precisely the message that John Paul II applies to the field of human work in the 1981 encyclical *Laborem Exercens*. In paragraph 15 (a section of the text that bears the title "The Personalist Argument"), the pope explains and defends his famous principles of "being over having" and the "priority of labor over capital." He focuses on the way people are so often treated as cogs in a machine in the modern industrial order, particularly in market relations and the processes of economic production, in such places as highly automated factories and the boardrooms of large corporations. These environments are not evil in themselves, of course, but the personalist seeks reforms so that they serve the full range of human needs and potentialities, rather than stifling the growth of people and thwarting the achievement of their deepest goals.

As ever, John Paul seeks to balance the relevant values as they relate to the core tenets of personalism and the entire body of Catholic social teaching. On one hand, the dignity of each person should not be dwarfed by the encroachments of runaway technology and huge economic structures that threaten to gobble up human individuality. On the other hand, we should not emphasize our individual rights so strongly that we lose all sense of social responsibility, including our willingness to make reasonable sacrifices for the good of larger groups. Because personalist thought helps us maintain this important balance, we should warmly welcome further explicit use of personalism in future Catholic social teaching documents.

As is true with the remaining three themes treated in this section of chapter seven, the increasing prominence of personalism in Catholic social teaching represents not something drastically new but, rather, the further development of a helpful strand that was already present in the inner logic of the Church's social message. Because the term personalism captures so many of the concerns the Church seeks to underline in its teachings about human society, it is certainly reasonable to expect the continued and deliberate use of personalist thought in future social encyclicals as John Paul's successors seek to build upon his rich contribution to social teaching.

2. Humility before the Data of Social Analysis

A second theme expected to continue into the future concerns the attitude and method of recent church social teachings. The growing trend worth noticing here is perhaps best summarized by the phrase "humility before the data." While an older style of proceeding might have favored making firm church pronouncements on social issues, with a strong sense of certainty about its positions, the style on display in recent social teachings emphasizes caution and modesty about the judgments that are drawn about contemporary world affairs.

As noted several times already, the Church is hesitant to lay down firm stances on complex societal issues, preferring instead to view its task in such matters as one of informing the consciences of people as they form their own prudent opinions. This observation becomes especially obvious when contrasting Catholic social teaching with the Church's more clearcut stipulations in the field of sexual ethics, where the emphasis tends to fall on an objective moral order and strict adherence to laws. All the documents of Catholic social teaching since the 1960s have recognized the possibility of legitimate differences of opinion and the need for ongoing social analysis, that is, the method of gaining knowledge about political and economic life that was described in chapter four as part of the see-judge-act schema.

Why is it safe to expect a continuation of this theme in Catholic social teaching? The lessons of history point to a need to retain a healthy sense of modesty about whatever judgments are reached at a particular historic moment. While there are indeed many eternal verities worth standing up for as moral absolutes, it is always wise to recall that a given culture or group may be limited in its understanding of the full meaning and impact of a particular moral principle. Especially on matters of social justice and relations in society, it is presumptuous to claim that we have nothing more to learn about a given topic or that our formulations have permanent and unalterable value. To foreclose the possibility of new learning based on updated social analysis is an irresponsible approach to social teachings. Fortunately, recent church documents on social justice reflect this awareness in a very consistent way.

This principle of the necessity of revising judgments on social issues is very much on display whenever historians look back, for example, upon the writing of the Constitution of the United States. At the time the founding fathers established the new nation's initial set of laws in the eighteenth century, few people would have argued for voting rights for women or for African-Americans, most of whom were slaves on the Southern plantations of that era. The Constitutional Congress that met in Philadelphia in 1787 consisted exclusively of white males. Far from the minds of most of these leaders was the thought that these categories of people, the great majority of whom were denied an education because of prejudice and social convention, could function as full citizens. Yet, within just a few generations, full civil and political rights were extended to African-American men and eventually to all women as well. Although each reversal came only after much hard work and even massive bloodshed, the nation had indeed revised its collective judgments about the crucial question of who merits full political participation. Luckily, the Founders had provided procedures for amending the Constitution, so that the fruit of new social analysis could find its way into law. Whether the new data includes updated assessments of human capabilities or novel findings from the physical or social sciences, it is the wise society that retains a stance of openness to the surprises revealed in the processes of history. While changes in the popular consensus do not always prove to be correct or ethical, it would be misguided to lock into place in a permanent way the transitory opinions of a particular historical moment.

Another way of explaining this second theme is to say that Catholic social teaching has grown toward a greater appreciation of the limits of natural law. Recall from chapter four that natural law is a source of ethical wisdom that includes the expectation that God's will is somehow discoverable in the structures of nature. In the past, the Church exhibited somewhat firmer confidence that the conclusions it drew from natural law reasoning were fixed and final. Recent decades, however, have witnessed such rapid social change that the need for ongoing social analysis and data collection can no longer be ignored.

A good example of this shift concerns the Church's stance on the legitimacy of private property. As noted earlier, the earliest social encyclicals cited natural law to affirm the general principle that private ownership of property is God's firm intention for the created world. Yet later documents came to recognize a number of legitimate exceptions to recognizing unlimited property rights. What accounts for this change is a growing awareness of the complexity of social relations in an increasingly interdependent world. Especially given the great diversity of institutions in various cultural contexts around the world, it makes little sense to expect a uniform set of principles to apply to property relations (or any other topic, for that matter) everywhere under the sun.

This shift is reflected in a basic change of style in the more recent documents of Catholic social teaching. Whereas the oldest documents used a *deductive* style (a top-down way of reasoning from universal principles to local applications), the newer ones are more *inductive* (using bottom-up reasoning that is more likely to respect local variations and special needs). This trend toward a more limited role for natural law reasoning in social teaching is likely to continue, if only because human society continues to undergo a dizzying rate of change. While all four sources of social wisdom and ethical insight—revelation, reason, tradition, and experience—are sure to have permanent relevance for Catholic social ethics, it is easy to support the prediction that social analysis and the entire category of experience will exert particularly strong influence upon future church social teaching.

3. Awareness of Social Sin

A third development that is likely to continue is the recent emphasis on social sin, a reality mentioned in earlier chapters. Since the 1970s, several of the documents of Catholic social teaching have expressed concern about structures of evil that surround all people and in which they all too often take part, generally in an unwitting way. In fact, paragraphs 35 to 37 of John Paul II's 1987 encyclical *Sollicitudo rei Socialis* refer to the notions of social sin or structures of evil over a dozen times.

Although some of the concepts surrounding social sin turn out to be rather complex in nature, the basic idea is quite straightforward. Living in an environment surrounded by many vices and injustices that are taken for granted makes it very hard to become a virtuous person. People easily become complicit with unjust structures even when they do not consciously choose them in the first place. Vigilance against unthinking cooperation with inherited evils is an urgent necessity but also a great challenge for contemporary people. Because of these tensions, the notion of social sin is emerging as one of the most important frameworks for adequately forming the consciences of people in our day.

A key example of such an evil social structure is racial discrimination—blatant unfairness toward minority groups and their members. Although we are free as individuals to reject this temptation, the accumulated weight of racial bias exerts an indisputable influence on our cultural environment. The sheer act of living in a society that perpetuates such destructive patterns of thought and action makes it quite likely that each person will somehow fall prey to the sin of racism, even if in subtle ways. Other evil structures treated in recent encyclicals include imperialism, colonialism, militarism, environmental degradation, and consumerism—patterns of activity that have harmed millions of people and in which billions of others have cooperated over many centuries.

The point of talking about social sin is not to make us feel guilty about injustices we are hardly responsible for and situations we merely inherited from previous generations. In fact, to truly qualify as a sin in the usual sense of the word, an act of racial bias or some other form of injustice must be deliberately chosen by an individual who acts with impure motives and at least some awareness of the harm being inflicted. Pope

John Paul II was particularly careful to issue a reminder that the root of social sin is always in personal sin and the evil choices of individuals, which precede the spread of evil to large social institutions and cultural practices. Nevertheless, since Catholic social teaching began addressing the topic of social sin, it has made a real contribution to shared reflection about the barriers to achieving true justice in the world today. Calling attention to the evils that are already present in social structures may help to motivate many people to make the desperately needed reforms that will benefit those harmed by destructive patterns of behavior. It may succeed in challenging us to move beyond the temptation of apathy to a sincere commitment to urgent social change.

By spreading the message about social sin, the Church invites all people to engage in some form of consciousness raising, that is, a change in attitude and a desire to learn more about the world's problems. Hopefully, this will lead all listeners to increase their awareness of evil social structures so that they will be increasingly motivated to take action to end these unfair situations. Few of us are called to be famous prophets who boldly denounce injustice in public arenas, but the Christian vocation always includes a call to practice the virtue of courage and to challenge an imperfect status quo in some modest way. In order to contribute to social justice in constructive ways like this, it is first necessary to expand the horizons beyond the narrowest sense of what is right or wrong and to consider the cumulative weight of unfair practices over centuries and ways to correct these injustices.

Sadly, the Church's call to resist social sin has so far largely failed to capture the imaginations of a majority of the faithful. After all, most people are tempted to evade responsibility for wrongs they are directly responsible for; all the more reason exists for ignoring the ways in which indirect responsibility issues a call for repentance. Rare indeed is the priest who, in the sacrament of reconciliation (also known as confession), ever hears a penitent express remorse over participating in evil structures, such as clubs or organizations that practice racism, sexism, or elitism. All too seldom do faithful Christians reflect on the indirect but important effects of their economic actions, such as purchasing garments sewn by child laborers or investing in companies that illegally dump toxic wastes. It is doubtful whether any advertising executive has ever stepped into a confessional to discuss his or her abuses of the public trust in promoting misleading commercials for an overly profit-hungry corporation. As the quip goes, when we think about sin, most of us imagine the bedroom, not the boardroom. In other words, the lion's share of the awareness of sin and the practice of sacramental confession remains squarely focused on the level of strictly individual or at most interpersonal acts, but rarely on the level of larger-scale involvements in social institutions such as corporations.

Nor is this situation likely to change anytime soon. It will be a constant challenge to future popes, bishops, clergy, and laypersons to find ways to talk to their neighbors about the need for a much sharper awareness of social responsibility. In the present climate of apathy, it is a tall order to encourage greater participation in movements to change the status quo by viewing the world with a keen eye for exposing injustices in large-scale structures. Of course, the easiest path for most people is to keep their faith private and to ignore the urgent need for Christians, as a necessary requirement of their faith in Jesus Christ, to increase their involvement in public affairs. In the face of these challenges, it is important to nurture the hope that leaders and all members of the Church will continue to use Catholic social teaching as a vehicle for expressing the call to both individual and social holiness. To ignore either dimension is to cut the faith in half. Future social teaching documents will continue to be a privileged place where church teachings might bridge the local and the global and express the need to examine ever more closely unjust aspects of the structures and institutions so often taken for granted even by people of immense good will.

4. Public Theology and Concerns about Credible Witness

The final item on this list of shifts in Catholic social teaching that are expected to continue is the renewed emphasis on the public role of Christian theology in the broader society. This development involves the task of engaging the whole society along with its largest structures, and not just Christians as isolated individuals, in order to pursue justice in the fullest way possible. This shift toward a more complete public face of the Church is neither a brand-new development nor an achievement that is close to completion. Rather, it is an ongoing task the Church has been pursuing since the beginning of Christianity. Recall that chapter two explored several aspects of this task of "doing public theology," including the questions and positions that naturally arise when any age tries to answer the famous metaphorical question of Tertullian: "What does Jerusalem have to say to Athens?"

A few particularly important issues have arisen in recent years concerning the way Catholic social teaching has been able to engage public life in contemporary society. One significant development has been a noticeable antagonism between some Christian voices and certain aspects of popular culture. In standing up boldly for important principles such as the dignity of all human life, spokespersons for Catholicism as well as Protestant Christianity have found themselves assuming a stance of denouncing certain currents of thought that have become common in the cultural mainstream.

The most ringing phrase that echoes in these recent public conversations is the accusation that the dominant culture amounts to a "culture of death." This phrase calls attention to the many ways that society has exhibited an attitude of callousness toward human life. This disregard for the sanctity of life unfolds on the level of public policies as well as private practices and includes support for abortion, euthanasia, capital punishment, and other threats to human life. The principle of the inviolable dignity of human life, so prominent in the documents of Catholic social teaching, seems to be under massive attack when decisions are made with increasing frequency to terminate lives that are considered a threat, an inconvenience, or a burden to others.

Perhaps the boldest denunciation of these horrifying trends appears in Pope John Paul II's 1995 encyclical letter *Evangelium Vitae* (*The Gospel of Life*). Here the pope reviews and extends arguments such as the "consistent ethic of life," a framework mentioned in chapter five as originating with Chicago's late Cardinal Joseph Bernardin. Pope John Paul's efforts to promote this approach are part of a passionate struggle, one that has fortunately outlived him, to speak a prophetic word against distorted values that end up favoring death rather than life. It is part of the vocation of all Christians to resist the culture of death by creating a culture of life grounded in the Gospel.

By challenging the culture of death, church leaders seem to be making a choice to play the prophet, not in the sense of predicting the future but in the sense of challenging injustice even at the price of their own popularity. But it would be a serious mistake to interpret this choice of the "prophetic option" as somehow eliminating the "dialogue option" that has for the most part characterized the relationship between Catholic theology and modern culture in recent decades. Even as it spends time and energy criticizing destructive aspects of secular culture, Catholic social teaching renews its commitment to engage, teach, and learn from what is helpful in that culture. This willingness to work within the dominant culture in a critical but still constructive way conforms very well to the historical pattern in which Catholicism has never been satisfied merely to judge and reject a culture, but seeks instead to transform it into something nobler and more hospitable to human values. Dialogue with the contents and agents of a given culture is the privileged route to this type of social progress. In fact, although they barely make an appearance in most official church documents, a number of pressing concerns regarding strengthening this dialogue option have received much attention in church circles in recent years.

Perhaps the best way to summarize these concerns is to say that many in the Church today are worried about the credibility of the Church's public witness. There is ample reason to ponder these anxieties with the utmost gravity. If hardly anyone is willing to take seriously what the Church says about peace and justice, then it becomes doubtful whether Catholic social teaching can really fulfill its mission. The solution cannot be, of course, to change the content of the Church's message just to win a more favorable audience. This type of compromise would amount to watering down the gospel message to fit the latest fashion and would constitute a serious betrayal of the mission of the Church. In other words, it is an important sign of vitality and fidelity to its mission that the Church keeps open the prophetic option, even when this might strain some relationships with those who are accomplices to the culture of death.

So, in looking to the future, what steps can the Church take to increase its public credibility without altering its prophetic messages about social justice? The most important steps involve measures that would, so to speak, take ammunition away from those who claim that the Catholic Church is guilty of blatant hypocrisy. These vocal critics find fault with the Church for not practicing in its internal policies and procedures all the elements of the justice message it preaches. Until the Church gets its own house in order, they warn, it will not have earned sufficient credibility to be an effective public witness to the Gospel. In fact, from time to time, voices inside the Church have publicly echoed this very concern. For example, *Justitia in Mundo*, the social teaching document from the 1971 Synod of Bishops, declared that "anyone who ventures to speak to people about justice must first be just in their eyes" (no. 40).

It remains a matter of debate whether a full-fledged credibility gap exists. But even to acknowledge the mere possibility of such a stumbling block immediately creates the priority of describing the possible credibility gap in full detail, with an eye toward preventing it or closing it, as the case may be. This chapter can provide only a brief and partial list of the problems highlighted by critics of the Church. Of course, all such complaints are a matter of perception; various people might look at the same facts and make very different judgments about their significance. While some observers would claim that rapid change is urgently needed in several areas of church life, others would respond that "if it isn't broken, don't attempt to fix it." In any case, the remainder of this section considers three of the issues that cannot be ignored as the Church attempts to win a fair and sympathetic hearing for its social teaching and to continue its important task of dialogue with the modern world.

At the top of any such list of credibility issues facing the Church today is the question of gender equality and the treatment of women within the Catholic Church. Charges about sexism in church practices are especially prevalent in the Western nations with the most advanced feminist movements and go far beyond the controversy over whether women are eligible to be ordained as priests or deacons. Both male and female critics of church practices accuse officials of excluding women from meaningful participation in ecclesiastical decisions and blocking their rightful access to positions of authority.

Even the very documents of Catholic social teaching are sometimes read as part of the problem, as they seem to some critics to belittle the contributions of women and enshrine an outdated family ideal that prevents women from advancing. It is not that the documents demean women in some blatant way. Unsympathetic reviewers of church documents often point out that what most inhibits the progress of women is the tendency of official church literature to praise the qualities of women so highly and to place women on such a high pedestal as selfless mothers and exemplary practitioners of virtue that their ordinary contributions to church and civil society are eclipsed. These critics urge the adoption of a new sensibility in church assessments of the possible accomplishments of women at all levels of society: as workers, administrators, and professionals fully worthy of a place of absolute equality alongside their male counterparts. Even without entering into the complex debate about the merit of these accusations, it is easy to agree with the proposal that the Church should work hard in the years ahead to change these perceptions and the realities behind them. Until women are able to recognize in Catholic teaching the real world of their daily struggles, the Church's social message will fall on many deaf and disbelieving ears.

A second cause for concern about the credibility of the Church relates to labor issues, an area where Catholic social teaching has been a beacon of light in professing the rights of workers. The problem is that, directly or indirectly, the Church employs millions of workers who do not always receive the best possible treatment. In recent years, specifically, controversy has swirled around the adequacy of the pay scales and fringe benefits received by those who work in schools, hospitals, and other institutions sponsored by the Catholic Church and its religious orders of priests, brothers, and nuns. In some cases, church officials have encountered unfavorable publicity when union organizers pointed out to them the discrepancy between Catholic documents supporting the right to form labor unions and the actual practice of some church-based institutions that discourage unionization. Until the values of worker rights and full participation (which are clearly proclaimed in the documents of Catholic social teaching) are fully reflected in actual labor practices within the Church and all its agencies, this stumbling block of perceived hypocrisy will remain.

A third challenge to Catholic social teaching involves the internal life of the Church, including the very procedures by which the teaching documents are written. Some critics claim that the Church needs to take a hard look at the way it conducts its study of social issues and shapes its response to the problems of today's world. They argue that achieving broader consultation in drafting the documents that become Catholic social teaching would enhance the credibility of the public witness of the Church. In order to understand these suggestions, let us take a look at some of the underlying concerns about the actual writing of the documents of Catholic social teaching.

Readers may have noticed that previous chapters of this book have been careful to refer to the teaching efforts of popes in terms of *publishing* encyclicals rather than *writing* encyclicals. These words must be chosen carefully because the issue of actual authorship of the documents of Catholic social teaching raises certain delicate issues. In most cases, we possess limited knowledge of precisely who it was that actually penned the final words. Scholars agree that a majority of the words and paragraphs of the social encyclicals were written by people other than the pope who signed his name at the end of the letter. Upon first glance, it may seem dishonest for a pope to claim credit for writing a document that contains words that did not originate with him. But recall that encyclicals appear in the form of letters addressed to members of the Church and are offered as pastoral and practical assistance in their lives. It only makes sense for popes facing this daunting task to consult with the appropriate experts and employ the most highly qualified writers so that the best possible letter may be composed and published over the signature of the pope himself, invoking the full weight of his authority.

Recall that table 3.1 includes a list of twelve documents. As explained in chapter three, two of these documents (*Gaudium et Spes* and *Justitia in Mundo*) are from gatherings of bishops. In the case of several of the other ten letters, certain clues have surfaced about how the document was actually written. Most often, popes seem to have relied on an inner circle of a few advisors who contributed to successive drafts of encyclicals, often over many months of work. It should come as no surprise to hear that most of these aides have been members of religious orders or priests or monsignors with specialized knowledge of economics, political theory, and the social sciences. In some cases, popes have given wide latitude to their chosen experts, asking only to see semi-completed drafts as they neared completion. Other popes, particularly those with more scholarly backgrounds, have preferred a hands-on management style and have undertaken a great deal of the actual writing themselves. In general, the research and writing of social encyclicals have progressed under the veil of strict confidentiality, with a prevailing policy of silence about the drafting process. Most contributors have been remarkably discreet about their assistance even decades after their involvement. To boast about serving as a ghostwriter of important church documents is considered bad form in the world of theologians.

Being aware of these procedures raises questions about the possible benefits of wider participation in the process by which social teaching is developed. Some ask whether it is desirable for a document that will represent the entire worldwide Church to be written in relative secrecy by just a handful of people who work at the Vatican. Various arguments for and against the current approach might appeal to different people. In the search for alternative models, one might turn to the history of four documents already mentioned.

Gaudium et Spes from Vatican II and *Justitia in Mundo* from the 1971 Synod of Bishops, as products of meetings of bishops, were written during the course of worldwide gatherings of church leaders by committees composed primarily of bishops and their advisors. At the end of the long deliberations over each of these two documents, votes were taken on whether to promulgate the final version. Previous chapters have also referred to two substantial pastoral letters from the Bishops' Conference of the United States: *Economic Justice for All* and *The Challenge of Peace*. Each letter went through a lengthy process in which several early drafts were released in order to invite public feedback. In a remarkable spirit of open dialogue, the select committee of bishops in charge of drafting each letter sponsored listening sessions in which dozens of experts were invited to comment on the subject at hand. Many people expressed great enthusiasm for such an unprecedented process that consulted broadly and publicly over such a considerable length of time.

Clearly, a happy balance needs to be struck between the extreme models presented by papal encyclicals, on one hand, and the American bishops' recent pastoral letters, on the other. One issue is timeliness; it took the U.S. bishops six long years to complete the two letters after an initial commitment to the task in 1980. While many people were genuinely excited about their roles in helping to improve each draft of the letters on peace and economic justice, it must be admitted that there is a diminishing usefulness to any project that lingers on for too long. It may seem like trying to hit a moving target; by the time the relevant parties agree to a shared description of the problem, the problem itself may have significantly changed. It is certainly true that Vatican II provided a tremendous service by adding to the traditional model of the *teaching Church* a new model of the *learning Church*. That worldwide gathering in the 1960s experimented with new models for collaboration and information-gathering that set the Catholic Church on a new path. However, the Church still struggles with the challenge of finding the most effective ways to accomplish its task of listening and learning from events and voices in the wider society.

Beyond these drawbacks, anyone who has ever worked on a drafting committee will acknowledge the perennial frustration of attempting to write any document by means of a committee. The sheer mechanics of committee work present serious obstacles to success in producing solid texts. The best insights and contributions tend to become watered down in a process of compromise that seeks to please all partners. This can become a major drawback when attempting to produce documents that exhibit a unity of vision and clarity of purpose, as do the best encyclicals. The desire for broader consultation on social teaching is clearly a genuine and constructive guide to future efforts. But it still remains unclear precisely how best to achieve wider participation in shaping the stance the Church will take on social issues in the coming years.

This completes the list of four significant and continuing shifts in recent Catholic social teaching as well as the list of three challenges the Church must face in order to be as credible as possible as it participates in public dialogue today. To this list of the three challenges may be added other areas where the Church might grow toward greater internal justice: eliminating abuses such as clericalism, excessively centralized hierarchy, and the exclusion of minority voices that are too seldom heard by high church officials. Addressing each of these items will contribute to the ongoing work of reforming church procedures and polices in the wake of the clergy sexual abuse scandal that rocked the U.S. Catholic Church in 2002 and absorbed so much of its energy for years afterwards. Of all the sources of concern about credible public witness, this betrayal of trust on the part of church personnel was perhaps the most grievous, and its effects will surely be felt for decades.

Until all these problems are addressed, we should avoid any uncritical celebration of the Church's contribution to public life and the ongoing debates regarding social issues. Only by making progress in all these areas will the Church in the years ahead find itself a truly effective advocate of the values it professes: freedom, democracy, human rights, the broad sharing of opportunities, and the equal dignity of all God's children.

TWO NEW CHALLENGES: THE ENVIRONMENT AND GLOBALIZATION

This chapter began with a promise to make some significant predictions about future directions for Catholic social teaching. The analysis so far hardly goes out on a limb in venturing forecasts, since the four trends treated above are merely continuations of already established themes and concerns in church teaching. That easy part of the job now gives way to the harder task of predicting some topics that will, without benefit of much advance fanfare, become important in future documents of Catholic social teaching. The paragraphs below wager on just two developments that might begin to loom large in the years ahead.

1. The Environment in Catholic Social Thought

The first is the area of environmental concern. Although care for the earth is a theme that fits easily with the call to social responsibility within Catholic social teaching, it is surprising how seldom ecological concerns are actually mentioned in the encyclicals. There are practically no sections within the twelve major social teaching documents that offer an extended treatment of what it means to practice environmental justice. In fact, the few sentences that dedicate any attention at all to the environment can fit on a single page, and they are gathered in table 7.1. Other social teaching documents tend to miss obvious opportunities to make rich connections between the themes they treat and the topic of ecological concern, such as the 1981 encyclical *Laborem Exercens* on human labor.

When critics of Catholic social thought compile lists of lacunae or flaws in this body of church doctrine, the paltry attention given to the environment is often the top criticism mentioned. Indeed, some observers are absolutely horrified that environmental concern is usually left off of lists of top themes in Catholic social teaching, such as the nine themes featured in chapter five of this book. So to predict that future Catholic social teaching will begin to tackle the topic of ecology in the years ahead does indeed constitute going out on a limb. This prediction involves an element of risk, since there are few previous signs of interest in this topic on the part of Vatican officials.

Yet this guess about this future direction for Catholic social teaching is a gamble that is likely to pay off for a number of reasons. First, there is a growing worldwide consensus that damage to the environment is reaching a critical point in the early years of the twenty-first century. Although there have been significant efforts and movements for ecological improvement for many decades, human abuse of the resources of the earth has left the world's waters, wetlands, and atmosphere crying out for renewed attention. Concern about global warming and climate change due to carbon emissions and greenhouse effects is only the most dramatic of many campaigns geared to promote awareness and change human behavior. This represents a set of urgent challenges that can no longer be ignored by individuals or the groups they belong to, including churches and faith-based nonprofit organizations.

Second, there are already some initial hints that the message of environmental concern is beginning to take root in the minds of some church leaders, especially on the local level. Many parishes and dioceses have

TABLE 7.1. CITATIONS FROM CATHOLIC SOCIAL TEACHING DOCUMENTS ON THE ENVIRONMENT

Gaudium et Spes (1965, Vatican II)
For man [and woman], created to God's image, received a mandate to subject to [themselves] the earth and all that it contains, and to govern the world with justice and holiness, a mandate to relate [ourselves] and the totality of things to him who was to be acknowledged as the Lord and Creator of all. Thus by the subjection of all things to man [and woman], the name of God would be wonderful in all the earth. (no. 34; see also no. 12 and no. 33)

Octogesima Adveniens (1971, Pope Paul VI)
Man is suddenly becoming aware that by an ill-considered exploitation of nature he risks destroying it and becoming in his turn the victim of this degradation. Not only is the material environment becoming a permanent menace—pollution and refuse, new illnesses and absolute destructive capacity—but the human framework is no longer under man's control, thus creating an environment for tomorrow which may well be intolerable. This is a wide-ranging social problem which concerns the entire human family. (no. 21)

Justitia in Mundo (1971, Synod of Bishops)
Such is the demand for resources and energy by the richer nations, and such are the effects of dumping by them in the atmosphere and the sea that irreparable damage would be done to the essential elements of life on earth, such as air and water, if their high rates of consumption and pollution, which are constantly on the increase, were extended to the whole of mankind. (no. 11)
. . . the richer nations [should recognize] the danger of destroying the very physical foundations of life on earth. Those who are already rich are bound to accept a less material way of life, with less waste, in order to avoid the destruction of the heritage which they are obliged to share. (no. 70)

Sollicitudo Rei Socialis (1987, Pope John Paul II)
Among today's positive signs, we must also mention a greater realization of the limits of available resources, and of the need to respect the integrity and the cycles of nature and to take them into account when planning for development, rather than sacrificing them to certain demagogic ideas about the latter. Today this is called ecological concern. (no. 26; see also no. 34)

Centesimus Annus (1991, Pope John Paul II)
Equally worrying is the ecological question which accompanies the problem of consumerism and which is closely connected to it. In his desire to have and to enjoy rather than to be and to grow, man consumes the resources of the earth and his own life in an excessive and disordered way. At the root of the senseless destruction of the natural environment lies an anthropological error, which unfortunately is widespread in our day. Man, who discovers his capacity to transform and in a certain sense create the world through his own work, forgets that this is always based on God's prior and original gift of the things that are. Man thinks that he can make arbitrary use of the earth, subjecting it without restraint to his will, as if it did not have its own requisites and a prior God-given purpose, which man can indeed develop but must not betray. Instead of carrying out his role as a cooperator with God in the work of creation, man sets himself up in place of God and thus ends up provoking a rebellion on the part of nature, which is more tyrannized than governed by him. (no. 37; see also no. 38)

adopted programs to raise awareness of pollution and to organize efforts to preserve our fragile ecosystem. Local campaigns to expand recycling, to encourage organic farming, and to raise funds to preserve the world's shrinking rain forests have often been started or cosponsored by churches. If one looks hard enough, it is possible to find church-based activism on the full range of ecological concerns: deforestation, soil erosion, overfishing of the world's oceans, ozone depletion, hazardous nuclear waste, acid rain, oil spills, threats to biodiversity, loss of aquifers and watersheds, and others. Programs and efforts to alleviate such crises have made an important impact on the lives of many people of faith, feeding their spirituality and rekindling their commitment to a life of discipleship. Many parishioners express hope that their grassroots efforts will capture the attention of high church officials and make their way into the teachings of popes and bishops.

In fact, there is already some evidence in church circles of the trickle-up effect that these local activists have long hoped for. Prompted by appeals from many of the faithful, several regional groupings of bishops have sponsored studies of specific environmental problems and published insightful pastoral letters to publicize their findings and concerns. Some of the boldest efforts of this sort have unfolded in North America in recent decades. On two occasions (in 1975 and in 1995), the bishops of the region of Appalachia featured the environmental degradation associated with coal mining in their joint pastoral letters. In 2001, the bishops of the Northwestern United States and British Columbia in Canada published the groundbreaking pastoral letter *The Columbia River Watershed: Caring for Creation and the Common Good.*

Further, the entire body of U.S. Catholic bishops in 1991 issued the very insightful twenty-page document *Renewing the Earth: An Invitation to Reflection and Action on the Environment*, summarizing the many spiritual and theological themes that feed Catholic concern about the earth. Although he mentioned environmental issues only briefly in actual social encyclicals, Pope John Paul II dedicated his 1990 World Day of Peace Message to the topic. The document he offered on that occasion bears the title *The Ecological Crisis: A Common Responsibility*, and it consists of a heartfelt appeal for all people to respect the integrity of creation. His successor Pope Benedict XVI set a fine example in 2007 by adopting plans for the Vatican to go green in very significant ways. Press releases of the Holy See announced a series of innovative measures, including reductions in energy use, the installation of one thousand photovoltaic solar panels on the roofs of Vatican buildings, and a commitment to engage in carbon dioxide offset measures such as the planting of trees in ecologically sensitive European locations. This greening of the Vatican signals the pontiff's sincere intention to make Vatican City the world's first carbon-neutral nation-state.

But there is a third reason supporting this confidence about a future flowering of environmental concern within the Church: given the core commitments of Catholic theology and spirituality, it simply stands to reason that this development of the tradition would unfold in a time of ecological crisis. Considering all the rich themes of Catholic social teaching in particular, it is a natural outgrowth of its messages about justice to extend the practice of social responsibility to concerns about the environment. That is why the relative silence of the Church on these matters until now is so disappointing.

Connections of ecological concern to prominent church teachings are easy to draw. Christian theology holds that the earth is a gift from God that humans share with all other creatures, and it is obvious that our relationships with other beings, human or not, are affected by the physical environment. To show disregard for the air that others breathe and the quality of the water they drink is to sin against God and against other people, who disproportionately turn out to be the poor who tend to live in especially polluted areas. Such disregard for ecological degradation damages not only inanimate objects but also humankind's overall relationships with living things. Wasting and polluting precious natural resources is justifiably deemed sinful, for it is an offense against all the things, living and inert, that God has blessed us with. To be concerned about the effect of all one's actions on the fragile ecosystem is to nurture an attitude of care for others that is most consistent with the core messages of Catholic social teaching.

It is interesting to speculate on the possible shape of future church statements about the environment. Some clues may be found in recent documents on the environment published by national and regional groups of bishops. Besides the pastoral letters mentioned just above, mostly from the U.S. context, there have been particularly excellent statements from the Philippines, Australia, Italy, and various parts of Latin America and Northern Europe. Intriguingly, some of these incorporate the contributions of native indigenous peoples and their insightful folk wisdom about the relationship of humankind to other species in the fascinating web of life. These letters, along with a few writings and addresses from the Vatican on this topic, seem to be struggling to make a transition from a somewhat inadequate older theory of the environment to newer and more promising approaches. The next several paragraphs describe what is at stake in these contrasting perspectives on ecology. Table 7.2 provides a summary overview of this analysis and also includes two extreme positions (the dominion model and deep ecology) that will not be considered in these paragraphs, as they have not figured prominently in Catholic social teaching.

Table 7.2. Models of Possible Christian Approaches to the Natural Environment

Model	Characteristic Stance	Emphasis	Dangers
Dominion model	Humans rightfully exploit natural environment	Humans are not at all at home in nature; stresses differences between humans and the rest of nature	Arrogant disdain for material world; tendency toward matter-spirit dualism
Stewardship model	Humans care for creation, which is intended to serve our needs	Wide gap between humans and the remainder of creation; anthropocentrism, in which the human person is the center of creation	Overemphasis on mastery, with focus on conquering and controlling nature; speciesism; no sense of solidarity with other species
Creation-centered approach	Humans are not so much caretakers as fully part of creation	Intrinsic value and sacredness of nature, so all species deserve protection; recognizes interdependence within the web of life	The call for sustainability leaves many unresolved issues; unclear how to balance human needs with solidarity with other species
Deep ecology	Radical revisioning of the relationship and boundaries between humans and the rest of creation	Calls for revival of asceticism, human renunciation, and mysticism; ecotheology views nature as a medium for the mystery of the sacred, which humans must not presume to know fully	Overly romanticized view may make creation into an idol; danger of totally neglecting legitimate human needs

The older approach is usually referred to as the *stewardship model*. It portrays humans as the rightful masters of creation, placed at the center of the world, and presented by God with the gift of nearly absolute dominion over the universe. In the few places where documents of Catholic social teaching mention the natural environment, they interpret the Book of Genesis in a way that encourages people to subdue the earth and claim its resources for the sole purpose of human improvement. For example, the section of *Gaudium et Spes* referenced in table 7.1 declares:

> For man [and woman], created to God's image, received a mandate to subject to [themselves] the earth and all that it contains, and to govern the world with justice and holiness. (no. 34)

Following this view does not necessarily make one oblivious to ecological damage, but it does tend to restrict the scope of concern exclusively to human well-being. As evidence that the spotlight is clearly on humans (although the noninclusive language of the original text of the document suggests a focus on only the male half of the human race), note this sentence from *Octogesima Adveniens*:

> Man is suddenly becoming aware that by an ill-considered exploitation of nature he risks destroying it and becoming in his turn the victim of this degradation. (no. 21)

The focus of concern is exclusively on humans; the effect on any other victims, such as particular species of animals or entire ecosystems, remains at best an afterthought.

A more adequate and updated approach would take more seriously the intrinsic value of nonhuman created things. Such a creation-centered perspective would reach beyond the inordinate bias, sometimes called *speciesism* or *anthropocentrism*, that may belittle the worth and beauty of nature. A more thorough reverence for creation would allow us to imagine a type of solidarity that extends beyond the limits of the human species to include other forms of life and the places they inhabit as well. The divine plan for the universe is frustrated not just when our acts boomerang and cause harm to humans, but whenever they destroy the environment in irreparable ways. The challenge is to begin to measure human acts, such as damming rivers, felling forests, and developing land for commercial use, in a more holistic manner in terms of their ecological impact.

According to a healthy, creation-centered approach, humans are not just caretakers of the natural world, but are fully a part of it. This insight necessitates a thorough recasting of traditional approaches regarding the uniqueness and even superiority of *Homo sapiens* within the biosphere.

The habitat humans share with all other species is more than an instrumental thing, but something with intrinsic value, just as each living thing is to be considered a good in itself. The search for sustainable practices that simultaneously promote the well-being of humans, other species, and shared habitats becomes a moral responsibility that falls upon all people. It is especially encouraging that the Catholic community will not be pursuing these momentous questions alone in the years ahead. Discerning constructive directions for ecological protection is an especially promising area for interreligious dialogue and partnership with secular groups, such as the network of nongovernmental organizations and advocacy agencies already working hard on these issues. All parties should be eager to take advantage of the fruits of reflection and knowledge already achieved by member groups collaborating in coalitions to promote environmental causes.

It is one thing to predict that Catholic social teaching will someday grow beyond the stewardship model to a more ecologically sensitive approach, but it is a much more difficult task to imagine what guidance a new framework will provide for balancing care for persons and care for the environment. After all, every step of any form of progress involves some costs, and every economic or technological advance gobbles up some share of natural resources. Discerning how to weigh the benefits of future economic growth against the costs of pollution and resource depletion is an especially difficult question and can become a rather divisive issue, pitting human needs against the well-being of the natural world as varying priorities are debated. Because such trade-offs are perennially difficult to ponder, making progress in this area will surely require the most careful retrieval of wisdom from the resources of all available traditions of reflection.

It would be a great contribution to both Church and world if future documents of Catholic social teaching would offer a set of insightful guidelines for taking up these important decisions. On the positive side, the Church's tradition of speaking so forcefully about the sacredness of life, universal solidarity, and the common good gives it a head start in forming constructive and credible teachings in the area of environmental concern. Because of its ability to draw upon rich themes such as sacramentality and the incarnational principle, Catholic theology is well positioned to make a solid contribution to future society-wide debates regarding ecological concern.

2. Globalization

Another major future challenge for Catholic social thought involves the evolving shape of the worldwide economy and the moral dimensions of these bewildering changes. The political, economic, cultural, and techno-logical transformations of recent decades are captured in the buzzword *globalization*. The paragraphs below offer a brief account of this multifac-eted phenomenon and then comment on how Catholic social teaching is beginning to come to terms with its ethical challenges.

Globalization refers to the many ways that people around the world are coming to share a single existence. Advertising catchphrases like "we are all connected" and "it's one world—ready or not" actually capture this fa-miliar insight quite effectively. What formerly separated individuals in various lands—geographical distances as well as humanly created boundaries of politics, language, and culture—are no longer so forbid-ding. Innovations in high-speed transportation and communication, in-cluding most prominently the Internet, have overcome the artificial barri-ers that previously kept people and cultures from mixing. In a way unprecedented in world history, every inhabitant of earth is now poten-tially in a relationship of some sort with every other person, since the bor-ders that once separated them are now so permeable. Someone in India may help me install a computer program; another person in China may be competing with me for a job; a Brazilian may be investing in my firm. These new relationships create enhanced opportunities for both good and evil. The potential for globalization to become either a great force for hu-man liberation or yet another excuse for exploitation of the powerless makes it the single most important ethical sign of the times in the twenty-first century.

Boosters of the trend toward globalization usually emphasize the mu-tual gains that may come to pass under optimal conditions of interna-tional exchange. As the world economy is more fully integrated, nations and regions specialize in those activities for which they have a compara-tive advantage over other places, and production becomes more efficient. With decreases in import tariffs, quotas, and other barriers to free inter-national trade, goods flow ever more freely from place to place. Depend-ing of course on patterns of the eventual distribution of new wealth, such gains from free trade hold the potential to make everyone better off. Un-der this rosy scenario, the only remaining challenge is to find ways to in-clude more and more people in the headlong rush to a better life.

But, like everything related to globalization, this interpretation soon finds itself treading on contested terrain. While the liberalization of inter-national trade may bring benefits to many, it may also be accompanied by unfair practices, such as the imposition of skewed commodity processes that favor those trading partners who possess the most power. Creating a single global market for goods, capital, and labor may lower production costs, but it may also spark a "race to the bottom." This phrase refers to the tendency of nations to compete to attract investments from powerful transnational corporations, which are always looking to lower their production and labor costs. In order to persuade these corporations to create jobs and build factories on their soil, these often desperate countries reduce their protections for workers or relax their environmental regulations. In response to such concerns in recent decades, several international trade meetings have witnessed violent demonstrations against the undesirable effects of global markets and predatory global capitalism. It is hard to forget the bloody street clashes that disrupted the World Trade Organization summit in Seattle in 1999, but that was only one of many such protests. Populists have protested the downward pressure exerted on wages for low-skilled workers, the inequities of the new global division of labor, the downsizing and outsourcing of production, and the numerous related concerns that accompany globalization.

In their honest moments, both pro-globalization and anti-globalization commentators recognize a mix of positives and negatives in the complex economic forces at work in the world today. The global interdependence that comes as good news for many also reveals a shadow side: to a greater extent than ever, we are all at the mercy of forces beyond our control, no matter how far away they may seem at a given moment. Nowadays, no single party is ever completely beyond the reach of potentially hostile forces, be they terrorist strikes, rapidly spreading financial crises, global drug traffickers, or the latest computer virus or highly contagious disease that leaps from continent to continent. This alarming reality is true for countries as surely as it is for individuals. Because nations can no longer expect to be able to wall themselves off from undesirable developments in the international system, the traditional notion of national sovereignty is greatly diminished. No country can single-handedly control its destiny or even its increasingly porous borders. The effectiveness of government policies in any nation now depends greatly on the decisions of other nations and even international organizations. Domestic politics is rendered primarily reactive, no longer proactive in determining priorities and strategies to advance the common good of the people.

A credible case can be made that globalization has introduced a large number of inequities and social injustices in society. Its detractors can cite a long litany of problems that it has created or exacerbated: runaway capital without a sense of social responsibility, volatile markets featuring cutthroat competition, dangerously low prevailing wages, a distressing homogenization of cultures. Yet as much as one might favor a movement to roll back at least some aspects of globalization, there is an indisputable air of inevitability about globalization. It would be utterly futile to attempt somehow to turn back the hands of time and reverse the process unleashed by the many forces that spawned the globalized economic order. Even those who are least enthusiastic about this worldwide phenomenon are reshaping their questions. It is no longer a matter of *whether* to global-ize, but rather *how* to globalize in a way that protects core values as much as possible.

How, then, should religious communities address the ethical short-comings of globalization? The distinctive voices of faith-based groups like churches surely have unique contributions to make to this discourse, since globalization involves moral issues beyond merely technical mat-ters of economic policy. Because these challenges are so new, it goes with-out saying that Catholic social teaching has no ready-made answers at hand to be applied instantly. Indeed, observers of the Church's response to these new ethical demands still await a full-throated statement of moral analysis from Vatican sources. While there have been partial and local responses in various parts of the world from groups of bishops or lay councils of concerned Catholics, as of this writing there is yet no pa-pal encyclical that takes up in detail the moral challenge of globalization. Except for a few brief allusions to globalization in the 1991 social en-cyclical *Centesimus Annus* and a few sentences on the topic in John Paul's 1999 apostolic exhortation *Ecclesia in America*, we still await substantial treatment of globalization in documents invoking the highest level of pa-pal authority.

Indeed, the most extensive authoritative text that brings up the ethical dimensions of globalization appears in the 2004 volume *Compendium of the Social Doctrine of the Church*. But this reference work, issued by the Pontif-ical Council for Justice and Peace, was not intended to break new ground, so for the most part it merely repeats the sketchy formulations of popes and church-based groups up to that time regarding how principles of Catholic social teaching may be applied to the new era of globalization.

Toward the end of his pontificate, in the early years of the new millen-nium, John Paul II did treat the topic of globalization in summary fashion, and it is primarily upon these brief addresses that the *Compendium* draws. Here are two typical passages that are cited frequently. In his World Day of Peace Message for 2000, John Paul stated:

> Globalization, for all its risks, also offers exceptional and promising opportunities, precisely with a view to enabling humanity to become a single family, built on the values of a single family, built on the val-ues of justice, equity, and solidarity.

And in his Address to the Pontifical Academy of Social Sciences on April 27, 2001, John Paul commented:

> Globalization, a priori, is neither good nor bad. It will be what peo-ple make of it . . . . and it is necessary to insist that globalization, like

any other system, must be at the service of the human person; it must serve solidarity and the common good. (no. 2)

Note how each of these assessments acknowledges a balance of positives and negatives, of risks and potential benefits associated with new economic conditions. The outcome of this massive process depends entirely upon how we manage globalization. Indeed, the two phrases most often repeated in John Paul's comments on the topic call for the "globalization of solidarity" and the "humanization of globalization." In calling for these lofty ideals to be accomplished, the pope was appealing to people around the world to add a values dimension to their economic activities in a renewed way.

John Paul II and other voices of the official church echo the sentiments of many other observers of globalization. From many quarters, those concerned about the morality of contemporary economic practices express the keen desire to see the unruly forces of globalization somehow controlled. It is even quite amusing to notice how often such ethical-minded commentators employ metaphorical language that likens globalization to a wild animal in need of being tamed. Inadvertently or not, the literature of this field is laced with vivid verbs that suggest precisely this insight, calling upon people to "harness," "bridle," "yoke," "curb," "circumscribe," "domesticate," "discipline," and "restrain" the forces of globalization. It is not often that ethicists use such colorful language, so this tendency is worth paying attention to.

The general shape of these common reflections on globalization should come as no surprise. Whether religious or secular in inspiration, anyone who clings to hope for a better, more humane world is likely to travel this well-rutted path of ideas. While there are some aspects of the modern economy that cannot be easily changed, there are many ways that ethical concerns can be pursued with likely success. While impersonal market forces must be reckoned with in a hardheaded way, it is important not to make too many concessions to the inevitability of appalling compromise. In other words, we are not doomed to live in a world horribly disfigured by the negative impacts of globalization. While respecting the insights of the discipline of economics, it is vital to focus on the legitimate requirements of integral development and human aspirations for a better life. For this reason, it is important to view globalization as a force that must be tamed so that it serves human needs. With adequate moral scrutiny and carefully measured interventions, the forces of global economic integration can indeed emerge as instruments of inclusion and opportunity for all.

People of faith in the coming years are well positioned to join broad coalitions to protect a whole range of important human values that are threatened by certain aspects of the globalized world economy. One focus is likely to be environmental sustainability, a topic treated in the previous section of this chapter. Another focus will likely be the issue of international trade agreements, such as NAFTA and other regional treaties that seek to open up national borders to commercial penetration. Especially where the parties to such agreements include developing countries that are at sharp disadvantages with respect to their trading partners, it is imperative to ensure that free trade is also fair trade. Enhanced accountability, transparency, and wider participation in all aspects of international trade and investment will be crucial goals in the years ahead. A closely related topic is the accelerating rate of international migration, an aspect of globalization that is intimately linked to the persistence of unequal levels of economic opportunity from country to country.

Other related issues regarding world economic patterns could be added to the list. But the main point is simply for people of conscience to be vigilant in advocating for an array of reforms and practices to ensure that social responsibility is never jettisoned in the name of economic progress. Protecting the most vulnerable people and preserving the delicate ecosystem we inhabit should never be mere afterthoughts in economic pursuits. If we reach the point where globalization tears the social fabric apart so violently that millions are made destitute and find themselves without hope, then we will have allowed the pursuit of wealth to rule over humankind, rather than serving it.

Of course, there will always be winners and losers in the global economy. However, the only morally acceptable version of globalization is one that includes a safety net adequate to protect all people from becoming profound losers whose very lives are threatened at every turn. The insights and values contained in Catholic social teaching—including its messages about human dignity, solidarity, and the common good—require no less. Very often Catholic social teaching is accused of being long on diagnosis but weak on cure. Addressing the need for constructive interventions to correct the flaws in the globalization process may well lead Catholic social teaching to a new level of specificity, perhaps regarding particular reforms in global financial institutions or codes of conduct for transnational corporations.

These are a few of the ideas that might form the outline for a future church approach to the challenge of a globalized economy. They stretch the message of previous Catholic social teaching so that it covers a new set of problems in an increasingly globalized context. These suggestions extend the arguments that have been cited in support of the preferential option for the poor so that they now address the needs of new categories of people around the world whose life prospects are being threatened by the market forces of the contemporary economy. Any future social encyclical or Catholic social teaching document that deals with globalization in a more thorough way than seen up to this point will surely touch upon these values and concerns in offering principles for the pursuit of social justice in the years ahead.

SPREADING THE WORD ABOUT CATHOLIC SOCIAL TEACHING

Chapter one of this book mentioned that Catholic social teaching is sometimes referred to as the Church's best-kept secret. In this final chapter, having surveyed possible future developments in this tradition of reflection about justice dimensions of life in human society, perhaps the most important message to emphasize is the importance of efforts to publicize the riches of Catholic social teaching. It is often said that what the Church most needs in this area is not another document or additional teachings on new themes (however welcome that might be in areas like globalization and the environment), but rather a systematic effort to implement the teachings it already possesses. Practical enactment is more the order of the day than further statements of principles. Indeed, even if popes and bishops suddenly decided to stop writing encyclicals and publishing documents on social issues, the work of the Church in pursuing justice would continue on unabated.

But precisely what does it mean to implement, enact, or publicize Catholic social teaching? What does such a commitment look like concretely? Those who are eager to see Catholic social teachings applied to the real world may direct their gaze in many different directions in order to see encouraging results. Although it is surely true that there is a long way yet to go, there are abundant and outstanding examples of people and organizations putting into practice the lessons and principles of Catholic social teaching. The following paragraphs describe just a few heartening directions and ways that people of energy and commitment have found applications of this message.

The broadest and perhaps most effective instance of the influence of Catholic social teaching in tangible ways has to do with movements for social reform. At particular pivotal moments in the history of a given society, powerful movements arise in order to correct imbalances, modify social priorities, address injustices, or simply to provide a viewpoint that has come to be overlooked. Examples include the civil rights movement in the United States in the 1950s and 1960s, the *Solidarnosc* labor movement in Poland in the 1980s, and a host of popular movements throughout the world in recent decades: anti-war, green, and feminist among others.

On the surface, it might seem that social reform movements arise completely spontaneously, in ways that are impossible to explain in terms of historical precedents. However, it stands to reason that people of conscience who are confronted with injustice draw substantial inspiration from established traditions of thought or academic study to which they have been exposed. New challenges prompt individuals and groups to reach into whatever toolbox of resources they have collected in order to shape their response. Social scientists say that the overall human repertoire of behaviors displays marked continuity over time and tends to replicate familiar patterns of thought and influence.

Very often in recent decades, the toolbox of pivotal leaders and movements has included a good dose of Catholic social teaching. In direct or indirect ways, the content of Catholic social teaching has found its way into some of the most courageous social reforms of the past century. One clear example involves Cesar Chavez, the California-based leader of the labor movement that sought protections for migrant farm workers in the 1960s and 1970s, most famously by its long-standing boycott of table grapes grown under objectionable labor conditions. Whenever he was asked about the wellsprings of his activism on behalf of exploited workers, Chavez quickly volunteered the names of the popes and encyclicals that inspired his work. This movement, which is far from outmoded in this age of fierce immigration controversies and persistent concerns about low-wage agricultural labor, actually reprised the concerns of nineteenth-century European social Catholicism, as they are described in chapter three.

Many other examples could be cited of social movements whose leaders were inspired explicitly by church teachings. The Polish *Solidarnosc* labor union and its Catholic leader Lech Walesa have already been mentioned, but the list of such movements for admirable causes could be multiplied many times over. Most often, Catholic social teaching is just one of many strands of reflection that influence leaders and participants in these reform efforts. Catholic teachings and sensibilities such as concern for the common good and commitment to the most vulnerable members of society have a wonderful way of finding common ground with people of conscience from many backgrounds. For this reason, social movements are usually rightly portrayed as multifaceted coalitions of people who weave diverse concerns into united action on urgent causes.

Besides the ways it touches dynamic social movements, Catholic social teaching also exerts an influence on the more stable organizations, agencies, and groups that one might find listed in a phone book. To coin a phrase, social justice organizations are where social movements go when they go mainstream. After the initial fervor of a given cause has died down a bit, it is necessary to establish an ongoing social advocacy presence for the long haul. Whether the movement has generally met with success or whether its reform agenda is incomplete, there comes a time to regularize its efforts. Symbolic gestures like street demonstrations and hunger strikes are replaced by routine activities such as research, publishing, and lobbying legislators to enact desired social change. Many such offices and agencies locate themselves in cities like Washington, DC, and New York, close to the corridors of business and governmental power, to settle into their valuable role as the conscience of society. Here, too, Catholic social teaching has served as a support for many social justice organizations, whether officially affiliated with the Church or not. In the literature and websites of a wide variety of advocacy groups for the poor, human rights watchdogs, and various other social justice agencies, it is common to find explicit or implicit reference to the principles of Catholic social teaching.

An even more routine presence of Catholic social thought exhibits itself in the life of schools where the topic of social justice has found its way into the course curriculum or into cocurricular programs and extracurricular activities. In many Catholic high schools, colleges, and universities, students now enjoy a wide array of opportunities to engage in service learning, immersion trips within other cultural settings, and volunteer programs during school breaks. Most of these opportunities focus on offering material assistance and other supports to needy people either in inner cities or in areas of grinding rural poverty, such as Appalachia. Increasingly, students at U.S. schools have ventured to Mexico, Haiti, and other Caribbean and Latin American destinations for service placements. Still others have focused on domestic priorities such as improving low-income housing and helping to clean up after natural disasters like Hurricane Katrina, which struck the Gulf Coast and New Orleans with such tragic results in 2005. The best of these programs feature theological reflection as a prominent component to complement the hard work of active assistance. The campus ministry offices that oversee so many of these programs also sponsor a range of social justice involvements that expose thousands of students every year to Catholic social teaching.

The campuses of secondary and higher education institutions are not the only places featuring offices dedicated to religious activism for social justice. Most Catholic dioceses maintain offices of peace and justice or social ministry commissions that serve as clearinghouses and resources for local efforts. States with more than one diocese within their borders often feature a state Catholic conference with a lobbying and information office located in the state capital. Similarly, most major religious orders of sisters, brothers, and priests coordinate their regional or national outreach on behalf of social justice through a central office of social ministries, sometimes preferring the label "social action." Some particularly excellent efforts proceed from two Washington-based organizations of this type: the national office of Jesuit Social and International Ministries (http://

jesuit.org/SocialJustice/default.aspx) and Network (www.networklobby
.org), a social justice advocacy organization founded by several orders of
Catholic religious sisters. Some parts of the country feature offices for the
promotion of social justice maintained by regional groupings of religious
orders. Perhaps the best example is the Chicago-based 8th Day Center for
Justice (http://www.8thdaycenter.org/index.html). This coalition pools
the efforts of over three dozen Catholic religious orders, mostly centered
in the Midwest, to promote the spirituality of justice through activism, in-
formation-sharing, and coalition-building for a variety of worthy social
causes.

The list of Catholic organizations working on issues of peace and social
justice is very impressive, but is so long that it is impossible here to offer
a comprehensive list. While only a fraction of such groups are officially affiliated with the United States Conference of Catholic Bishops, the national coordinating organization introduced in chapter three, the website
of the Bishops' Office of Social Development and World Peace (http://
www.usccb.org/sdwp/) is a good place to start in compiling helpful web
links to track issues and gain knowledge of the field. Various think tanks
and advocacy offices publish informative newsletters and maintain websites on topics from labor rights to peacemaking to corporate responsibility to international development. Many Catholic periodicals and publications from Catholic presses also offer at least occasional analysis of social
justice issues. Prominent national publications of this type include *America*, *Commonweal*, *National Catholic Reporter*, and *Church* magazine. A quick
search of Internet resources and print libraries reveals that there is practically no field of human social relations to which Catholic social thought
has not been applied.

Amidst the bewildering number of opportunities to become involved
in work for social justice, a few commonsense principles are well worth
bearing in mind. Above all, it is vital to remember that most worthwhile
efforts unfold on the most local of levels: with individuals or local congregations detecting a need for social action, assessing their ability to
make a difference, and mobilizing to act. These efforts to embrace the
Gospel's message of charity and justice start small and, indeed, usually
remain quite modest in their scope and impact. While national and international programs tend to garner most of the media attention, it is the regular, local, and even quite mundane efforts of small groups of parishioners and volunteers that actually make the most difference in the long
run. Without the grassroots of what is called "congregational activism,"
more high-level efforts for social justice would founder for lack of a base
of support.

The natural focus of any group project is on the effect it is having on
the outside world—whether that is the delivery of social services,

changes in social policy, or any other goal of volunteer work for social justice. However, it is also crucial to keep an eye on the effect that this same work is having on the workers themselves. Is the effort taking too high a toll on those responsible? Are they able to maintain a sharp focus, recalling the original purpose of the project and holding true to the work as a type of ministry? Has the project gone on too long, perhaps beyond the point of usefulness? Is it time for a reassessment of goals and strategies so that a proper fit between resources and expectations can be maintained?

A very common peril in this type of activism involves overwork, burnout, or compassion fatigue, so it is very important to guard against situations where social justice ministry has started to do damage to the very people who initiated it. Because none of us are superheroes, it is impossible to be of much help to others when the work is sapping us of vital energies. This is an especially valuable lesson garnered by generations of activists. It is crucial to find ways to build into such ministries opportunities for prayer, renewal, healthy companionship, and ordinary recreation so that the work becomes sustainable and even joyful rather than mere drudgery. Careful attention to patterns of leadership, planning, and broad participation will also be repaid many times over.

Work for social justice is a part of every Christian vocation, but it is far from easy. Becoming overwhelmed by the seemingly insatiable needs of our world is a frequent outcome of even the most sincere efforts to live out the faith that does justice. The only way around these traps of discouragement and disappointment is to stay on mission by means of maintaining clarity about one's efforts and involvements. There is no substitute for constant reflection and review of the sense of identity and sense of calling that draws individuals and small groups of companions into service to their neighbors and to God.

THE SURPRISING FUTURE

This chapter has attempted to peek into the future and predict some of the future concerns of Catholic social teaching. Notice that this endeavor is only partially a matter of new documents and novel themes. The success of this vital aspect of the Church's service to the world depends increasingly on ordinary people implementing these teachings in daily life. The center of gravity of Catholic social teaching is shifting from the universal to the local, from principles to implementation, from documents to people. Perhaps what is most needed today is a greater commitment on the part of many of the faithful to live out their beliefs about social justice in a courageous yet prudent way.

No progress toward these goals will be possible unless people of many talents apply their efforts in advancing the social mission of the Church. Those who participate will learn to work together like the many parts of a body. Some will play the role of the tongue, teaching and preaching about the themes of Catholic social teaching. Others will be the hands of this faith-based justice, lifted up to God in prayer or thrust down into the earth, grinding soil under the fingernails as our collective social involvement grows deeper. Others may be the eyes, gathering new information about this fragile world and contributing to projects of social analysis that will illuminate the footsteps of all on the paths of justice. Catholic social teaching will only be as effective as the many varieties of practitioners who put it into action.

Above all, Christians today should feel encouraged to go about these tasks with confidence rather than with any kind of trepidation. The Christian view of God includes a most consoling affirmation that God is always active in the world and never abandons disciples in their moment of need. The God of justice is present wherever Christian people, motivated by their faith and acting on convictions about the proper ordering of political and economic life in society, engage in efforts to make the world a place of greater fairness and peace. This is what makes the pursuit of social justice so open-ended and unpredictable. Just as no one may limit the actions of the Holy Spirit, it is impossible to shackle the Gospel of peace and justice. Indeed, the only thing that would be completely surprising is if God ceased to send any new surprises.

Each one of us may be reassured that we are not alone and need not reinvent the wheel as we discern our personal calling. Instead, we are already, in a sense, standing on the shoulders of giants. Catholic social teaching offers us an extremely helpful tradition of thought about why and how to practice justice and to follow the call of Jesus to care for the least among the human community.

QUESTIONS FOR REFLECTION

1. Does the concept of personalism add anything new to Catholic social teaching? In what ways is it a helpful word to use when we think about social justice?
2. As you think about your daily activities, how helpful do you find the concept of social sin as it appears in recent Catholic theology? What benefits do we derive from thinking about our participation in large social structures as sometimes having a sinful dimension? Or is this somehow a misleading idea?

3. Can you relate any significant experiences of the ways, positive or negative, that women have been treated within the Church? What changes in church structures, procedures, and opportunities would you suggest to achieve greater gender justice?

4. What suggestions would you offer for improving the process by which encyclicals are written? How can wider participation be encouraged without sacrificing the unity and integrity of the documents of Catholic social teaching?

5. Do you think that concern for the health of the natural environment is mostly consistent with the themes of previous Catholic social teaching, or do ecological priorities generally conflict with this worldview that has tended to place humans at the center of creation? How can we resolve the tensions? Are there any trade-offs to consider in the task of accommodating traditional theology with new environmental awareness?

6. Describe the major ethical challenges associated with the new realities of globalization. Who are the winners and the losers in this process? What specific contributions may the Church make to the worldwide search for guidance in responding to the realities of this new era?

TOPICS FOR FURTHER RESEARCH

1. The history of personalism, including the tradition of Boston Personalism exemplified by the work of Protestant scholars Borden Parker Browne, A. C. Knudson, E. S. Brightman, and Walter G. Muelder

2. Voices of personalism in European Catholicism (Emmanuel Mounier, Jacques Maritain, Louis Janssens, and Bernard Häring)

3. The history and significance of the concept of social sin

4. Pastoral letters on the environment from groupings of bishops throughout the world

5. The contributions of various ecotheologians: Matthew Fox, Thomas Berry, Sallie McFague, Leonardo Boff, Rosemary Radford Reuther, John Cobb, Larry Rasmussen

6. Free trade agreements (such as NAFTA) and the record of their effects on the poor

7. The history of anti-globalization protests (starting at the World Trade Organization meetings in Seattle in 1999)

8. The work of The Interfaith Center on Corporate Responsibility, a leader in the movement for corporate social responsibility (see http://www.iccr.org/)

9. The social justice programs on any secondary or higher education campus in any of the following categories: service learning; course offerings; extracurricular and cocurricular activities
10. The tendency to burn out in ministry and social service work and proposals to alleviate this pitfall of social justice work

Annotated List of Resources
for Further Study

Note: This resource has been compiled with an eye toward helping readers of this book continue in their study of Catholic social teaching. What follows is by no means a comprehensive listing of relevant materials but simply a user-friendly account of where to find helpful information to take the next step in exploring this topic. The items are grouped together in appropriate categories. Brief commentary describes the merits of each item and provides an assessment of what the entry accomplishes.

REFERENCE WORKS

Dwyer, Judith A., ed. *The New Dictionary of Catholic Social Thought*. Collegeville, MN: The Liturgical Press, 1994. In dictionary format, this reference work offers entries on practically every topic associated with Catholic social teaching. This unique contribution to the field is quite readable.

Massaro, Thomas, and Thomas A. Shannon, eds. *American Catholic Social Teaching*. Collegeville, MN: The Liturgical Press, 2002. This work focuses exclusively on the U.S. context from 1792 to 1999. It contains two parts: (1) a CD-ROM with the fully digitalized and searchable texts of 23 pastoral letters from U.S. bishops, and (2) a book containing 20 articles on those teachings by diverse scholars of the twentieth century.

O'Brien, David J., and Thomas A. Shannon, eds. *Catholic Social Thought: The Documentary Heritage*. Maryknoll, NY: Orbis Books, 1992. This volume contains the English translations of all twelve texts listed in table 3.1 as well as the U.S. bishops' pastoral letters *The Challenge of Peace* and *Economic Justice for All*.

Pontifical Council for Justice and Peace. *Compendium of the Social Doctrine of the Church*. Washington, DC: United States Conference of Catholic Bishops, 2005. In about 200 pages of text, this reference work offers a remarkably succinct summary of the content of Vatican social teaching documents. It resembles a catechism in style and sacrifices some desirable historical sensibilities but is still a major achievement.

GENERAL COMMENTARIES

Byron, William J. "Ten Building Blocks of Catholic Social Teaching." *America*, 31 October 1998, 9–12. A frequently used magazine article that offers a helpful summary of major themes in this tradition.

Dorr, Donal. *Option for the Poor: A Hundred Years of Vatican Social Teaching*. Maryknoll, NY: Orbis Books, 1992. This volume includes detailed treatments of the contents and contexts of all the major social encyclicals. It contains reliable commentary but is not nearly as complete or as scholarly as Himes's *Modern Catholic Social Teaching*.

Coleman, John A., ed. *One Hundred Years of Catholic Social Thought: Celebration and Challenge*. Maryknoll, NY: Orbis Books, 1991. One of the best collections ever assembled of diverse essays on themes of Catholic social thought. Its publication coincided with the century anniversary of *Rerum Novarum*.

Curran, Charles E. *Catholic Social Teaching: A Historical, Theological, and Ethical Analysis*. Washington, DC: Georgetown University Press, 2002. A highly respected scholar explains the tradition in terms of theological categories in a way that most undergraduates will be able to understand. The analysis in terms of themes, rather than document-by-document descriptions, is unsurpassed.

Curran, Charles E., and Richard A. McCormick, S.J., eds. *Readings in Moral Theology No. 5: Official Catholic Social Teaching*. New York: Paulist Press, 1986. This is a very rich collection of diverse essays on aspects of Catholic social teaching, including both historical and theological perspectives.

Henriot, Peter J., Edward P. Deberri, and Michael J. Schultheis. *Catholic Social Teaching: Our Best Kept Secret*, third edition. Maryknoll, NY: Orbis Books, 1992. The unique contribution of this volume is a series of very clear outlines of each document of Catholic social thought with additional resources and analysis.

Himes, Kenneth R., Lisa Sowle Cahill, Charles E. Curran, David Hollenbach, and Thomas A. Shannon, eds. *Modern Catholic Social Teaching: Commentaries and Interpretation*. Washington, DC: Georgetown University Press, 2005. A masterful and very comprehensive collection of essays by the very best scholars on this tradition. There are fourteen essays that treat each of fourteen Vatican documents; another seven long essays are dedicated to themes and foundational considerations.

Kammer, Fred. *Doing Faithjustice: An Introduction to Catholic Social Thought*. New York: Paulist Press, 1991.

Kammer, Fred. *Salted With Fire: Spirituality for the Faithjustice Journey*. New York: Paulist Press, 1995. Many groups have made excellent use of these two companion volumes by a noted practitioner of social justice advocacy. Each is written in a vivid and straightforward style.

Krier Mich, Marvin L. *Catholic Social Teaching and Movements*. Mystic, CT: Twenty-Third Publications, 1998. This book describes some of the concrete expressions of Catholic social teaching in organized movements for social change, such as the struggle for worker justice and human rights in the twentieth century.

Land, Philip S. *Catholic Social Teaching: As I Have Lived, Loathed, and Loved It*. Chicago: Loyola University Press, 1994. This book offers a rare glance inside the process by which Catholic social teaching documents come to be written. The author worked for many years in Rome as an advisor to commissions that were responsible for some of the documents surveyed in this volume and gives a firsthand account of the pivotal decades after World War II.

Merkle, Judith. *From the Heart of the Church*. Collegeville, MN: Michael Glazier Books, 2004. This book gives attention both to the content of the social teachings and to the way these teachings are rooted in spirituality, theology, and the lived historical reality of the church.

National Conference of Catholic Bishops. *Communities of Salt and Light: Reflections on the Social Mission of the Parish*. Washington, DC: United States Catholic Conference, 1994. This is the major document of an initiative of the U.S. Bishops Conference in the 1990s. Additional resources still available from the bishops' publication service include resource guides and parish resource manuals to encourage local outreach for charity and justice.

National Conference of Catholic Bishops. *Sharing Catholic Social Teaching: Challenges and Directions—Reflections of the U.S. Catholic Bishops*. Washington, DC: United States Catholic Conference, 1998. A document from the Bishops Conference that offers its own list of major themes and suggestions for ways to publicize them more broadly.

WORKS ON SPECIFIC ISSUES AND TOPICS

Bernardin, Joseph. *Consistent Ethic of Life*. Edited by Thomas G. Fuechtmann. Kansas City, MO: Sheed & Ward, 1988. This is just one of several collections now available of Joseph Cardinal Bernardin's insightful addresses and writings on the topic of the "seamless garment" of human dignity. For readers new to the topic, this is perhaps the best place to start.

Bokenkotter, Thomas. *Church and Revolution: Catholics in the Struggle for Democracy and Social Justice*. New York: Image Books-Doubleday, 1998. This is a valuable study of the historical roots of Catholic social thought. The author covers material regarding nineteenth-century social Catholicism that is found in few other places, but maintains a lively and accessible style throughout.

Christiansen, Drew, and Walter Grazer, eds. *"And God Saw That It Was Good": Catholic Theology and the Environment*. Washington, DC: United States Catholic Conference, 1996. Perhaps the best single source of information on the Church and its regard for environmental justice, this book includes both church documents from bishops' conferences around the world and scholarly articles on ecology.

Fahey, Joseph J., and Richard Armstrong, eds. *A Peace Reader: Essential Readings on War, Justice, Non-violence, and World Order*. New York: Paulist Press, 1992. A fine collection of very diverse materials on the importance of peace and the many paths to achieving it.

Henriot, Peter J., and Joe Holland. *Social Analysis: Linking Faith and Justice*. Maryknoll, NY: Orbis Books, 1983. This brief book is still the single best source of information about the technique of social analysis, the process by which observers of social relations learn from firsthand or historical experience.

Hogan, John P. *Credible Signs of Christ Alive*. Boulder, CO: Rowman and Littlefield, 2003. This very lively volume, replete with case studies, describes the work of the Catholic Campaign for Human Development, an agency of the U.S. Catholic Bishops treated in chapter one of this book.

Phan, Peter C., ed. *Social Thought: Messages of the Fathers of the Church*. Wilmington, DE: Michael Glazier, Inc., 1984. The most comprehensive collection of citations regarding social justice from patristic documents.

Ryan, Maura A., and Todd D. Whitmore, eds. *The Challenge of Global Stewardship: Roman Catholic Responses*. Notre Dame, IN: University of Notre Dame Press, 1997. This book includes essays on how Catholic social teaching may develop its treatment on a series of topics that are currently underdeveloped or inadequate, including the environment, immigration, human rights, population policy, economic development, the global food system, children, and racism.

WEBSITES

8th Day Center for Justice. http://www.8thdaycenter.org/index.html A coalition of over three dozen Catholic religious orders pooling their resources to promote principles of nonviolence and the spirituality of justice. The website contains statements and endorsements regarding social justice causes and the challenge of maintaining a critical alternative voice for social change.

Catholic Studies Database. http://www.stthomas.edu/cathstudies/webindex/ This valuable resource is maintained by the John A. Ryan Institute for Catholic Social Thought at the University of St. Thomas in Minnesota. It lists a wide variety of institutes and organizations working in the area of Catholic social thought around the world.

Catholic Media Report. http://www.catholicmediareport.org/ Updated daily, this is a project of Catholics in Alliance for the Common Good and allows users to track news stories pertinent to Catholic social teaching as well as religion and politics in general.

Education for Justice. http://www.educationforjustice.org/ This informative website is maintained by the Center of Concern, a Jesuit-sponsored think tank in Washington, DC. Most services are available by paid subscription only, but it has no equal in its coverage of Catholic social teaching resources.

The Holy See. http://www.vatican.va/ The website of the Vatican contains the texts of Catholic social teaching documents in many languages and much more as well. It is surprisingly easy to navigate.

The Interfaith Center on Corporate Responsibility. http://www.iccr.org/ This leader in the movement for corporate social responsibility helps to organize shareholder resolutions and other strategies to advocate for social justice in the operations of large companies. Many of its goals are based on the principles elaborated in the social teachings of the Catholic Church and other religious communities represented among its participants and sponsors.

Interfaith Worker Justice. http://www.iwj.org/ Formerly known as the National Interfaith Committee for Worker Justice, this Chicago-based office spearheads campaigns to promote labor justice throughout the United States. Its advocacy of workplace reforms is grounded in the social teachings of many faiths, including Catholicism.

Maryknoll Office for Global Concerns. http://www.maryknoll.org/ This extensive website represents all Maryknoll affiliates and addresses issues of peace, ecology, and economic justice in a global perspective. Users may follow links to track legislation and discover a variety of organizations working on key initiatives to advance social justice.

National Office of Jesuit Social and International Ministries. http://jesuit.org/ SocialJustice/default.aspx The website of what is called the Jesuit Conference in Washington, DC, includes this treasure trove of resources for tracking social justice issues and advocating for social change. Regular updates on domestic and international issues and legislation.

Network. www.networklobby.org Network is a social justice advocacy organization founded by Catholic religious sisters. Its work, based in Washington, DC, includes tracking issues and legislation pertaining to social justice, with a particular emphasis on gender equity and budgetary priorities.

The Office for Social Justice of the Archdiocese of Saint Paul and Minneapolis. http://www.osjspm.org/ Of all the dioceses in the United States, the Archdiocese of St. Paul maintains the most comprehensive collection of web resources for the pursuit of social justice. Includes many texts and helpful guides to other resources for activism and education for justice.

Office of Social Development and World Peace of the United States Conference of Catholic Bishops. http://www.usccb.org/sdwp/ This office of the U.S. Bishops Conference covers a host of international and domestic issues involving social justice and peace. It includes up-to-the-minute analyses of developments as well as archives of social teaching documents.

Sojourners Magazine. http://www.sojo.net/ Besides publishing an award-winning magazine of progressive Protestant thought, the Sojourners community in Washington, DC, seeks to live out the biblical call to social justice and social transformation. This site contains valuable writings on faith, politics, and culture that address service opportunities, community organizing, and public witness for justice.

Theology Library at Spring Hill College. http://web2.shc.edu/theolibrary/index .htm. The theology library at Spring Hill College in Alabama has assembled links to a wide variety of documents of the Catholic Church, far beyond social teachings.

Index

Italicized page numbers indicate that entries are found within tables.

abortion, 81, 153
advocacy groups, 4, 172–3
Amish people. *See* sectarianism
apathy, 28, 116, 142, 151–2
Aquinas, St. Thomas, 30, 45, 69–71,
    91–2
Augustine of Hippo, St., 30, 68, 70–1,
    104

base Christian communities, 49
Basil the Great, St., 68–70
Benedict XVI, Pope, 37, 51–2, 161
Bernardin, Cardinal Joseph, 81, 153
Buckley, William F., 93–4
burnout, 72

canon law, 38
capital punishment, 81, 105, 153
casuistry, 135, 139
Catholic Campaign for Human
    Development, 10–11, 15
Catholic Charities, 4
Catholic social teaching: and church
    morale, 7–8; application of, 75–6,
    134–40; as committed to engaging

culture, 153; as "our best kept
    secret," 8; continuities in, 18,
    145–58; critics of, 152–58; growth
    and writing of, 5–6, 156–58;
    implementation and publicizing
    of, 171–75; modesty within,
    148–50; official documents of,
    34–38, 46–51; purpose and limits
    of, 119–26; unofficial sources of,
    39–40
Catholic Worker, the, 5, 105, 111. *See
    also* Day, Dorothy
CELAM (Spanish acronym for Latin
    American Conference of Bishops),
    49–51, 113, 117
Centesimus Annus (On the Hundredth
    Anniversary of *Rerum Novarum*),
    35, 48, *51*, *80*, 84, 114, 133–4, *160*,
    168
The Challenge of Peace, 39, 71, *80*,
    110–11, 157
charity: and justice, 9–14, 115; and
    works of mercy, 45
Chavez, Cesar, 172
Chrysostom, St. John, 68–70

church: as advocate for the poor, 25, 115; as godmother of the nonprofit sector, 8–9; awareness of its social mission, 12

Claver, St. Peter, 141–2

colonialism, 41, 48–9, *80*, 97–103, 129, 141, 150

common good, *80*, 85–87, 116, 131, 165, 170, 172

Communism, 122–3, 125–29, 147. *See also* socialism

compromise, 25, 70, 136, 138, 169

conscience, 147, 150, 170, 172–3

Constantine, Emperor, 19

consumerism, 102, 131, 150

crusades, 23–4

"culture of death," 153

Day, Dorothy, 5, 40, 111

Dei Verbum (Dogmatic Constitution on Divine Revelation), 71

development (economic), 97–103

Deus Caritas Est (God Is Love), 37, 51–2

Dignitatis Humanae (Declaration on Religious Freedom), 43, 53

discernment, 5, 72

Economic Justice for All, 35, 115, 157

education (schools), 9, 66, 85–6, 130, 173

encyclicals: and scripture, 60–1; continuity and change in, 48–9; defined, 34; table of, *35–6*; timing and release of, 46–50; writing and authorship of, 156–58. *See also individual titles*

environment, 84–86, 116, 150, 159–65, 170

episcopal conferences, 38–9, 162. *See also* USCCB

Evangelii Nuntiandi (Evangelization in the Modern World), *36, 51*, 100

Evangelium Vitae (The Gospel of Life), 153

experience, human: as a source of ethics, 71–75; in the pastoral circle, 73, 76

family life, *80*, 87–89, 116–7

Francis of Assisi, St., 40, 111

French Revolution, 42, *52*, 53

Gaudium et Spes (Pastoral Constitution on the Church in the Modern World), 27, *35*, 37, 41, *51*, 72, *80*, 88, 94, 100, 110, 112, 120–21, 156–7, *160*, 164

globalization, 102, 116, 165–71

government: and labor justice, 95; and the principle of subsidiarity, *80*, 89–91; as agent of the common good, 86–7; constructive role of, 131–2; in scripture and early Church reflection, 18–9; participation in, 86–7; policies toward families, 88

Gutiérrez, Gustavo, 49

human persons: and personalism, 146–7; as body and soul, 29; dignity and equality of, 80–84, 123, 153; qualities of, 131

human rights, 4, 41–43, *80*, 82–84, 124, 128, 146–7, 158, 173

humanitarianism, 4, 21, 25

Hurtado, St. Alberto, 13

Inquisition, the, 23

inter-religious dialogue, 6, 165

Iraq, war in, 108–10, 117

Jesus: addresses politics, 18; and the poor, 112–3; as a worker, 97; in the New Testament, 58–60

John XXIII, Pope, *35*, 47, *51*, 73, 83, 85, 93–4, 99, 105, 108, 113, 124

John Paul II, Pope, 34, *36*, 48, *51*, 60, 84, 88, 94–5, 97, 101–2, 108, 114, 121–23, 133–4, 146–7, 150–1, 153, 161, 168–9

justice: and charity, 9–14, 115; Church's mission to, 13–4; in human relationships, 137; in scripture, 59
"Justice and Peace," Papal Commission on, 38, *51*, 53, 168
Justitia in Mundo (Justice in the World), 14, *36*, 37, *51*, 53, *80*, 154, 156–7, *160*
Just-war theory: as a necessary concession to imperfection, 37; criteria of, 105–10; critiques of, 110–11; origins of, 71, 103–4; questions regarding, 117

Ketteler, Archbishop Wilhelm Emmanuel von, 44–46
King, Jr., Martin Luther, 12–3, 111, 142
Kingdom of God: advancement of, 4, 28–9; and the imperfect present world, 20–1; in the New Testament, 60; righteous order of, 13

labor unions, 9, 40, 45–6, *80*, 89, 95–7, 130, 155
Laborem Exercens (On Human Work), *36*, *51*, *80*, 84, 88, 95, 97, 147, 159
laity, 27, 40, 68, 105, 168
Leo XIII, Pope, *35*, 41, 43, 46–7, *51*, 67, 95
liberation theology, 28, 49–50, 53, 114
libertarianism, 130–33
Lincoln, Abraham, 89
lobbying, 10, 173
love (of God and neighbor linked), 5, 57
Luther, Martin, 30, 64

magisterium, 39
Manifest Destiny, 24
Manning, Cardinal Henry Edward, 46–7
Maritain, Jacques, 146
Marx, Karl, *51*, 113, 126–28
Mater et Magistra (Christianity and Social Progress), *35*, *51*, 73, *80*, 85, 93–4, 99–100
Millennial generation, 8

Montalembert, Charles de, 45
Mother Teresa. *See* Teresa of Calcutta
Mun, Albert de, 45

natural law, 65–67, 70, 149–50
nuns, 9–10, 68, 173–74

Octogesima Adveniens (A Call to Action on the Eightieth Anniversary of *Rerum Novarum*), *36*, *51*, 75, *80*, 100, 128, *160*, 164
option for the poor (preferential), 50, *80*, 112–17, 125, 170
ownership. *See* property ownership
Ozanam, Antoine-Frédéric, 45

Pacem in Terris (Peace on Earth), *35*, 47, *51*, *80*, 82–3, 105, 108
pacifism (or nonviolence), 70, 103–4, 105–11, 137
parishes and parish life: and ecological concern, 159–60; as locus of Catholic social analysis, 75; disillusionment from activities of, 7
participation, *80*, 85–6, 94–5, 123–4, 126, 170
pastoral circle, 73–75
Patristic figures, 68–70
Paul VI, Pope, *35–6*, 37, *51*, 75–6, 92–94, 100–02, 128
Paul, St., 18, 60, *63–4*
Pax Christi, 4, 111
peace (and disarmament), 37, 49, 53, *80*, 103–12, 161, 168
personalism, 146–7
pilgrimage (as metaphor), 29–30
Pius IX, Pope, 42–3, 128
Pius XI, Pope, *35*, 47, *51*, 60, 67, 89–90
Pius XII, Pope, 108
Populorum Progressio (The Development of Peoples), *35*, 48, *51*, *80*, 92, 94, 100–1
poverty: alleviation of, 132; causes of, 2, 44; during nineteenth century,

44–46; global, 99–102; relation to pollution, 162
Prohibition (of alcoholic beverages), 24–5
property ownership, *80*, 91–95, 116, 149–50; access to, 115; and natural law, 94–5; in Aquinas, 69–70, 91–2; Patristic positions on, 69
public theology, 152–58

Quadragesimo Anno (After Forty Years, or The Reconstruction of the Social Order), 35, 47, *51*, 60, *80*, 89, 92, 128

racial discrimination, 115–17, 150
relativism, ethical, 67
religious liberty, 42–3, 86, 128
Rerum Novarum (The Condition of Labor), 35, 41, 46–48, *51*, *80*, 92, 95, 114
revelation, 57–61 65–67, 104
revolution, 6, 125–27
Roman Empire, 18–9, 30
Romero, Archbishop Oscar, 49
Ryan, Msgr. John A., 53

Saint Vincent de Paul Society, 4, 45, 91
Scripture: and option for the poor, 112; as related to tradition, 71, 104–05; as source of Christian ethics, 57–61; citations (in table 4.1), *62–64*
Second Vatican Council (or Vatican II), 26–7, 30, *35*, *51*, 88, 100, 110, 112–3, 120–1, 157
sectarianism, 20–1, 27
secular humanism, 20
separation of church and state, 10, 18, 22, 42
service work, 3, 73, 173
sexual ethics, 148, 151
sexual-abuse crisis, clerical, 7, 158
"signs of the times," 33, 72, 111, 121, 166

slavery, 60, 141–2
social analysis, 73–76, 148–50
Social Catholicism (in nineteenth–century Europe), 43–44, 95, 114, 172
social ethics: as open–ended, 2; and law, 55–6
social justice: and charity, 9–14; as a goal of welfare state policies, 129–30; as a new term, 41; convergence of many religious voices around, 6; definitions of, 1; in scripture, 57–61
social sin (and structures of evil), 98, 102, 150–52
social reform movements, 1, 9, 21, 152, 171–2
socialism, 45–6, 92–3, 122–3, 125, 128. *See also* Communism
socialization, 93–4
solidarity, *80*, 84–87, 99, 101–2, 113–16, 121–23, 126, 128, 130, 165, 170
Sollicitudo rei Socialis (On Social Concern), *36*, 48, *51*, 60, *80*, 84, 102, 121–2, 150, *160*
Suárez, Francisco, 71
subsidiarity, *80*, 89–91, 116
Syllabus of Errors, 42

Ten Commandments, 56–7, 65
Teresa of Calcutta, Mother (or Blessed), 40, 141
Terrorism, 22–3, 71, 109, 117, 137, 167
Tertullian, 19–21, 33, 68, 152
theocracy, 22
totalitarianism, 90–1, 127, 133

United Nations, 38, 82
U.S. Bishops. *See* USCCB
USCCB (United States Conference of Catholic Bishops): advocacy efforts of, 10, 174; description of, 38–9; documents of, 157; on peace and war, 110–1; on environment, 161;

option for the poor and vulnerable, 115; website of, 39, 174, 183

utopia, 14, 26, 128

Vatican, the: commitment to environment, 161; offices and Secretariats of, 37–8; website of, 37

Vatican II. *See* Second Vatican Council

Walesa, Lech, 40, 121, 144, 172

World Council of Churches, 65

women: aspirations for equality, 49, 177; in the church, 154–5; in the workforce, 88; in writings of St. Paul, 60

worker justice (and wages), 44–46, 67, 80, 95–97, 155

About the Author

Thomas Massaro, S.J., a Jesuit priest of the New England Province, is professor of moral theology and director of the Licentiate in Sacred Theology (S.T.L.) Program at Weston Jesuit School of Theology in Cambridge, Massachusetts. He is a founding member of the new Ecclesiastical Faculty of the School of Theology and Ministry at Boston College.